Fat Is the New 30

The Sweet Potato Queens' Guide to Coping with (the crappy parts of) Life

JILL CONNER BROWNE

To the Very Precious Memory of my All-Time Favorite People: The Bountifully-Breasted, Never-Boring, Queen of Us ALL: Maryln Schwartz; and Booneville, Mississippi's Favorite Son: Michael Rubenstein. We'll know if they have any Say in Things now because if they DO—Oprah will be off the air and Vanderbilt will win the BCS Championship.

Acknowledgments

The last few years have afforded me much experience in Coping with the Crappy Parts of Life referenced in the title of this book. However, it must be said that the Crap, plentiful as it has admittedly been, is overshadowed still by the Amazing, the Humbling, the Gratifying, and the Nifty. My prayer for us all is that we're always able to pay more attention to those things in our lives and laugh our way around the Crap.

This book was made possible by the brilliant and easily amused Terry Goodman at Amazon Publishing, along with the beautiful and talented Katie Finch and Nikki Sprinkle. Sarah Burningham at Little Bird Publicity and Marika Gunnels Cackett with the Jackson, Mississippi Convention and Visitor's Bureau are True Queens.

As always, nothing good would ever happen without Kyle Jennings and the entire staff at Bad Dog Management.

The wheels would have long since fallen off if not for the constant vigilance of Alycia Jones and Sarajean Babin. I am ever grateful for the once-a-year loan of their husbands, Russell and Mike, who help me survive Parade Weekend.

The wildly successful First Annual ZIPPITY DOO DAH®
PARADE took place in 2011 in the Jackson, Mississippi Arts
District of FONDREN. This was nothing short of a Miracle,
wrought by: Jeff Good, Merrill Tenney McKewen, Jim Wilkirson,
Jennifer Emerson, Erin McKewen, David Waugh, Lee Norris,
Erica Speed, Stacy Callendar, Kathy Clem, Ron Aldridge, Bill
Scruggs, Mary Jo McAnally, Belmont Trapp, Lisa Hathorn,
Amanda Overby, Jim Burwell, Sumati Thomas, Tanyalyn Burns,
Melissa Flanders, Maggie Briscoe, Dan Blumenthal, Jon Pixler,
Max Barron, Jennifer McHenry, Adam Brown, Danielle Davis,
Betty Strait, Linda Kay Russell, and Brenda Tillman.

Special thanks to John Rein and Dexter Blanchard at Southern
Beverage Company for making it possible for us to have THE
CLYDESDALES in the Zippity Doo Dah Parade in Fondren—
and also to visit Blair E. Batson Hospital for Children. What a
gift, thank you!

I am profoundly grateful to the Fondren Association of
Businesses, the Fondren Renaissance Foundation, Our Fondren,
and SoFo for totally Getting It and supporting this event.
FONDREN ROCKS!

Mayor Harvey Johnson, the Jackson Convention and Visitor's
Bureau, the Jackson Police Department, the Hinds County
Sheriff's Department, American Medical Response, University of
Mississippi Medical Center, the Jackson Chamber of Commerce,
and the State of Mississippi—WOW! THANK YOU!

Major smooches to our Benevolent Sponsors: Patty Peck Honda,
BancorpSouth, Brown Bottling Group, The Cirlot Agency,

Comcast, Southern Beverage Company, Cathead Vodka, The McKewen Company, Sal & Mookies, McGraw Gotta Go, Clear Channel Radio, Jackson Free Press, County Connections, Portico Magazine, Richard Schwartz and Associates, PA, Central Surgical Associates, Beau Mad Wines, Waste Management, Southerndrawlen, Ben Nelson Golf, Studio Chane, Find It In Fondren, Northside Sun, and Gulf States Golf Cars. BLESSINGS BE UPON THESE FOLKS AND ALL THEIR KIN.

With the help from all of those people, we were able to give to Blair E. Batson Hospital for Children over $65,000—our very first year. We are thrilled and grateful beyond measure.

Liza and Rick Looser, Chris Swann (E-vil Henchman), Steve Erickson, Greg Gilliland, Ashley Strange, and Lynda Lesley at the Cirlot Agency—I can personally testify that I have not ever done anything in this life to deserve your generosity. And y'all know that and STILL do it. Lovin' y'all SO!

Clear Channel Radio—Kenny Windham, Jan Michaels, and Crew—couldn't do it without y'all—wouldn't wanna try.

Patty and Jeff Christie, Bob Aubrey, and Donna Ransdell at Patty Peck Honda—THANK YOU ought to be covered in sequins and rhinestones!

Dr. Carolyn Meyers and David Hoard at Jackson State University—Welcome to Jackson and to the QUEENDOM! The Sonic Boom of the South is THE O-fficial Marching Band of the Sweet Potato Queens—"the quintessence of contemporary sounds and maneuvers, the summa cum laude of bands." We will have no other bands before us.

Sweet Potato Queens Cynthia Speetjens, Pippa Jackson, Melanie Jeffreys, Katie Werdel, Leigh Bailey, George Ewing, Martha Jean (by Gawd) Alford, Robin Mitchell, and Ellyn Weeks—love y'all more than a fat kid loves cake and since I AM a fat kid who loves cake, I can tell you—that is a BUNCH.

Sweet Potato Queen Wannabes™ from all 50 states and 37 countries: YOU make my heart sing!

Fat Is the New 30!

*P*ossibly the very best survival tool ever devised is the Concept of Complete Denial. My seester Judy and I have made this our Life's Work. (Judy would like for it to be noted that she also has a minor in "Lolling.") Someone once told me that if you study and practice something diligently for five years, you can become a bona fide expert at it. I shared this tidbit with Judy and we decided that we would commit ourselves to doing whatever it took to accomplish that in our chosen field, and I am happy to report that we were 100 percent successful, and also, it didn't take us anywhere near five years. We are, as far as we can tell, the World's Leading Authorities on Denial. No, we didn't do much—OK, ANY—research into the possibility of the existence of other authorities and/or their potential superiority to us in this, our chosen field. We decided that we are the best, and if anybody says otherwise, well, we will just deny it. So, there. Done.

We come from good stock, denial-wise. If there was a breeding program for Denial, our parents would no doubt have been the world champion. What? Stud and mare? If anything unpleasant EVER came up, Daddy's immediate and consistent response was always, "Let's talk about WATERMELON." Or if it happened that someone was upset about something, didn't matter much what it was, he would suggest that they THINK about watermelon.

If you're trying to make sense of that, you are wasting your time. It makes no sense. Except that it does actually work. Watermelon is the perfect, totally neutral diffuser for practically any woeful situation. Just offering that up in response to any form of verbal infelicitousness is the perfect soft answer that turneth away wrath—probably due, to a large degree, to the fact that it is such a surprising non sequitur.

Rambling around on AOL, I happened across an article about chronic pain and all the ways sufferers are treated and mistreated. A really smart fellow (M. Cary Reid, MD, PhD) said that he totally believed the "old adage" that "the best analgesic is an occupied mind." I Googled the quote to see the origins of the "old adage," but there was no record of anybody having ever said those words but M. Cary Reid, MD, PhD. So am I crazy or does that not sound an awful lot like thinking about watermelon to divert one's attention from anything unpleasant? I mean, if you're thinking about watermelon, your mind IS occupied, yes? I am calling that scientific proof.

And MAMA. Well, Mama's approach to any and everything was simply to declare victory, no matter what the outcome. Whatever happened was just the way she planned it by the time it was over. It was like saying you're going to Texas, telling everybody far and wide of your travel plans for the Lone Star State, and shopping for Texas clothes—maybe even a new pair of cowboy boots and a HAT—to wear in TEXAS because that's where you're going. Only, you somehow end up in Vermont. JUST THE WAY YOU PLANNED IT. And she would never waiver on this stance. It's an advanced version of "That's my story and I'm sticking to it," which has always been a personal favorite of mine.

So, for Judy to come up with "FAT IS THE NEW 30" is hardly even an exercise for us. We are seasoned pros at denial.

We must admit, though, that we do feel that somewhat of a gauntlet has been flung down before us whenever we peruse the latest installment of *People of Walmart*. Surely you've seen those photos online? I cannot imagine that there is anybody alive on Planet Earth today who has NOT seen this truly stunning and ever-growing collection of photographs—but if not, well, then pause now and go look. I warn you—it is a serious time drain, nearly impossible to tear yourself away once you begin. And I can't say that you will be a better person for having done it, either.

I am particularly taken by the fact that they have it broken down state by state, and I admit I have done a few comparison studies, pitting our own homegrown Mississippi Walmart train wrecks to those of other presumably more cosmopolitan locales, and the results are at once shocking and predictable.

I used to wonder where that artiste with the Raw Meat Dress came up with her costuming ideas—well, mys-te-ry SOLVED. One must allow that her physique is sadly not replicated in the ranks of Walmart shoppers—but her outfits certainly are. She would totally BLEND; nobody would even notice her in there. It's kinda like there is one big giant family of hideous people, with relatives in all 50 states, and they have at least two things in common—the only two things we can stand to consider, really. They WILL go to the store wearing ANY-THING and the store they are going to is Walmart. Oh, and their last name is "Gaga." (I wonder if they all sing and dance. Wouldn't THAT be festive?)

At your very own local Walmart, you can see every size and shape of butts and boobs, quite often in their entirety—and you will no doubt note, with alarm, the increasing occurrence of the reversal of these two distinctive physical characteristics. Where once we expected to see—might even say we relied on it—the butts on the BACKside of the person and the boobs on the front, now, more and more, thanks to the ever–more revealing outfits worn by unbelievably unfit Walmart shoppers all over the United States, we are subjected to the sight of back boobs and belly butts, in various stages of undress and display.

Based on their cornea-searing guises, we are ASSUMING that these Walmartians are Denial Devotees, out practicing their craft. Either that or they are all the visually impaired victims of an enormous, nationwide practical joke, and really, that just seems too unwieldy to actually carry off, so we're going with the denial theory of the crimes against fashion, decency, and/or humanity. I mean, they can't ALL be blind and they can't ALL be totally mirror-less so we have to assume from there that they are, in fact, taking their time in dressing like that and then looking in the MIRROR and saying to themselves, "Uh-HUH—I am lookin' SO FINE," and waltzing out the door, into the unprotected eye of the unwary and, for the most part, undeserving public.

So, all that is to say, there are at least SOME contenders for the State of Complete Denial World Championship, but as I said, Judy and I deny that we have any competition worthy of our worry. That's our story and we're sticking to it, and as the self-proclaimed Deities of Denial, we think we have something to offer you for your own personal arsenal in your attempts at avoiding acceptance.

It appears to me that we (the Baby Boomers) are the first generation in the recorded history of igmos to be so completely terrified of age that we make up silly maxims to repeat to ourselves, and to each other, in hopes of quelling the quavering in our hearts and minds as we contemplate growing older. I can tell you for a fact my mama lived to be 85 ¾ and I never heard her, even one time, say that 80 was the new 65 or anything like that.

Gray is not the new black—it's GRAY. But we had all bought so much black stuff we weren't gonna need any more in this lifetime and the clothes folks were needing to make some sales and so...voyola! A new star is born on the color wheel. And so it goes, every year—some color becomes the "new black," to be worn all the time, with everything. Except in New York City, of course, where actual black will forever be the only black because they're all too afraid to wear anything else. Every time my daughter Bailey is headed to NYC, I chide her for packing "outfits" and cute shoes. It falls on deaf ears, though, when I remind her that the ONLY people in New York City who EVER dress like *Sex and the City* are Bailey and her friends on vacation there. I personally have never seen one single New Yorker on the street dressed in anything but assorted black items and running shoes.

Whatever Age We Are is not actually the New Ten Years Younger—and we all know that. However, denial is nine-tenths of the law, so I say have at it but within reason. And by "reason" I mean that you do have to be aware of the fact that you are in denial and are actively CHOOSING it. You don't have to admit that, of course—that's why it's called "denial"—but there is a difference between "denial" and "delusion." The difference is that denial is a fun game and delusion is pitiable and requires meds that you will be too delusional to enjoy.

You can think of this book as sort of a "Sweet Potato Queens' Stimulus Package and Survival Guide" and my ultimate goal will be to help you sparkle—plenty and often—no matter what.

OK, I made up the Stimulus Package part—there is no giveaway program associated with this book, nor is there any low-interest loanage to be had. Not that I am stingy or unchari-table. To the contrary, I would love to give away a free pony with every book or even free books. However, sadly, my personal defi-cit is only slightly less than our government's—not that that has slowed those guys down a bit. If I had a printing press like theirs, I'd have money, too, I reckon.

How about this—y'all buy a couple million of this book, and my next book will be free. That's a great deal, yes? And it doesn't even have to be a couple million sold to a couple million different people; if you know somebody with more money than sense and can talk them into personally ordering a couple million copies—I don't care if they use 'em for mulch—then a deal's a deal and the next book will be free. That's the closest thing to a Stimulus Package that I can come up with, and it appears to be fair, square, and beneficial to all—or close enough. But if I think of anything Stimulating as we go along, rest assured I'll throw it in here at no extra charge.

Survival Guide part is true. Whatever crappy thing is going on in your life, old as I am, I'm pretty sure it's already happened to me, and hey, here I am, still ambulatory, cognitive, communi-cative, and more than willing to share my experience, strength, and hope with you—or at the very least, help you laugh through your tears.

Times are tough all over—and pretty much all the time, from what I can tell. It's a global problem and a personal problem—al-though, in my opinion, EVERYthing is personal. If somebody is screwing up on the other side of the planet, in no time a-tall, it's gonna be ruining MY day way over here in PoDunk. You cannot GET far enough away to avoid it—the universe is simply not big enough.

So, right off here, we are acknowledging that Escape Is Not an Option, and as much as I hate to dash your hopes so early on, I guess it's really for the best. Just pause for a moment and try to accept that you ARE here, in THIS life, and there is nothing you can do to avoid whatever has been designated as Your Personal Raft of Shit for this lifetime. It was assigned to you upon arrival, it cannot be exchanged, and no refunds have ever been issued, to my knowledge.

There MAY have been times in the History of the World when laughter was needed more, but I wasn't alive for any of them, so it's really not my fault that I couldn't be of any help then. However, NOW is another matter altogether—because, well, Everything Pretty Much Sucks, as far as I can tell, and well, here I AM and so there is nothing for it but to Pitch In and Do My Part.

I am uniquely unqualified to do absolutely anything else— you name it, I cannot do it—but I AM funny. That's it—that's all I got. Oh, I HAD ambitions, all right—I WANTED to be a diminutive, large-breasted, incredibly sexy (natural) redhead with a spectacular vocal talent and tiny feet, and I am quite certain that if I had only been granted that opportunity, I would probably have cured cancer and brought about world peace a long time ago. I would have already saved GM and the American Way—there would definitely be a chicken in every pot by now— and the ozone hole would have been fixed, better than new, I'm sure of it.

But NO. I was denied this opportunity—through no fault of my own—and just LOOK at the mess we've got on our hands. NOT MY FAULT is all I've got to say about THAT. I was WILLING to alleviate all human suffering with my stunning looks and unforgettable soprano voice, but nooooo, they didn't WANT MY help—so, fine.

What I CAN offer you is some much-needed relief from the overwhelming stress we are all mired in (as a direct result of my not turning out to be the World-Saving Little Redheaded Singing Sensation), by making fun of all the messes and the people who made them—even if they are us, which, truth be told, they occasionally are. I will make you laugh even if you don't want to—I can do that. It will feel good and you will feel better even though most everything will still suck.

I will teach you how to have some fun with No Money A-tall, if need be. And if all else fails, I can teach you how to make a halter top out of your boyfriend's old tighty-whiteys, thus providing several of Life's Essentials: clothing, good use of resources readily on hand, and belly laughs.

If Change is What is Needed (nobody's disputing THAT), I can help you Change your Attitude—and I will because I am a Proud American Patriot and it is My Duty to Serve My Country. I live to Serve. Just don't ask me to sing. (Oh, and also, don't ask me anything about algebra—other than that, we're cool.)

Daddy always said, "There are very few situations in life that we really and truly canNOT change, but when we do encounter one of those, then the task at hand is to figure out how to either make fun OUT of it—or to make fun OF it." That advice has served me well in this life, so I offer it to you. But you don't have my daddy to help you figure out how to actually DO it—and it does take practice. I got personal training from Daddy, plus I've had lots of experience at Spinning Crap Into Fun (also known as "Shit to Shinola"—similar in theory to the storied Spinning of Straw Into Gold—only, actually possible), so I think maybe I can help you with that.

We are fortunate to have many tools with which to fend off everything from boredom to disaster, but remember, no matter how bad it is, it's much better to laugh than to cry—or to maim and kill, which will only make more trouble for yourself, so I discourage it, no matter how tempting it may be.

What? No Watermelon?

"Thinking about watermelon" is by no means the only method we have for dealing with Life's Little (or Big) Unpleasantnesses. Hyperbole is also helpful.

If you've ever watched any of those "funniest videos" shows on TV, you gotta admit there is some REEEALLY funny stuff on there sometimes. One of my personal favorites featured a little girl, about five or six, at her birthday party, which featured a piñata. Birthday Girl did not seem to grasp the piñata theory, or I guess she grasped it perfectly well and just did not appreciate it—at all. As one attendee after another took a turn taking blindfolded swipes at the spinning papier-mâché donkey, BG watched in horror and she did not sit silently by, stewing in her consternation at the scene before her. Indeed, she was quite vocal, dramatic, and even physical in her attempts at rescuing HER piñata. As the camera calmly recorded the festivities, BG could be seen (and heard, definitely heard) pouncing on whatever kid was wielding the stick at the moment, trying to wrest it from their grasp, and hollering to high heaven the whole time: "STOP IT! YOU'RE HURTING HIM! DON'T HIT HIM! I LOOOOVE HIM! STOP! STOP! STOP!" She was sobbing and yelling and flailing at the stick-bearers. Then she seemed to almost accept defeat and she collapsed into a pile, clutching her face, but she stepped up the wailing as she turned her face to Heaven and bawled, "THIS IS THE WORST BIRTHDAY E-VER! STOP HITTING HIM! WHOSE IDEA WAS THIS? I HATE THIS PARTY! THIS IS THE WORST DAY OF MY LIFE!"

I don't know who it is, but there is SOMEbody in that house who is a major drama queen besides her. This little bitty girl did not come up with all this angst in a vacuum. She has clearly seen and heard a similar performance prior to this fifth or sixth birthday party of hers. The language, the tone, the drama, the whole performance has got to be looking oddly familiar to some-body around there; it's way too sophisticated for a preschooler. Or perhaps she watches a lot of "reality TV." It was like a five-year-old auditioning to be a "Guidette" or a "Real Housewife" or something.

Well, then somebody finally succeeded in breaking the pi-ñata open and the whole performance up to this point was pale, bland, and lifeless compared to the scene she unleashed as the party guests scrambled for the treats that rained down. "ARE YOU HAPPY? AAAAUUUUGGGHHH! HE'S BROKEN! I LOOOOVED HIM! I HATE YOU! I HATE YOU! THIS IS THE WORST BIRTHDAY PARTY E-VER! OOOOH! GIVE HIM TO ME!" (As she gathered up pieces of the shattered donkey, clutch-ing them to her heaving bosom, you would have thought they were her children, crashing to the earth around her from the flaming *Hindenburg*—so extreme was her grief.) "THIS IS THE WORST DAY OF MY LIFE!" was her parting shot as she sank, once again, to the ground, impervious to the gaiety being en-joyed by her guests all around her.

I found that to be quite odd and telling as well. I've personal-ly observed that, under normal circumstances, if one person in a crowd is behaving in a banshee-like manner, it tends to definitely get the attention of the more subdued segment of the population and quite often has a dampering effect on the general mood of the group. And yet, in this video, one person—the honoree of the whole thing—is in a state of total hysteria, complete with choreography, and everybody else is just happy, happy, happy, all around her. The other children did not appear to be sightless and deaf, judging from their movements and interactions on the screen, but neither did they betray the slightest hint of awareness of her presence, let alone her histrionics.

The only plausible explanation is that it was just her everyday MO and it's happened with such frequency and regularity that it now just blends in. Like how if you live next to a railroad track, after a couple days, you no longer hear the CITY OF NEW ORLEANS as it rumbles and roars and rattles the rafters of your house and loosens the fillings in your teeth.

My friend Blanche's mama, Lorise—we call her "Big L," but not to her face, of course—has her own version of "THIS IS THE WORST DAY OF MY LIFE," although, granted, it's not nearly so splashy and it is certainly not ever LOUD. Big L is no longer a spring chicken—she's not exactly a winter chicken, maybe more of a late-autumn chicken—yet gets around pretty well, hasn't lost a step exactly, but occasionally misplaces one or two. We don't discuss age—Blanche and Big L are fond of saying that "a woman who will tell you her age will just tell you ANYTHING," and therefore, such a woman is not to be trusted. (If you're reading this, you just have to imagine the very B R O A-D E S T Southern accents you can fit inside your brain—that'll put you fairly close to Blanche and Big L.) ANYWAY, now that Big L is an autumn chicken, she gets tired more easily than she did back in her springtime. But she's never just "tired" anymore. Today, if she's tuckered, it's front-page news and it's a mystery, to boot. Any announcement concerning the exertion and resulting fatigue of Big L is preceded by a swift and dramatic lowering of her person into a chair (preferably overstuffed), followed immediately by the going limp of her neck—causing her head (with the perfectly coiffed hairdo) to flop either back against the chair (overstuffed is best for this, obviously) or to pitch forward, chin to her chest. In either case, just prior to the head flop, her perfectly made-up eyelids flutter rapidly for a second and her eyeballs can be seen rolling back ever so slightly in their sockets. Her hands might move independently, one to her perfectly made-up forehead or elegantly dressed heart area and the other flung loosely off the cushy arm of the chair, or they might move in concert, both clasping her perfectly made-up cheeks, displaying perfectly manicured nails. Along with this dance comes the now-familiar refrain, "Oh, ME! I just don't know WHEN I have been SO TIRED!"

Besides the elegant use of exaggeration, there's a bonus in this one. The "Big L Lesson" that Blanche and I have gleaned from the many stagings we have seen of this performance is this: You may not always FEEL good and you may not always BE good, but, hunny, there is just no EXCUSE for not LOOKING good. Big L has always taught by example. (And, of course, it goes without saying but must nonetheless BE said that Blanche and I added in the part about "not being good" in reference to ourownselfs on account of we have not/are not always measuring up in that regard. Absolutely NO inference should be made about Big L's behavior, which, as far as we know, has always been/will always be Above Reproach and we readily concede to her superiority in every conceivable area of life.)

Daddy used to tell of an old man "up home," meaning in the vicinity of Ethel, Mississippi, who was known to imbibe a bit—OK, a lot. And when he did, which was often, he became even more morose than he was sober, which, truth be told, he hardly ever was—sober, that is. Anyway, Daddy had been off to war for some years, and upon returning "up home," he was not surprised when he encountered this man in the same place and in the same condition as he did before he left—on the park bench in the town square and drunk. But time and Ezra Brooks had done nothing to the old man's memory, and when he saw Daddy, he sprang—or I guess, lurched—from his seat and threw his arms around him and burst into tears, shouting, "Lawdamercy, John Albert, I ain't seen ya in s'long I don't care nuthin' about ya!"

We have pondered that greeting for some years in our family: "What the fuck did that mean?" We have often asked ourselves both individually and as a group, and we have not ever come up with anything like an answer, but we USE it, just the same.

Blanche and I use all three of these on a nearly daily basis now. If there is the slightest hiccup in our day, we go immediately to "THIS IS THE WORST DAY OF MY LIFE!" If the day has been the slightest bit taxing, we go to "Oh, ME! I just don't know WHEN I've been SO TIRED!" And if she can't reach me on the telephone on her first try, when I finally do answer, I can expect to be greeted with, "Lawdamercy, Baby Girl, I ain't seen ya in s'long I don't care nuthin' about ya!"

So, I offer them to you now. Feel free to use them at will as the need arises and always remember: Nobody can argue with nonsense, and if it brings a momentary pause and a chuckle, it's done its job. And good grief, go put on some lipstick.

Fair and Square

*I*n our family, "fair and square" is only used when we have done something that is neither, but for various and sundry personal reasons, we felt it was right or at least somehow justifiable.

As with so many of Life's Lessons, we learned this one from our own personal mother who INVENTED "fair and square." Mama loved to travel—anywhere, anytime. She was pretty much always packed and ready to go. Daddy always traveled in his work, so when he took time off, the very last thing he wanted to do was GO. He wanted only to be completely horizontal on the den couch and share long naps with the brown dog purloined from the unworthy neighbors.

Not deterred in the slightest by the selective sloth of her spouse, Mama would decide where she wanted to go and then browbeat a sufficient number of other folks into going along that she would get her own trip for free. Of course, this meant that she had to shepherd all those other travelers for days or weeks at a time, but she (not unlike myself) was always at her happiest when Bossing Others, so this was a bonus in her eyes.

Stateside, she organized countless bus trips, always utilizing the same bus company and requesting her favorite driver each time. At her instigation, at the end of each day, the group would put all their change into a box. On the last day of the trip, one traveler's name was drawn from a hat and was the lucky winner of the "pot." On more occasions than for which the law of averages would grant permission, the winning name was that of the unbelievably "lucky" bus driver—because he did a great job and Mama thought he deserved a little something extra. THEREFORE, he won, in Mama's terms and mind, "FAIR AND SQUARE."

Now, I have no earthly idea why I started telling you that. I like the story—I think it's hilarious—but it was definitely not where I intended to end up. When I started it, there had been some moment of inspiration, and that story seemed to be the perfect segue into the real point of Something, but as luck and advanced middle age would have it, I had to pee. No one, regardless of the alleged import of the words they are attempting to put to paper, can long resist the clarion call of a full bladder, and though I forestalled the trip until the last-possible moment without risking dampness of a personal and unpleasant nature, I was, at last, driven by a force unseen, but definitely felt, to take the very briefest of potty breaks.

I swear, I was gone from my desk for under two minutes. Indeed, my swift peeing action is a source of endless amazement and wonder to my husband, The Cutest Boy in the World. What can I say? I pee quick. But upon my return, I looked at the words on the screen—the ones you see preceding these, the ones about "fair and square"—and my mind was a complete and total blank concerning them.

Brain rackage has yielded nothing—whatever was in there is, at the moment, gone or at least unavailable to me. There are two full pages of notes open in front of me and I have reason to believe that some scribbled notation therein was the trigger for the story I set out to relate to you. Naturally, I have reread all of those chicken scratches at least four times and…I got nothin'.

So, I guess what I NOW need to tell you about is one of the many indignities of aging with which you will, sooner or later, unless you die young, be forced to cope: You Cannot Remember Shit. And you can read that with emphasis on any word in the sentence and grasp the nuances of the effect this will have on your life. YOU cannot remember shit. You CANNOT remember shit. You cannot REMEMBER shit. You cannot remember SHIT! I think the last variation best suits my frame of mind at this moment. It is maddening and I am mad. I had a really great story to tell you and it's just flown out one of the many holes in my head—which sometimes feels like a wind tunnel.

But since this is a book about SURVIVAL and the aging process is definitely something for which we are all ill-suited and completely unprepared, I will offer you the dubious benefit of my experience, strength, and hope, and armed with that, plus a few bucks, you can, well, get a few bucks' worth of something.

It doesn't really matter that your memory bank has turned into more of a memory sieve. All that matters is HIDING IT, along with other portents of your impending Geezerdom.

Denial is not only the main symptom of many things; in my experience, it's also the best line of defense in just about any case. Although there are many occasions that do call for explicit and vehement denial, the concealment of short-term memory loss is best accomplished by more subtle means. As pertains to stored thoughts, or rather, the lack thereof, you're not looking to overtly declare that you have NOT forgotten stuff, because to do that only invites others to seek substantive proof of that which, of course, you cannot provide.

So the plan is to deny by deception and deflection. Let me illustrate this with a story from my youth. It involves alcohol, the overconsumption of which can have the same effects on memory and behavior as getting old sober. For example, my friend Chip and I used to enjoy going to baseball games together. Let me rephrase that: Chip and I used to like to sit in the third-base bleachers AT baseball games and drink beer together. The fact that there were other people in attendance, some of whom were engaged in playing baseball, was pretty much immaterial.

By the time those other people quit playing baseball—thus forcing the cutoff of the beer taps—we would emerge from the stadium to discover that the parking lot now held about 10,000 more cars than had been there when we entered. You can see our problem, right? Nobody in our group (the two of us) knew WHERE the car was. But we were loath to allow our behavior to broadcast this fact to the world, by wandering slowly and unsteadily up and down the row upon row of automobiles, obviously searching for our vehicle.

Admittedly, our favored plan of action would have been to sit down, in the parking lot, and continue drinking beer until all the other cars were gone, making our own far easier to spot (in theory). But, as previously stated, the beer hut was closed, so that was out.

We hit on what I still think was an outstanding idea: Act Not Lost. And that's what we did. We would walk out of the stadium at a brisk clip—not unlike people on a mission, one that they both understood and felt equipped to accomplish. We walked out quickly, as if we'd just realized we had to be somewhere important in five minutes. We walked purposefully, as if we KNEW WHERE OUR CAR WAS.

Up and down the many rows we strode long, powerful strides, wearing facial expressions that said, "Don't get in our way, can't you see we're headed somewhere important?" Occasionally, one of us would start to laugh at the other one for any one of a thousand handy reasons, which would lead to a howling guffaw fest amongst the group (the two of us), and that would endanger the process, since then we no longer looked like purpose-driven people so much as fast-walking, giggling drunks.

But you see my point here. As long as we kept up the charade, nobody outside the group (the two of us) KNEW that we were, in fact, wandering aimlessly in that sea of cars. And so, utilizing that principle here, I have completely forgotten what I started out to tell you, but I just went RIGHT ON TALKING and told you SOMETHING ELSE entirely, but I've done it with such a confident, competent air that you completely forgot that I had forgotten what I was saying in the beginning.

So, as you age, which I hope you will do sober—I truly cannot imagine trying to negotiate all these pitfalls drunk—and you find yourself starting a sentence but forgetting the targeted end before you even get to the middle, just keep talking, about anything, it doesn't really matter what, just keep talking and nobody will notice that you're lost. If you can REMEMBER to do this, it will serve you well.

All We Need Is Love and Maybe a Dyson

*H*ow do the Dogless do it? At some of the absolute lowest points in my life, my dog Randy was the only thing on this side of Heaven that kept me from trying to storm those Pearly Gates. She was my first rescue dog, and on the day that I found her, I promised her I would never leave her. So, you see my problem/salvation? I could not, would not, betray the trust of that most loving and devoted of all creatures by leaving her—which would certainly be necessitated by suicide. I know when they say, "You can't take it with you," they're usually talking about money, but as far as I know, the policy extends to dogs as well. So, I couldn't leave her—and I sure as hell couldn't kill my DOG. In my depressed state, I could actually conceive of taking my own life—but my DOG? I was depressed, not demonic. And stuck. Saved by my dog.

It should be noted that, at that time, I did also have a cat—Joyce. She was a very fine cat and she was also a rescue, but Joyce exacted no such blood oath of lifetime loyalty as had Randy. She may have wanted to, may have even thought about bringing it up, but you know how cats are—they're very private about their feelings. Unless they are hungry or want you to move over. While a dog might grieve himself to death over the loss of your company, a cat will miss you but will mostly be irritated because the only one in the house with thumbs is no longer available to do her bidding.

Life is hard on a good day. It's just not safe to be dog-free. We are well protected in all respects at our house. As most everyone knows, there are currently three people of the canine persuasion holding court here at Coochie Sprangs. We only got one of them on purpose (Sostie); God sent us another when we least expected it, as, in His infinite wisdom, He is wont to do.

I had just turned in the complete manuscript for my seventh book—*The Sweet Potato Queens' Guide to Raising Children for Fun and Profit*—and I was so happy and relieved to be finished with it and I was so looking forward to just the briefest of times off. After a two-month book tour, returning home just in time for the Million Queen March™ festivities, and then plunging straight into writing the book—well, I was just thinking that I might even DESERVE a minute or two just to sit on the back porch and mouth-breathe. Apparently, I was mistaken.

The stork paid us a visit. Oh, not the one that brings BABIES— mercy, no. He could see, I guess, that I'm a tired old woman and not up to any more young'uns of the human persuasion. No, the DOG stork visited us—or more likely, some heartless, hell-bound wretch who picked our cul-de-sac in which to dump his pathetic, tick-covered, heartworm-riddled shell of a sweet dog. So, you know, whaddya gonna do? We done got ourselves a new dog—a bonus dog—to go with the three-legged one we already had and our three cats.

Yes, B.D. joined the fambly. B.D.—Boy Dog, Big Dog, Bad Dog, Baby Darlin'. Many names apply at a given moment, but he seems happy with B.D. and his big ole face lights up when he hears it. He was just about dead when he showed up at our door, but he picked a good cul-de-sac to nearly die in; between us and our neighbors, Laura and Angie, he was guaranteed a good home. Indeed, we know many PEOPLE who would like to come and take up life as a dog in our homes. After numerous vet visits and thousands of dollars later, B.D. had a full recovery in his sights, and I don't know who was happier about it—B.D. or us.

Then our precious baby girl Bailey "gifted" us with the third. When Bailey was a sophomore at the University of Mississippi, an on-campus housing shortage developed and we decided to buy a condo near the school for her to live in. One of the very first House Rules we so firmly laid down was "NO ANIMALS." So, naturally, when one of her Kappa sisters came by the condo with the tee-niny brown baby dog that she had purchased from some guy in a parking lot, Bailey fell deeply in love with the doglet. As the two girls oooed and goooed over the pup, it dawned on the friend that, well, she currently lived in the sorority house and she actually couldn't HAVE a pet there, so she guessed she was just gonna have to take this infant to the POUND.

Bailey could not bear to think of that and she thought we could not POSSIBLY object to her having such a wee little "purse" dog (especially one that we did not know about), and so, without hesitation, she clasped the mite to her bosom, named her "Edie," and claimed her for her very own. By the time we learned of Edie, she had outgrown not only Bailey's purse but her condo as well. Welcome to Coochie Sprangs, Edie.

Who's Yo' Daddy?

Sostie (rhymes with "toasty") is our three-legged Border Collie (in our opinion) mix, B.D. is the big giant (we think) German Shepherd/Lab combo, and Edie APPEARS to the naked eye to be pretty much a Chocolate Lab. Because we're idiots with too much time on our hands and (it would seem) too much money backing up in our checking account, we saw a catalog offering test kits for testing doggie DNA and we promptly ordered off for three of them, anxious for some unknowable reason to discern the actual ancestry of our cuddly mongrels. As if it matters— they're adorable, they love us wildly, and they provide endless entertainment. Who cares where they came from? They're here and they're Perfect.

It took us a while after we received the test kits to get around to actually doing the cheek swabs on our wild heathen bunch, but we finally did it and dutifully packaged them back up and returned them to the "lab."

I say "lab" because what we got back from them would (to our minds) indicate something more along the lines of some dude with a book of dog breeds doing the "old blindfolded open-to-random-pages-and-point technique" of "testing" our mutts' DNA. In this case, DNA would actually stand for "**D**on't really **N**eed **A** lab for this!" Suffice it to say, we were less than impressed with the "results" of the "tests."

I ran a contest on all three of my Facebook pages with photos of the three dawgs and had people guess the breeds of each. People postulated that the pups could have any number of possible parents—including my seester's dead ex-husband, who was admittedly somewhat of a hound—but nobody got anywhere close to guessing what our "lab" results claim.

OK, just picture B.D. He's huge, in every way: tall, barrel-chested, legs like tree trunks, big ole feet, long upright tail like a brush, massive head, thundering bark. He's a big, black, lumbering giant of a dog is what he is. Imagine a black Shetland pony that barks.

So imagine our UTTER surprise when we eagerly ripped open our "results" packet from the "lab" and discovered that the "tests" revealed that B.D.'s number-one ancestor is none other than the West Highland WHITE TERRIER. Google that dog and check it out. You'll see tiny. You'll see snowy white. You can surely imagine the high-pitched yap that goes with those short little legs and stubby tail. We have not shared this with B.D. As far as he's concerned, we adopted him and WE are his parents and we think it best to leave him with that notion.

Maybe there are actual doggie DNA labs out there somewhere that can actually tell you the ancestry of your beloved fur babies, but we're pretty sure we wasted valuable money and dog spit—both of which could have been better spent on DOG TREATS.

This big pile of unconditional love does interfere with the one thing on my Bucket List. I suppose if there is only one thing, it can't really be called a "list." I just have one thing in my Bucket— one unfulfilled wish or dream, if you will. I just want to sit on my back porch and do NOTHING and that is not working out at ALL and these dogs are to blame.

This is quite a hairy problem I'm facing—literally. You have never seen so much hair in your life. I'm telling you, with these three dogs, PLUS three CATS, in the house, there is not this much hair in the First Pentecostal Church and Wig World, combined.

All six of these animals should be egg-bald, as much hair as I vacuum up every day. And trust me when I tell you, I am SO NOT a clean freak—I would never DREAM of vacuuming every day under "normal" circumstances. But here's the kicker: Five minutes after I put the Dyson away, I walk through the den and I see them; there are drifts of hair under the table, wafting gently to and fro in the breeze from the ceiling fan, and the casual observer would swear the house had not been swept in a month.

How is it they can lose so MUCH hair, but still have so much on their bodies? Is there any kind of market for this stuff? If there is, please let me know. I may never write another word; I'll just make my living peddling hair. I may get rich yet.

DOGdog is Love

We're big on adoptions in our family—babies, animals, causes— you name it, we're for it. My mama and her sister were adopted. The Cutest Boy in the World and The Cutest Sister in the World were adopted. TCBITW and I adopted Sostie. But then, one day, we found that WE OURSELVES had been adopted by B.D., with no advance notice and very little ceremony. It's always surprising when that happens. You walk outside one morning to get the paper and a New Guy follows you back inside and never leaves. We didn't so much adopt Edie as STEAL her from Bailey.

And now it came to pass that TCBITW's parents, The Cutest Mama in the World and The Cutest Daddy in the World, were adopted. Clearly, they were specifically selected for this honor after great deliberation because they live on the side of a mountain several miles past the center of nowhere. It is not easy to find them is what I'm telling you, and yet, this four-legged GPS homed in on them—and made himself AT home.

They feigned resistance, initially—Mom blaming the dog's continued presence on Dad when he was out of earshot and Dad returning the favor when Mom was in the next room. Neither of them would admit to the slightest bit of growing fondness or even interest in the mutt, but both insisted that the other one was secretly feeding and petting "her."

Oh yeah, in the beginning, they both constantly referred to the dog as a female—in spite of the fact that "she" required neutering shortly after they decided they were definitely NOT going to keep "her."

And yes, The Dog We Are Definitely Not Keeping has now been taken to the vet—regularly. AND she(he) was given the most sacred name from the childhood of TCBITW—the name of his "lovey," the 45-year-old stuffed POODLE, which has no remaining hair and the remnant of what clearly was once a fancy nylon net HAT on its head (haven't given him much ribbing about THAT!)—"DOG-DOG." The Dog We Are Definitely NOT KEEPING, even though we have taken him to the vet (regularly) and bought collars and leashes and beds and crates and ICE CREAM for—we are DEFINITELY NOT KEEPING THIS DOG—is named "Dog-Dog" and it's embroidered on the collar that she(he) will, I suppose, be wearing when she(he) is finally successfully run off the premises. Uh-huh.

I told Mom they had been adopted and that there was nothing they could do about it. She begged to differ—or at least she insisted that This Dog We Are Definitely NOT KEEPING will not EVER set any of those four feet INSIDE the house. No, ma'am. Nosireebobtailcat. On the porch will be good enough for This Dog We Are Definitely NOT KEEPING. On the porch, in the crate—with the down bed and several blankets—will do just fine, especially since WE'RE NOT KEEPING HER(him). "But, Mom," I said, "HE'S KEEPING YOU, and where's Dad, anyway?" Out walking Dog-Dog.

When I called to check on Dog-Dog's progress after her(his) neutering surgery, Mom reported that she(he) was doing fine—and I quote, "BUT SHE STILL WON'T COME IN THE HOUSE! We even left the storm door propped open and put the ice cream down just inside, and she just got it and took it outside." (Bwahahaha! "Outside dog," my hind leg! I'm betting Dog-Dog is sleeping IN the bed with them by the time you read this.)

I told Mom I guessed they hadn't really counted on having another baby at this point in their lives—but apparently God and Dog-Dog knew better. How wonderful it is when someone PICKS US to love? That's the wonder of adoption—Being Chosen.

Gloom, Despair, and Agony on... Thee and Me

*U*sually followed by "deep dark depression, excessive misery"—all words from one of the inimitable *Hee-Haw* theme songs. There were lots of verses—mostly dealing with the many and varied ways we can and do humiliate ourownselfs as we traverse the pothole-ridden roads of life. Somehow, someway, it happens to us all, and it's best to have a Snappy Comeback ready, if at all possible. Let us dredge up a few samples for consideration and dissection.

Can't very well tell off on other folks and spare myownself, so here you go, here's something REEEALLY stupid I did—not so very long ago. I enjoy cooking and I'm not too bad at it, although it must be said that I am constitutionally incapable of producing anything Pretty. The ONLY thing I ever made in my EN-tire life that turned out gorgeous is my daughter. That holds true no matter what the medium: I cannot draw or paint, cannot arrange flowers or table settings, cannot pleasingly decorate either my surroundings or myself, my gift-wrapping ineptitude is legendary, and I cannot cook anything that "presents" well. It will taste good, but you'll have to taste it on a leap of faith because it will look like absolute crap.

Being thoroughly and happily Southern, I mastered "gravy" at an early age. There is hardly anything in life that cannot be improved by gobs of gravy. So, one night, not so very long ago, I was cooking supper, and gravy was going to be required. Into a boiler I poured the liquid from whatever the meat du jour was—I can't recall ALL the details, but one very important one was that the sauce contained some incarnation of vinegar.

As the pot heated up, I reached for my yellow box of cornstarch, dumped a few tablespoons of the white powder into a cup, added enough cold water to dissolve it, and set it on the counter while I stirred the pot, and decided it was hot enough. In goes the cornstarch mixture, and to my everlasting surprise, the entire contents of the pan immediately leapt straight up and out directly at me, cascading in a veritable fountain of gravy, all over the stove top and the surrounding counters, flowing gushingly down the front of the cabinets and onto the floor in a rapidly widening pool in which I stood, bewildered—all in the span of a single nanosecond. I seem to recall saying something to the effect of "WHAT THE FUCK?"—repeatedly, for some moments, that being the only remotely pertinent comment I could come up with under the circumstances. It took quite some time to restore order—largely because it was several minutes before I could manage any reaction at all beyond the aforementioned "What the fuck?" And actually, it was The Cutest Boy in the World who sprang into action and full-mop-mode as I stood there repeating my useless profanity over and over, until finally I tore my gaze away from the inundatory au jus and saw in the cabinet before me not one but TWO—very different—yellow boxes. One containing the cornstarch that I had INTENDED to use and the other containing the BAKING SODA that I actually DID use, thus recreating everybody's favorite third-grade science fair project—the vinegar and baking soda VOLCANO. So, I've made a complete mess of the kitchen and an even more complete fool of myownself, but—grave insult to grievous injury—now there was NO GRAVY. Agony.

My seester Judy remembers well her first week of work and her very first plunge into the pool of the Gainfully Employed—at the Hinds County, Mississippi, Sheriff's Department. Whatever task she'd been hired to perform was clearly under-stimulating, because as the afternoon wore on, her interest and energy levels were sorely flagging. She had started the morning with eyes sufficiently bright and tail adequately bushy, I suppose, but shortly after lunch, she found her chin migrating to her palm in a propped, but still mostly upright position. Before afternoon break time, her cheek had moved to her arm, which was stretched over the desktop, and within minutes of that relocation, her bright blue eyes, which had been struggling to read the papers that were now only an inch or so from the tip of her nose, were completely sheathed in their lids, her mouth was agape with drool, and soft snores were escaping, plus she was in danger of sliding completely off her chair.

She was spared that final mortification of smacking onto the cool linoleum like a large dropped ham, as her boss happened upon the Van Winklette and roused her. It wasn't a tricky discovery to make—Judy certainly didn't have an office and the cubicle had not yet been invented. She was out in the middle of a room with several rows of desks containing other supposedly busy high school students. Personally, I think the only thing keeping them awake was their hilarity at her upcoming predicament—which, given the situation, promised to come up pretty quick-like. The moment the boss walked out of his office and looked over the sea of worker bees, that one who looked more slug than beelike was pretty easy to spot. Sore thumb, turd in a punch bowl, RuPaul at a NASCAR race—select your simile—Sleeping Beauty stuck out and was summarily roused from her slumbers. She awoke to a level of mortification not heretofore experienced, surrounded as she was by her wide-awake coworkers, finding herself totally bereft of anything like plausible deniability, nor was there any readily apparent way to shift the blame to anyone else—although it must be admitted that her suddenly alert brain did fly first to the one and, finding nothing useable there, fled rapidly on to the next but equally empty bucket.

She was simply Caught and she found the sensation to be singularly unpleasant at best.

OK, moving on from high school humiliation to some High-Falutin' Hollywood Humbling. (Were you aware that one cannot simply do a basic falute? They only come in "high," for some reason.) See the brilliant, young, newly minted television producer, Randall Wallace.

OK, lemme backtrack a little bit here and explain, for the uninitiated and/or under-rock dwellers, that Randall Wallace is currently a Very Big Deal in Hollywood, and actually, in the world at large. The man has written and/or directed a slew of films you know and love—*We Were Soldiers, Man in the Iron Mask, Pearl Harbor,* and most recently, *Secretariat.* He also stumbled around and somehow wrote *Braveheart,* for crying out loud—which means he's practically a god in Guyworld, for sure. But at our house? Nah, not so much. He's just Randy at Coochie Sprangs. And how did he come to ever wind up at our house? That would be a very good question.

It was on September 11, 2004, and he and I had never met at this point, but we were both speaking at the Southern

Independent Booksellers Association (now "Alliance") annual meeting in Atlanta. Mr. Wallace was promoting his newest book, *Love and Honor*, and I was promoting *The Sweet Potato Queens' Field Guide to Men: Every Man I Love Is Either Married, Gay, or Dead*. Randy spoke first and he's a very powerful speaker. Not only was it 9/11—a terrible day for all of us forever—it was also the third anniversary of the death of his father, and well, his emotions just got the better of him, and while he didn't actually break down and bawl or anything, there was a definite break in his rhythm with some tears and a catch or two in his voice. If I were talking about anybody else, I'd say it would qualify as a "snivel," but at this point in our relationship, I know Randy well enough to know that he would bow up big time at that term, so I'll refrain. (Truth be told, he will prolly take issue with the way I did tell that. And you know what? We will just let him tell it however he wants to in HIS book.) HOWEVER, there was plenty enough emoting going on; that, coupled with his already moving words, and the whole room was SOBBING by the time he finished.

When it was MY turn to speak. Oh yay.

As he made his way back to his seat and they began introducing me, I was sitting there going, *Oh fuck ME. This is going to be a DISASTER. Even I'M crying!* But there was nothing for it but to get on up there and do my best to (a) stop sniveling myownself and (b) try to get a chortle outta this crowd.

I lumbered up onstage and took command of the podium. Looking out at all the tear-stained faces and struggling to be heard over the sound of all the nose-blowing, I said, "WELL! I am, in fact, Jill Conner Browne, THE Sweet Potato Queen, and for those of you who are not familiar with me and my work, let me tell you THIS: Of all the people here who DO know me and my work, HALF of them are PRAYING that I don't say "fuck" or "blow job" and the other half is HOPING just as hard that I DO."

I can tell you, without fear of exaggeration, the room did, as they say, explode, and over all the ruckus, what could be VERY CLEARLY HEARD was the HOWLING laugh of one Mr. Randall Wallace. I have seldom heard anybody laugh quite that loudly—or for as long—to the point that he, once again, became the focal point in the room as we all turned to watch to see if he would fall off his chair and/or wet himself. And, of course, that kind of laughter IS totally contagious, so within seconds, the whole room exploded AGAIN over his laughing, and I really coulda just gone on back to my seat—clearly, My Work HERE Was Done—but by and by, he did calm down, as did the rest of 'em, and I finished my little part.

When it was over, my tablemate Jill Flaxman said, "LOOK at the WOMEN lined up to meet Randall Wallace!" Seriously, every woman in the room was in a big, long line, snaking around the room, waiting to fawn over him. I assured Jill that—oh yes, ma'am—we, too, were getting in that very line, and I hauled her over there with me. It prolly took the better part of an HOUR to get within earshot of Himself, and as we neared The Presence, the little girls who were directly in front of us all but fell at his feet, and you never heard such gushing and gooing. They said, "OH! MR. WALLACE, you just really TOUCHED US!" And I can see he is doing his dead level best at Appearing Humble— but, clearly, he's beaming like halogen headlights—and since, at 6'3" or so in the heels I was wearing, I could look right over the tops of their sweet little heads, I caught his eye after the "you just really TOUCHED US" line and said to him, "And we want you to TOUCH US, TOO—and WE'LL SHOW YOU WHERE!"

So again with the howling laughter he goes—totally spoiling The Moment with the little worshippers. (But I did him a favor, really. They were not so young as to send him to prison, but definitely young enough to be a health hazard for him.) So, off they went, and from that moment on, Randall Wallace and I have been pretty much Best Buds. We talk on the phone every single day and he is a regular at the parade each year and also at our home, Coochie Sprangs.

The first time Randy came to visit our home was actually during our move from our lovely home in the lovely Dinsmor subdivision out to what we had initially bought to be a "weekender"—our house at Coochie Sprangs. I picked him up at the airport—he's out at the curb, looking very handsome and Hollywood, and I am, as pretty much always, in rags and Stage 4 dishevelment—and I whisk him off to our erstwhile lovely Dinsmor home, where he gets to meet, for the first time, my husband Kyle, The Cutest Boy in the World, who is equally nasty and in tattered overalls. Kyle's first words to him after the introduction are, "Go put your shit in the house and come on—I'm hauling this crap to the dump!"

So, on his first visit to Mississippi and to our home, we took Randall Wallace, writer, director, producer, Hollywood honcho of the first water, to the Madison County Landfill—and the tone was set for future reference. Kyle dubbed him "Rando, Dump Commando."

So, that's how we know Randall Wallace, and NOW, here's one of my favorite stories that he tells on himself—it clearly demonstrates that Karma is watching us all the damn time, so it's best to fly as low as possible.

Randall Wallace's first act, upon learning he had just been tasked with the production of his very first TV show—and a struggling TV show, at that—was to go out and buy himself one of those cords to attach to his ubiquitous Hollywood sunglasses so that when Coolness was called for, he could respond by either whipping his shades off or on, and having spent some time in LaLa Land, he already knew which to do when, so he was ahead of the game. Or so he thought.

The program Randy was given was struggling and everybody involved was unhappy for one reason or another and none so much as the star who, as luck would have it, was a still-stunning former Miss Universe. Poor Randy, hate it for him, bless his heart.

So, his plan (now that he had his Hotshot Hollywood Producer Sunglasses AND Neck Strap) was to approach Missy Universe, wearing his shades, and say, "I'm Randall Wallace. I'm the new producer and I know you're unhappy and I know what to do about it"—whipping OFF the shades here—"You haven't been given enough to do and I am going to change all that, so from now on, if you have any problems, you just come to ME." And at this point, he figgered he would whip the shades back ON and stride away, exuding all the power and confidence he was gifted with at birth, plus whatever came attached to the producer's office, chair, and parking space.

So, he did all that—and it all went according to plan, as they say, UNTIL. See, somewhere during the time between the Whip OFF and the Whip ON, in his brief conversation with the buxom beauty, he had been somewhat bumfuzzled by both her beauty and her bux, and that caused him to commence fiddling nervously with his tie; thus, unbeknownst to him, it had become entangled with his Hotshot Hollywood Producer Sunglasses Neck Strap. The result being that when he performed the Whip ON, his tie got whipped along with the shades so that he was now wearing his Hotshot Hollywood Producer Sunshades, but the tail of his tie was inside 'em and it was hanging down over his nose, thereby totally tearing asunder any trace of Hotshottedness, not to mention credibility. We won't even THINK about his poor pitiful pride. I will say this about that, though: Since it always seems to prance out in front of us before we fall off in a big hole, it's a good thing we've got SO MUCH of it, isn't it? Maybe it makes for a softer landing.

On occasion, humiliation and/or embarrassment come to us through no fault of our own—except for maybe the company we choose to keep.

My dear, dear friend Blanche is something of a dandy—or whatever the girl version is of that. While I will, without a moment's thought or hesitation, go pretty much anywhere looking like the dog's dinner, if Clairol and Maybelline went belly-up, Baby Girl would sit in her house and starve to death before she'd run to the Kroger without her roots touched up and her mascara on. I might have on a 35-year-old pair of nearly crotchless Umbro shorts, a big giant T-shirt (stains optional), hair (liberally streaked with gray) in a ratty ponytail, and Merrell sandals that the dog chewed on, yet feel perfectly comfortable running errands to just about anyplace I can think of at the moment. But if she's got to go to the POST OFFICE, even, Miss B is gonna have that hair whipped, that makeup on, AND if it's summertime, she is gonna be head to toe in starched linen that will put your eyes out it's so white. Her shoes will have heels at least four inches tall and her sunglasses will be big enough to shade the patio. Our deep and lifelong friendship is conducted primarily on the telephone or at one of our houses because, well, obviously, we can't really go out anywhere together.

SO, Miss Fancy Pants Blanche is all duded up, naturally, and on a long flight with her very own Cutest Boy in the World, Jim. It's kind of a longish flight and she has had herself a most excellent nap for the duration. He has awakened her gently and sweetly before the landing and helped her gather up all her "supplies." As you might imagine, Blanche requires an arsenal of accoutrements if she's going to be away from home base for any length of time. Truth be told, her plane seat could be mistaken for a corner of her bedroom at home—so much crap has she hauled with her on the plane and spread out around her (and Jim). Pillows, blankets, slippers, eye masks—she's got everything but a cozy fireplace in front of which to curl up.

They get everything reined in and repacked just in time for her to fumble for her lipstick (red-red-red, of course) and dab some on (without benefit of a mirror—but she's well practiced at this) before it was their turn to exit the aircraft. It seemed to Blanche that the flight crew was perhaps a tad more friendly than usual as she passed them, smiling and thanking them all profusely for their kind attentions during the flight—but she mostly took that as her due and didn't dwell on it.

As they made their way down the Jetway and through the terminal, however, she noticed that nearly everybody they passed was smiling and nodding at them. Now, they do make a striking pair, Jim being every bit as meticulous about his toilette as she, but of course, Blanche thought that the throngs were surely responding favorably to her particularly darling outfit and adorable shoes. The prancing was just really reaching its zenith when she noticed that they were approaching a ladies' room and she thought she might as well duck in there for a moment, use the facilities, and do a proper touch-up to her hair and makeup—just to make sure that she was, in fact, 100 percent as Cute as Possible.

The big grins continued unabated from passersby as she made her way to the line in the ladies' room. Post-pee, she was rifling through her purse for her brush and makeup bag as she approached the sink—and the MIRROR. Brush in hand, she looked up at her own reflection, studying first the condition of her coiffure, but something caught her eye.

There was Something Amiss, Something Different about the face she had had first thing that morning—the one that she had oh so carefully and artfully applied makeup to, worn out to the car, to the airport, and onto the plane—and the face that was looking back at her from the mirror at this moment. Whole 'nuther face in there. THIS face did not look like Blanche at all; it actually looked remarkably like Sammy—HER CAT.

While Blanche slept the sleep of the Just (and the Unsuspecting), happily nestled on her big, strong, handsome husband's broad shoulder, HE took that opportunity to take pen in hand and adorn her beautiful, peaceful, trusting little face with long blue whiskers, freckles, and a perfect little blue kitty-cat nose.

Queen Lora and her "good" friend were guests at a Tupperware/Sex Toy party. (Please note the "/" between those. The hostess was offering both food storage ware AND tools of titillation, and the products were from decidedly different manufacturers. Just so we're clear.) OK, so at the time, Lora was manless and her "good" friend expressed her totally unsolicited opinion that what Lora needed was that very fine-looking RABBIT—with the rotating colored balls and vibrating tongue and all. As a matter of fact, "G"F went so far as to suggest that Lori should not even bother with the formality of placing an order for one but prodded her to simply filch the festive floor model. Our Lora demurred on all fronts and "G"F finally gave up and wandered off in search of additional cocktails and snacks.

By and by, Lora left, having ordered lots of Tupperware (and ONLY Tupperware), and being low on fuel, she whipped into her favorite gas station—which was made her favorite by the constant presence of the cutest little attendant boy ever seen in those parts. As she prepared to pay, she naturally opened her purse, and what do you reckon was sitting there, bigger'n Dallas, smack in the top of her wide-open purse, staring at her and the cutest little attendant boy ever? It was, of course, Mr. Rabbit, obviously planted there (with the Best Intentions) by that very "good" friend.

There was no pretending, for either of them, that they didn't SEE Mr. Rabbit—although it was plain that both were giving it their best shot for a fairly long and incredibly awkward moment. That moment was extended and exacerbated by the realization in the subsequent moment that Lora's wallet was underneath Mr. Rabbit's rotating balls and there was simply no way to extricate the funds for the fuel without first extracting Mr. Rabbit.

And THAT is how and why Lora came to find a NEW favorite gas station.

How best to survive a spell in the spotlight that is not of our choosing? Laughing at ourownselfs, especially at our own extreme discomfort and/or embarrassment, is not the easiest thing in the world, but I reckon it's a sight easier than spontaneous evaporation, which would, naturally, be our first choice. I recovered fairly quickly—after all, I had The Cutest Boy in the World to clean up after me and it was hardly the first stupid thing he'd ever seen me do. The only really bad part of that was, as I said, NO GRAVY. Sad but survivable, at least in isolated incidences.

In Judy's case, "Damsel Dozing on the Department's Dime," if she could have willed herself to drop dead on the spot, I think she might have given it a shot—especially since she was the only summer intern from Provine High School and all the others were from crosstown rival Murrah. Even today, some 40 years later, she feels certain that they could and should have awakened her before the boss caught her, and she is equally sure that they would have done it for One of Their Own. She doesn't remember a single one of them, and yet, nearly half a century later, she's still convinced "they did it on purpose because she was from Provine."

I hope you didn't think I was going to reference my seester as a role model in this area; grudge-holding is her hobby, she's a Life Master (just like in Bridge, only crabby and without cards), and last time I checked, she was the Louisiana state champion for several years running—amid some pretty stiff competition. But I think our takeaway from her experience is that you absolutely cannot sleep on the job at work until you have your own office to do it in.

It must be acknowledged that the shameful stories I shared about myself and my seester Judy are pretty innocuous. These should not lead the reader to think that we have led or are leading smart, shame-free lives. No sirree, we are way stupid and I COULD prove it, but this is my book, and if I prefer to paint myself favorably, it's certainly my right. I am still more than a little terrified of my big seester, and thus, I chose the tamest tale ever told about her. (You should know that I HAVE told you any number of DOOZIES on her, but due to the aforementioned terror, I changed her name. Snort!)

As for Mr. Wallace, he seems to have snapped back pretty well; I mean, the guy wrote *Braveheart* and wrote and directed scads of other fabulous films, he writes books and songs, he's single and gorgeous—he's fucking FINE, OK? His producer pride was pruned back considerably early on and it was prolly for the best—truth be told, he needs to revisit them lower pegs every now and then, lest he become, as my daddy used to say, "biggity-speckled." I told him just today, in fact, in reference to something or other, that I thought he needed to "remember who you ARE," while I assured him that I consider it one of my most important life-callings to make certain that he remember "who he ISN'T!" It is one of my more entertaining vocations, I don't mind telling you.

As for the hapless Blanche, whose only "mistake" was falling in love with that man, we all know what happens when we are in such company—otherwise known as "sleeping with dogs"—and yet, we are continually surprised by the fleas. Jim Richardson is a bad, bad dog, to be sure, but Blanche has always been pretty tickled by her "fleabites." Lucky for him, he's darlin'.

Ahhh, Queen Lora—her lessons were several and varied. First of all, she learned to always be on guard around that "good" friend if there was any possibility of alcohol and sex toys being in the room. She learned that if attending a sex toy party, one should carry either a purse too tiny to accommodate a Rabbit or large enough to obscure one. And last, but most assuredly not least, she learned that Mr. Rabbit is a very fine product.

If you can laugh at the misery of any of the aforementioned individuals, then you may imagine that WE would find YOUR embarrassing tales equally hysterical. So maybe that's how it all evens out—you laugh at mine, I laugh at yours, and we all strive to find some more important things to take more seriously than ourselves.

Tough Times, Tight Money

The following presents a multifaceted demonstration regarding two of our most basic human needs—Fun and Revenge—and it shows that both can be achieved with literally no budget whatsoever.

When times are tough and money is tight, prudent people pare their budgets, and dollars designated for entertainment are likely to be the first ones pruned—and this, at a time when it is probably most important that we have ample divertissements from our daily tasks and/or troubles. We may not readily embrace that concept—especially if we're cruising the "Recipes Under $5" website every day and cooking with packets of soy and barbecue sauce from China Belle and Wendy's. It's all well and good to accept that actual university studies have proven that PLAY is AS important to our health and well-being as food, clothing, and shelter, but it's less likely to be given the top billing it deserves if the lone peanut butter jar is sitting on empty. Personally, not a lot is funny to me if my stomach is growling—hence the adage "FAT and happy," yes? And sure, I've heard the weight-loss gurus spouting their "nothing tastes as good as being thin feels" mantra, and as I've said before—BULLSHIT. The times in my life when I have been thin, I enjoyed it well enough, but trust me, PLENTY of stuff tastes WAY better than being thin feels. For that matter, come to think of it, FEELING FULL FEELS better than being thin does.

So, right after we eat, it's time for laughs, and the worse our situation is, the more we need it. My dear departed daddy was some kind of world champeen at cooking up a big pile of fun with next to no ingredients, one of the few, if any, benefits of having grown up rich in family but cash-strapped. He could make a little machine that would crawl across the floor using only an empty thread spool, a skinny nail, a wooden match, and a rubber band. (These can no longer be made because spools aren't made of wood anymore and the cheap plastic they use for them now is too lightweight—the thing just flies up in the air one time and is done. Sigh.)

I grew up with a bunch of boys—Tommy, Davee, Timmy, and Harry—and we were entertained for WEEKS one summer when Daddy made us each what he called a FART MACHINE, using a section of a wire coat hanger, two rubber bands, and a washer. The rubber bands ran between the ends of the wire, and the washer was in the center of the bands. You would twist the washer until the rubber bands were coiled up as tightly as possible, then put the device under one of your butt cheeks. To operate it required only that one lean to one side, slightly lifting that cheek, which would allow the washer to spin rapidly on the rubber bands, creating a most delightfully authentic and impressively loud fart noise. It didn't hurt that the entire world was upholstered in Naugahyde back then. Yes, it was a simple time—with furniture that could be wiped down with a sponge AND greatly enhanced the sounds of flatulence, whether real or fabricated.

As you may recall from my earlier books, my daddy was a bit of a scatological scamp. "Funny as shit" seems to have been coined with him in mind, although "funny WITH" might be even more apropos. He had a knack, what can I say?

There was no such thing as "playground equipment" in rural Attala County, Mississippi, in the 1920s when Daddy was growing up. Instead, there was an abundance of basic ingenuity and also possibly an excess of spunk. The three Conner sisters—Alma, Moggie, and Lottie—and their younger brother John Albert (the baby brother Bub was as yet too young for this particular caper) worked diligently to craft for themselves a marvelous slide. This was accomplished by simply acquiring (pilfering) a very long and wide plank, which they leaned up against the roof of the barn. All they had to do was climb the tree next to the barn, hop over to the roof, sit on the board, and WHOOSH down for a thrilling ride.

Of course, the whooshing was not possible on the plank when they first got it. If one had attempted to whoosh on it in its original condition, one would have been rewarded with a hiney full of splinters. The getting of the board and the leaning of it against the barn were not the ingenious part of this deal; it was the creation of the Whoosh Factor that was brilliant.

At a time when Santa was known for bringing little more than an orange and new pair of socks, the Conner children had experienced a Christmas bonanza in receiving a box of eight Crayola crayons—each. This was riches beyond glory. They had in their collective possession 32 crayons, which, even by summer, had scarcely been used—so prized were they by the children. Not a single one had even been broken yet.

Childish imaginations were fired up. What mere mortals saw as an ordinary board, this gang saw as a potential rocket ride—lacking only in lubricity to send them flying down its slope. And so, the Crayolas were sacrificed to the slide. The four of them labored tirelessly for days and days, coloring every inch of the plank until half of the precious waxy crayons were worn to mere nubs and the slide was shiny and slick.

Every day, all summer, as soon as everybody's chores were completed, the slide provided hours of fun for the crew. They happily took turns, never quarrelling over who went first or anything—each just happy when their turn came. Any adult observing would have thought this was surely Utopia—the kids had made it all by themselves at no cost and they were playing on it all afternoon, with no supervision required. How often has that even happened in the world?

So, you just KNOW there's trouble brewing, right? This is just going too well. It's like watching a horror movie and the heroine/victim starts looking in the dang mirror. You KNOW, beyond question, any second now, the MONSTER'S face is gonna pop up right beside hers in there.

By and by, Daddy's big sister Moggie did something that caused him to feel an overwhelming desire for retribution and revenge. What She Did has been lost to the ages, but What He Did is still percolating right along in infamy. He would tell this as if it were the Most Logical Thing Ever—like, what else WOULD one do in such a case? Who WOULDN'T do this? You've got "A," and it is therefore followed by the requisite "B."

Daddy said that Moggie did (whatever it was), and "so, what I did was, I went in the barn and shit in a bag." Just like THAT, it made PERFECT SENSE. Oh? She did that? So, then what happened? Did you go in the barn and shit in a bag? Well, DUH, ye-ah!

He went in the barn and defecated into a paper sack, and then he skulked around with it in the general vicinity of the slide (which, as you recall, was leaning against the barn, so he was not required to transport this "package" over much distance). The sisters, including the dastardly Moggie, had forgotten whatever her grave transgression had been, and in gleeful innocence, they foolishly paid no mind to their little brother, who, bag in hand, was standing idly beside the barn as they took turn after turn on the slide.

Moggie, breathless with exertion from climbing the tree repeatedly, paused for a moment just before taking her place on the slick plank. The next scene unfolded as if in slow motion, although it was all over in mere seconds. Past the point of no return in her descent, she looked down to see her brother, my daddy, grinning at her with a demonic gleam in his eyes as he hurled his smelly sack onto the slide, where it exploded its dreadful contents directly in her unavoidable path, and through it she did slide. And all the arm and leg flailing she performed in panic, as the full import of what was befalling and befouling her became apparent, availed nothing except additional guffawing on the part of the perpetrator. It must be told that the perp was swiftly caught and soundly switched, after which he was forced to scour and re-crayon the slide, and he lost slide privileges for the remainder of the summer. It must also be told, however, that he was never repentant. No matter how severe his punishment, they could never take from him the sight of her freaked-out face as she realized that payback was, indeed, hell, and it also stunk to high heaven, but it didn't necessarily cost much at all. "Vengeance is mine," saith the mean-ass little boy.

≈≈≈

Pleasant Diversion for a Late Summer's Eve

≈≈≈

*I*n trying times, such as the ones we currently find ourselves mired in the middle of, one wants a distraction from one's troubles, and I find it most helpful to plan and engage in a pleasant outing or two with close and like-minded friends. Or you could go gator huntin'.

What follows are my personal journal entries describing how it was that we came to do such a thing. To this day, however, I really can offer no suitable explanation as to WHY.

AUGUST 2005

Today in Mississippi it is, as they say, hot as the hammered-down hinges of you-know-where and trying not to sweat to death is Job 1 for most of us, but in a matter of weeks, as the days grow shorter and at least a little bit cooler, we'll detect a decided spring in the step of a small group of our citizens. This happy bunch would be the "winners" in the latest lottery offered by the state. Yes, it is alligator-hunting time down South and a randomly selected fifty (50) of our own will be granted permission to grab themselves an alligator.

The news of this stellar "opportunity" rendered me temporarily agog and the announced rules of the state-sponsored "harvest" did little to un-gog me. It seems that the gator must be at least 4 feet long and it must be captured alive and restrained "in a manner that the alligator is controlled." Hmmm. All of the acceptable restraining methods clearly put the hunter in extremely close proximity to the beasty. I didn't dwell on the sanctioned means for "dispatching" the animal—is it no longer PC to call it "killing"?—except to note with interest that all firearms are required to be cased and unloaded until the restraining maneuvers are completed. All of this adds up in my mind to Advantage: Alligator. Sounds fair enough to me.

I immediately entered the lottery, hoping to win just to see for myself people who are dying (quite possibly literally) to go out in the dark and try to tie up an alligator. (The randomness of the lottery concept seems boring to me. What an excellent pageant opportunity this would be—complete with mandatory talent, swimsuit, and interview competitions. And then we would truly know that only the Best were selected. But as usual, nobody asked my opinion.)

To prepare myself for a win, I went online and I must admit to being somewhat surprised to learn that the popularity for this particular fool's errand is not restricted to the South. As of August 18 of this year, there was a giant alligator loose in a Los Angeles lake and the city had hired a "gator wrangler" to capture (but not "dispatch") the reptile. Apparently the wrangler is so giddy over his unbelievable good fortune at landing this gig he's said if he can't land the gator, his services are free.

At the time of this writing, his fruitless efforts had included the use of fishing nets, floured tortillas, and a squad of herpetologists armed only with raw chickens and electrical tape. At one point, the dauntless wrangler waded around, neck deep, using his own body as bait and was utterly rejected by the alligator. Little wonder *that a crowd of gator supporters gathered.* [Note: There was never a follow-up to that story that I could find, so I have no idea what became of either the gator or his hunter. Sorry.]

Our state-sponsored alligator harvest purports to be managing the burgeoning size of the gator population. I'm thinking it's more of a veiled attempt at thinning the human gene pool.

Oh, and by the way, I did not "win."

OK, so that was way back in 2005—WAY before the History Channel even THOUGHT about *Swamp People*. Moving ahead a few years now—all this time and STILL no better sense, it seems.

SEPTEMBER 2009

By the time anyone reads this, I will have been on my first (and one can only hope, last) gator hunt. Yep, after all these years, the lottery gods smiled on us (or spat on us, depending on your point of view), and we "won" a permit that will allow us the great and glorious "privilege" of going out, from 6 p.m. one night until 8 a.m. the following morning—on TWO consecutive evenings—in a small boat, unarmed, to see if we can't hunt us up some live alligators to mess around with.

Whee.

Yes, indeed, on our Ship of Fools, we will embark in darkness and head up the inky waters of the Pearl River, no doubt covered head to toe in a solid mass of mosquitoes, with actual AIRCRAFT LANDING LIGHTS strapped to our HEADS (and hooked up to car batteries), to find the appropriate gator for our initial encounter. The first one must be, according to the rules, a "runt," of 4 to 7 feet in length. Now, let me just go on record as saying that I don't see how anything that's as big as I am can seriously be considered to be a "runt" in any litter. But them's the rules—and obviously, I wasn't consulted on them. So, first, we must find and subdue us a "runt." Only THEN are we allowed to go for a big 'un. Again, whee.

This will involve getting wet—I don't see any way around it. And I don't like water I can't see through in the DAYTIME—we're talking PITCH-BLACK NIGHT HERE and I can already feel the heebies and the jeebies running up and down my spine. Somehow, we have got to get this "runt" into the boat WITH US and tie him up. I am at a loss as to how this might be accomplished without some human body part being snacked on by the intended victim. I myself, while I would admittedly give serious consideration to liposuction, am not at all interested in having any parts—even the fat ones—CHOMPED off and eaten before my very eyes. Nor would I find it particularly entertaining to observe anybody in our party being nibbled away at by a big giant amphibian—whose eyes, by the way, really do glow as red as Rudolf's nose at night. Eww.

Since I've not been able, personally, to come up with an answer to the "WHY" of this whole shenanigan, I've not even begun to address the "HOW" of it. But at some point, if we are to be "successful," I suppose it will be important to figure out HOW to get close enough to a live, fully awake alligator to engage in trying to get him into our boat.

We have been told, by folks who conduct swamp tours in Louisiana, that alligators like marshmallows. Now, doesn't that sound like malarkey to you? Who discovered this and how? Poodles—I know they like poodles—but marshmallows? I just find that hard to swallow, so to speak. I think SOMEBODY is trying to make us look STUPID. AS IF we don't already look like complete morons for signing up for this gig to begin with.

If I, and all my fingers survive, details will follow.

Sure enough, here we are:

LATER IN SEPTEMBER 2009

Since I am typing this myself and not dictating it to someone else, you may assume that I as well as all my digits survived the Great Gator Hunt of '09. I am proud and pleased to report that there were no (0) human casualties recorded, on our boat or any others.

On an earlier hunt—for which I was not in attendance, thank you, God—The Cutest Boy in the World did somehow manage to pull a big, giant treble hook out of the hide of a gator and stick it into his arm, which, as you might imagine, is Not a Good Thing to Do.

Fortunately, one of the other Hunters that night is an anesthesiologist in real life, Dr. Derick Marshall, and so he simply called up the 24-hour pharmacist and asked for the top-rated antibiotic to combat this bacterium with an unpronounceable name 4 miles long. TCBITW, bless his dyslexic heart, was nearly knocked unconscious by the next action of the doc: SPELLING, off the top of his head, the name of the unpronounceable bacterium for the benefit of the apparently confused pharmacist. Said confusion was unacceptable to our doc, who immediately said, "Never mind," hung up, and called the home number of the HEAD of pharmacy at the hospital where he practices. Did I mention it was 3:30 a.m.?

It was not unlike an episode of House, *with the two docs engaged in Deadly Serious Discussion, weighing the pros and cons of the various treatment options available. Once pharm doc was satisfied that the hook had merely come out of the HIDE of the beast and that it had not ever been anywhere near the MOUTH of it, he and our doc were comfortable with the drug selected as Most Likely to Prevent the Necessity of Amputating the Arm of TCBITW.* [I know Kyle's mom will really get a bang out of reading this, since it will be the first she's heard of Kyle's brush with

amputation and/or death by gator poisoning! Hi, Mom! Look!
He still has two hands! YAY! I know it will also be especially
meaningful to her that the gator was successfully captured,
after all—what a relief. I know that would have been her first
question.]

*The following week, when I WAS along for the festivities, we
had one actual HUNT boat—a comparatively small craft where
there were only a total of 4 igmos trying to physically catch live
alligators. The Igmo Hunters were, of course, my own personal
husband, The Cutest Boy in the World; our very own bloodthirsty
Queen TammyLeigh Bailey and her then-fiancé-now-husband,
the equally bloodthirsty Jamie Redmond; and their guide, hunter/
sharpshooter extraordinaire, the inimitable Shambeni Watts of*
Outdoors With Shambeni.

*On the Hunt Boat, there was no food, no alcohol, and most
significant in my opinion, no BATHROOM. The lack of facilities
was of no real concern to the boys on the boat, obviously, since they
can and do pretty much just stand and pee anywhere, anytime the
urge strikes 'em, guys being guys and all. (If Nature had sent them
a Higher Calling, you can bet your ass they'da been hightailing
THEIRS over to the Squealer Boat. No, scratch that, we'da prolly
had to go all the way HOME if one of them had developed an urge
to make umps.) But one woulda thought that Queen TammyLeigh
might be the slightest bit squeamish, if not about peeing in the presence of penis-bearers, most of whom she was not engaged to, then
certainly at the thought of hanging her hind quarters off the side
of a low-riding boat—in the dark, over alligator-infested waters.
Apparently not. Perhaps she was wearing Depends and just not
fessing up to it?*

*The OTHER boat—where I and quite a large party of our
friends gathered—was known as the SQUEALER Boat, with the*

infinitely patient and jovial Captain Victor Watts at the helm. The Squealers were me, our darlin' neighbor Angie Gray, Spud Studs Allen Payne, Little Jeffrey Gross, Charles Jackson, and Scott Caples, along with Queen TammyKatie Werdel, Queen TammyEllyn Weeks, Queen TammyPippa Jackson, and our intrepid videographer Craig St. John. Yes, there is video. (Queen TammyGeorge Ewing was unable to participate, having a prior theatrical engagement. This was a source of irritation to us all, in that we could avail ourselves neither of the pleasure of his company nor his performance. We're still pissed.)

OK, so you've got your choice of Hunt Boat—no food, no bathroom, and a high probability of sharing limited space with a large, live, and deadly amphibian. Or the Squealer Boat—roughly 400 pounds of food (including mounds of perfectly fried catfish that OWS Pro Staffer Trevis Banks and Shambeni hisveryownself cooked up for us on the dock before we boarded, Scott's famous deviled eggs, and a gift from the sweetest woman in the world, Barbara Whitehead, Barbara's Beautiful Cornbread, for which I WILL give you the recipe later); a potty chair zip-tied in a back corner of the double-decker pontoon boat, surrounded by a shower curtain suspended from a hula hoop (for the ultimate in boating pleasure, especially in a swamp in the dark of night, with NO CHANCE WHATSOEVER of being boarded by a gator); PLUS we all had extremely large plush alligator HATS.

We felt the envious eyes of all the other "lottery winners" on us as we pulled out after our Hunt Team. No other hunting boat had a luxury liner full of spectators following THEM and they most certainly did not have a deluxe potty and absolutely no cute outfits with matching hats were to be seen. But then, they also did not have their own videographer on board, so they were not exactly what you would call "camera ready."

We imagined that they were envious. It is remotely possible, I suppose, that they were looking askance at us. We refuse delivery on askance, preferring to interpret any glance from others that is not openly admiring to be envious. It works for us—saves us from any possibility of embarrassment. I recommend it to you.

Food + potty + safety + outfits? The Squealer Boat was DEFINITELY the place to be. But even in the comparative cushy luxury of our big-ass Squealer Boat, the night—well, it did drag on. We ate and we ate and we ate 'til the novelty of that eventually wore off, and by and by, some of us began to feel a bit nappish. One of us, anyway. The one who had left behind in California her two-month-old baby (not to name any names) in order to participate in this little divertissement. That one nodded right on off—which is to say, she, with no preamble or fanfare, simply withdrew quietly into a coma. Given our current circumstances—we were in a moving boat, in a stiff wind, on the water, in the DARK, actively seeking live alligators on their home turf—it was fairly amazing that anybody could just casually doze off, and so we did check regularly, closely, and often to be sure she was still breathing. Although, after a bit, she did begin to emit snores that were soft enough at first but gained respectable volume as the depth of her slumbers progressed. Nobody falls asleep faster or sleeps harder than a new mama who is allowed to sit in one spot without a crying baby for longer than 25 minutes. We do have some nice photos of her as well as some charming video footage. It must be noted that there is little difference between the still shots and the video—since she was, well, still. And not in what would readily appear to be a particularly soporific position. We're still amazed that she didn't slide off onto the deck—it was like she had no bones.

She did wake up when the hurrahs began erupting on the Hunt Boat, indicating that they had a line on their requisite runt for the night. The hurrahs and assorted sanguinary shouts would probably have passed unnoticed by our sleepyhead, but the chorus of spontaneous squeals from our crew could not be ignored or slept through. We sounded like a pack of piglets stuck in a fence.

We had to keep our distance until the beasty was snared and subdued on their boat—and we were cool with that. Well, all except for Allen, who was dancing a jig to get over there and SEE IT. From our vantage point, we could see and hear much thrashing about as the surprisingly strong "runt" was hauled on board.

Once it was on their deck, Captain Victor maneuvered our craft next to the Hunt Boat so that Allen and Little Jeffrey could have their photos made HOLDING the live gator. Truth be told, Little Jeffrey was not dying for this opportunity; he only did it (like he does so many, many things in this life) to please and appease Allen. Not totally satisfied that the quality of the live action shots would be up to his exacting standards, Allen asked Kyle—who is not only The Cutest Boy in the World but also The Most Prepared for Any Possible, Even Remotely Imaginable Potentiality—if there might be an auxiliary light source available to ensure that Allen's gator-holding photos were sharp and well defined.

Well, within a two-second time period, Kyle had leapt from his spot on the Hunt Boat over to the railing of the Squealer Boat, sprung over to the generator he had (unbeknownst to us) deposited in the aft, cranked it up, and flipped a switch, which caused not only our two boats but at least 20 square miles of the river and surrounding areas to be flooded with brilliant, blinding light. Allen got his very clear photos and we all got flash-blind for the next hour and a half.

Allen would have been content to hang out and continue posing bravely with the live gator (which had a few yards of duct tape around his bone-crushing jaws, although he could still send you flying with that tail), but the Hunters were like wild dogs at this point. NOW, runt in hand, they could go after a BIG 'UN and they were all a bit mouth-frothy at the prospect.

Lights were extinguished, leaving us in a dark that was impossibly darker now, lines were cast off, and away they went—in search of Godzilla. Our own adrenaline levels really couldn't compare to that of the would-be assassins, and as we followed their boat at a quiet distance—to avoid spooking the intended prey—the fun began to wear off for us. We felt we had gotten all the good outta this deal that there was to be got. Pippa and Ellyn got cold. That's never good—when the women start to get tired and cold, you just know nothing good will happen after that. Pippa had on Scott's jacket, which amounted to a sleeping bag on her tiny self, and Ellyn looked like a bag lady, wearing, as she was, every other spare piece of clothing available on the boat. All she needed was a shopping cart and half a cigarette.

Allen would have happily joined the Hunt Boat, but they had their legal limit of bodies on the boat and would be penalized for any additional crew members, so he grudgingly agreed to let us all go the hell on home and go to BED. Emphasis on the "grudgingly."

The plucky Hunters stalked around upriver until the permitted hunting time completely expired—around breakfast time for normal people—without bagging a Big 'Un. (Allen was less-than-secretly pleased that he had not missed out on anything but hours of mosquito bites in the dark.)

So, imagine our surprise when, over a YEAR LATER, after the Coochie Sprangs Gator Huntin' Club had made our virgin voyage, we see that the History Channel has launched a new reality show—*Swamp People.* As usual in this life, we were well ahead of the curve.

Naturally, we were instant fans of the show, feeling, as we do, a kinship with Troy and Jacob and alla dem down dere in de swamps, donchu know? We also felt pangs of jealousy at the apparent complete lack of RULES governing their hunts.

THEY get to hunt in broad-ass daylight, they get to set baited hooks for them, and they get to "CHOOOT IT!" right then and there—no trying to "restrain" a 14-foot monster and haul it, live, into the boat with them.

We also have yet to see any of the Swamp People, even the hapless Tommy, try to lure the gators with marshmallows. Even us lowly Squealers are relieved we didn't fall for that.

Ooohhhmmmigod, I'm Never Going Hooomme

I recently read an online article that put forth the idea that the whole Spa (spa-a-h-h-h) Experience has, or at least should be, moved from the realm of Luxury to that of Absolute Life Necessity. No arguments here. We all need to be submerged in hot water, spoken to lovingly, patted dry, and rubbed on—frequently. But, as I write this, there is something hatching in the back of my brain and it is working its way forward, I can tell.

In a previous writing, I recall describing to y'all a Most Satisfactory Birthday Party Experience that had been provided for me by some friends of the particularly jolly variety: They rented out TON 'O' FUN and we climbed on all the stuff, slid down the slidey things, and spent hours laughing hysterically in the Big Ball Pit. I postulated at that time that many, if not all, of the world's problems and certainly all of our individual ones could be solved by spending some quality time in the Big Ball Pit with our friends—100 percent as effective as any medically prescribed antidepressant and no dry mouth, loss of libido, or weight gain. Doctors' offices should forget installing aquariums to calm their patients during lengthy waiting periods—put in a Big Ball Pit instead. Patients might be a little sweaty by the time the doc sees them, but they'll be a lot happier.

OK, so we've already got this: Laughing and playing relieve stress and anxiety.

Now, who DOESN'T love a NAP? If anybody is ever recounting the events of their day to you and a nap was one of those events, the raconteur will doubtless wax nostalgic and perhaps even a bit misty-eyed as The Nap is mentioned and then described as to degree of satisfaction, as well as the location and duration, along with what was eaten immediately before and after it. With few exceptions, when a nap has occurred in a given day, it is nearly always given premium Highlight status.

Most of us can't consciously remember when naptime was strictly ENFORCED on a daily basis, along with a bedtime that seems, in retrospect, deliciously early—although most of us can clearly recall lodging vehement protests against that dictated time for retiring. At some point, though, when we least expected it, and really without having any concept of what we were being robbed of, both these precious commodities were snatched from us, without ceremony or explanation. Just one day it seems that, from that day forward, we were expected to remain upright and alert all dang day and into the night. Some of us have contemplated moving to any remaining Latin American country that still observes the sacred siesta time each day. Here's hoping that, as our Hispanic population grows, this lovely custom can be introduced and embraced here.

And now come we to the notion of Spa—where our actual physical bodies are lovingly caressed by the hands of others and we are soothed to a state that hearkens back to that perfect time in our lives when all we had to do was Play, Take Naps, Have a Bath, and Go to Bed: CHILDHOOD. We don't want to return to the womb—too cramped, dark, wet, noisy, and no active snacking—but the time shortly after that and up until around age four?

THAT'S our goal and a worthy one it is. We struggle and kick and claw our way out of The Nest and only too late do we realize the true cost of our freedom: no naps. And if you want a body scrub and a massage, you're gonna have to pay for it. Yourself. Play Time is equally scarce and expensive, too. Sigh. Just never know what we've got 'til it's gone. No wonder we're all so stressed out. We have all made the same HUGE and apparently irrevocable mistake—we grew up and left home. Damn! What were we thinking?

So, yes, I would agree with the essayist: Spa time should be considered a Life Necessity and there should be legislation introduced to provide it.

In my opinion, a satisfactory Spa Experience is one that, by the end of it, I am completely sick of people fooling with me. It takes a lot—and some folks seem to think it's impossible to GET "too much" at a spa—but I am here to tell you, IT CAN BE DONE. One must be dedicated, of course, and willing to adhere to a rigorous schedule of lying in assorted positions on assorted tables nonstop, for several days at a stretch, interrupted only by the occasional meal (OK, the mealtimes are honored as sacred), potty breaks, and showers/baths/whirlpools, etc. Once or twice every year, I am invited to the Spa at Lake Austin, where I am joined by my dear friend and fellow Queen, Katie, and so far, we proudly hold the standing spa record for the Most Number of Spa Services in the Shortest Amount of Time—and we defend our title fiercely. Upon arrival, we march grimly up to the appointment desk and map out our days so that every single available minute that can be spent on a treatment table is appropriately scheduled. We adhere so strictly to this regimen that we usually require assistance in entering the limo when it's time to leave—it's almost like trying to load two dead, greasy bodies into a backseat.

The first spa I ever went to was in Summit, Mississippi—an unlikely spot for a spa if ever there was one. It was in a big, giant house—formerly owned by an alleged drug dealer—out in the very center of nowhere. I think somebody finally noticed that there was a 20,000-square-foot house out yonder and didn't nobody livin' in it have any kind of visible JOB to speak of, and well, questions were asked and, I suppose, answered—on account of, presently, it got turned into a spa by some new owners. I heard that, later on, it got turned into a drug rehab place, which was what you'd call some of your "irony," I reckon. (Funny thing, irony. Met a guy once who had just broken up with the cutest girl in three counties—way too cute for the likes of him, in my opinion—and he had dumped her for the fact that "she had no irony." I still don't know what he meant by that, but I'm thinking he did her a favor.)

Anyway, this drug-lord's-lair-turned-spa was very fine, indeed, and as luck would have it, on that first visit, I was accompanied by my seester Judy. We checked out the entire facility and handily identified the Very Best Amenity on the Premises. It was an enormous box, big enough to hold two jumbo-sized humans at the same time, and me and Judy were and are just that—both jumbo-sized and human—so in we went. It was some kind of enviro-chamber or something; I can't for the life of me recall what they called it, but I do vividly recall that we nearly died in there—from uncontrollable and very ill-timed laughter.

Wearing swimsuits (take a moment and try to rid your mind of THAT visual), we clambered inside and parked our giant selves at opposing ends of the box, which had a wooden-slat floor. There was plenty of room for us to lie down, side by side, but height-wise, it was clearly designed for long-legged, but extremely short-waisted individuals. We could not sit upright; the most we could achieve in the way of head elevation was roughly equivalent to propping up in bed with an extra pillow.

Neither of us was wearing our contact lenses, so reading the instructions on the control panel was a bit of an impossibility, and being, as we were, anxious to get on with it, I simply pushed a green button, which we interpreted as meaning "go," and in fact, it did, because things did get going pretty fast from that moment on. It was pretty much around (and around) the world in 30 minutes, in your bathing suit, in a big box.

First, the blazing desert sun came out and baked and broiled us at the same time. It was very bright, very dry, and very, VERY HOT. Just when we thought we about to star in a Butterball® commercial and be served up, perfectly roasted, on a platter to a happy cannibal family, the monsoons came, complete with thunder and simulated lightning. It rained—real hard, straight down, more like your massive waterfall than your summer rainstorm, really—and it did not slack off for quite some time.

We have BEEN waterboarded, and I can tell you, it's pretty scary. Except nobody was holding us down in an attempt to extract any kind of information from us—since clearly we were nearly too stupid to live, given that we had voluntarily entered this chamber—so it was actually pretty funny. Too funny. Nearly fatal funny.

Remember, we could not SIT UP in there and the water was coming down in Niagara-ic proportions, and unfortunately, we got tickled. I have lived to tell you that if you ever find yourself on your back underneath a waterfall, you should definitely think very sad thoughts until it is possible for you to roll over onto your stomach. Only at that point will it be somewhat safe for you to have your mouth gaping open with guffaws. If you attempt to belly laugh while you are belly-up underneath a raging torrent, you are very prone to drowning. Just FYI.

When I said earlier that there was plenty of room for the two of us to lie side by side, head to toe, in the big box, I should have been more clear: There was plenty of room for us to lie STILL in that position—not so much room, as it turned out, for moving around without a great deal of cooperative choreography to our movements, which, being reduced to uncontrollable howling as we were, proved nearly impossible to achieve. Had we KNOWN there was going to be a flash flood, we might have agreed ahead of time on a rotation plan, but as it was, we were caught not so much flat-footed as flat-backed, and between the thundering and the roaring downpour, our hysterical laughing, and our combined rollover attempts, one can only imagine what the whole thing looked and sounded like to the unsuspecting passerby. Rather like two hysterical manatees in a front-loading washing machine, I should think.

I Left My Heart...on the Porch, Actually

And I like my ass parked out there, too, frankly. Travel is a source of anticipation and pleasure for lotsa folks, but I am not amongst 'em. Not a wayfarer, me. A lot of folks, perhaps even most of them, like a nice sojourn to "get away from it all" every now and then. Not me. To the contrary, I want and work diligently at being able to "stay here with it all"—all the time. At one time, I didn't HATE travel. That would be about the best thing I could say about The Prospect of Travel today: "I used to not despise it like I do now." Eight book tours would sour anybody on it, I believe, but it really only took one to put me off of it forevermore, amen.

Thus, it is a mystery to me how I, the biggest homebody I ever heard of, got on so many travel-related mailing lists. I get every cruise brochure printed, plus all manner of travel magazines from "girl trips" to extreme luxury getaways. I have never requested any of this literature—printed or online—and yet I receive endless entreaties to venture out into the big, wide world.

I am not interested in the big, wide world. I like my little, tiny world. I like my back porch, I like looking out at our little corner of the lake, I like drinking my own coffee, wearing my own robe, sitting on my own rocking chair, mouth-breathing my own fresh air.

One of the top-ten commandments perennially issued by travel gurus is that We Should Not Expect Things in Foreign Countries to Be Like They Are at Home. And that's a deal-breaker for me right there. That's one of my very favorite things in the whole big, wide world: familiarity. I looooove me some same old, same old! I can't get enough of it, actually.

A recent travel article caught my eye. It was concerning some little-known laws in some foreign countries. I read it, only to further bolster my own convictions regarding Staying My Self at Home. I'm in the minority here, I realize. Most everybody I know just LOOOOVES to go running off to the various ends of the earth, and I know they have no idea the risks they are so blithely taking by doing so. Oh, I guess they get the necessary shots and all—the government makes 'em do that—but I guarantee you not a one of 'em has bothered to brush up on the laws in the assorted countries they are gadding off to. I guess the movie *Midnight Express* meant nothing to them. Scared the pure-dee crap outta me, I tell you what.

I was shocked, to say the least, to learn that, in certain regions of Italy, women of ill-repute or evil looks are forbidden to enter cheese factories. There was no information as to how these things are judged or by whom. How bad does one's reputation have to be to get one banned? Who decides if one has an evil look about them? I can tell you, cheese is important to me, and if, by some fluke, I were somehow persuaded to go all the way to some cheese-making section of Italy (which is FAR), I would definitely WANT to go to the very home of the cheese, and if, upon arrival at the doorstep, I was denied entrance because my looks and/or demeanor did not suit some unidentified individual—well, I would be severely miffed. One more reason to just stay safely home, where hardly anybody cares what I look like, including me.

Surely everybody knows by now that one of the basic tenets of Sweet Potato Queenism is Never Wear Panties to a Party. (If you don't, then you're just gonna have to go back and read *The Sweet Potato Queens' Book of Love* and all my earlier books; I cannot be expected to retell every little thing in every single book. And for God's sake, BUY YOUR OWN, don't BORROW them—I will NEVER get all my plastic surgery done if y'all are BORROWING my books. My tits will be hanging to my knees and it will be YOUR fault. I don't think you want that on your conscience.) Anyway, we have this No Panties Rule—well, I discovered that there is a little-known law on the books in Thailand that says it is AGAINST THE LAW to leave home without underwear.

So what possible fun are you gonna have over there—without risking Thai prison, that is? You just need to stay your little nek-kid hiney at HOME in the good ole US of A, where, thank God, we are FREE to go about panty-free. God Bless America.

Should you venture over to Lebanon, you might discover that your boyfriend would be allowed to copulate with any female ANIMAL of his choice, but you might be called for bail money if he were to mount a BOY animal. Ewwww. And now, you need a new boyfriend when you get home—where you ought to have STAYED.

If you get drunk in Scotland, you can't have your cow with you—so what's the point?

After 10:00 p.m. in Switzerland, men are required to sit down to pee. Not sure who investigates and/or enforces this one. Would you be expected to rat out your date if he failed to assume the dictated position? Would you be hauled in as an accessory if you failed to file a report?

And lest you think you'd be any safer traveling around in THIS country, let me disabuse you of that notion right now, because what you don't know can get you thrown in the pokey, with your name in the paper and your family disgraced. ALL of these were actual laws at one time, right here in our own back-yards—and some of 'em are likely to still be in effect, for all I know—so mind yourselfs out there:

- In Alabama, you can't drive a car blindfolded.
- If you go to Washington, you can't pretend your parents are rich.
- A guy in Wisconsin is expressly forbidden to fire off a gun if and when his female partner has an orgasm (no mention of protocol if partner is a guy). So how's any-body supposed to know?
- Hotels in South Dakota must have twin beds—at least two feet apart. And don't be thinking you can do it on the floor in between 'em, 'cause it's against the law.
- You can shoot whales—BUT ONLY WHALES—from a car in Tennessee. If you shoot anything else, you're gonna get caught and there will be hell to pay.
- If you plan to commit a crime in Texas, you MUST give your intended victim 24 hours' notice of the particular nature of the crime you intend to perpetrate on them. Shit, where's the fun in that for anybody? No surprise a-tall.
- Don't be walking across the street on your hands if you're in Connecticut. (So how are we supposed to get over there?)

- You may not sit on a curb and drink beer from a bucket in St. Louis. This has no doubt hurt their tourism industry. Where does one sit, pray tell?

- New Hampshire does not want you to, in any way, shape, or form, attempt to keep time to the music that might or might not be playing in public places. No foot tapping, no head bobbing. Just sit there and listen. You prolly clap on one and three anyway, which would mean it's a Good Law.

- Funerals suck in Massachusetts—there is a strict three-sandwich-per-person rule at wakes.

- A plus for Massachusetts—goatees require a special permit. And if it were up to me, none would be issued. Never trust a man with a goatee; clearly, he cannot commit to anything, one way or the other.

- If you're going to bite somebody in Louisiana, make sure you use only your natural teeth—that's just simple assault. If you forget and use your dentures, you're looking at aggravated assault—and possibly Angola.

- If your husband takes you on a "surprise" trip and it turns out to be to Jonesboro, Georgia, for God's sake, DON'T SAY "oh boy"—it's against the law. That seems like a pure trap for racking up fines from unsuspecting tourists, to me—on account of you just KNOW they all say "oh boy" when they get there. I know I would.

- Idaho sounds nice—no man can gift his woman with a box of candy weighing less than 50 pounds. I have always found that to be the perfect size. Let's move there. They seem sensible.

- No hanky-panky while hunting and fishing on your wedding day in Oblong, Illinois. Some honeymoon that's gonna be.
- I am surprised that Chicago—the Big-Shouldered City—is so trifling that they won't let you eat in a restaurant if it's on fire. Even if you already paid.
- Gotta make it snappy in Iowa—no kiss can last longer than five minutes. UP TO five minutes—but there's a mandatory break in the action at that point.
- BIRDS have the right of way on ALL Utah highways. (But they never signal.)
- ATTENTION WOMEN: Do NOT have sex with a guy in a Utah ambulance. You will be arrested and they will put your name in the paper. There is no penalty for the guy, though. So not fair.
- OK, next GLBT Convention has GOT to be in Florida. Men can't wear strapless gowns in public. Define "can't."
- While we're in Florida, only MARRIED women can parachute—no single, divorced, or widowed women allowed. AND your cats and dogs MAY NOT smoke. Anywhere.
- In Kentucky, "No female shall appear in a bathing suit on any highway within this state unless she be escorted by at least two officers or unless she be armed with a club." An amendment to the above legislation: "The provisions of this statute shall not apply to females weighing less than 90 pounds nor exceeding 200 pounds, nor shall it apply to female horses." Well, duh.
- Also in Kentucky, if you shoot the tie off a cop, you're in big trouble. Just so you know.

- NO SEX IN THE WALK-IN FREEZERS at stores in Wyoming. Even if it's hot outside? Geez.
- In parts of California, you must actually OWN a minimum of two (2) actual cows before you are allowed to wear COWboy boots. And if you've got MORE than 2,000 sheep with you? You can just forget about driving them down Hollywood Boulevard. They WILL count them.

So now, really, after you consider all these things that—once you leave your own home—you are no longer free to do, WHY BOTHER? How much fun are you gonna have? You're just gonna spend a whole buncha money and be wishing you were home smoking with your dog.

The Divorce Porch
I mentioned my preference for parking my personal parts on my back porch, I believe. Let me share with you a couple of my journal entries regarding my outer sanctum:

SEPTEMBER 2008
Even as I sit in my office at the front of the house typing this, I am vaguely aware that there is Progress Being Made in My Backyard. Only vaguely aware because there are no actual hammering sounds or sawing sounds or other equipment-related noise, but I can hear him thinking, I can sense the wheels in his head turning, turning, turning—and that is SOMETHING, I suppose.

I am referring, of course, to the mind of The Cutest Boy in the World, and the wheels in his punkin' head are spinning in regards to the Divorce Porch. Begun as a mere regulation, standard-issue back porch, in earnest and under the blazing sun by

TCBITW three (3) YEARS ago [Remember, this was written in 2008!], *only to be interrupted, like so much of life, by Katrina—it came to be known as the Divorce Porch as time marched on and at some point commenced flying by—and construction remained at the halt to which it slammed after that fateful August 29, 2005, storm.*

To his credit, it's not the kind of project that can just be given a cursory hour or so's worth of work here and there and eventually get finished—well, not the way TCBITW does things, anyway. I suppose a mere MORTAL could have/would have slapped some kind of porch together out there long ago—but not my boy, nosiree-bobtailcat, whatever that means.

This is not so much a PORCH as it is an open-air bomb shelter. This thing will be here way past the end of time. Whatever the building codes might be for structures to withstand major earthquakes and/or Cat-5 hurricanes and any other disasters, God- or man-made, this thing exceeds those requirements by a minimum of 400%. Seriously. I am not kidding. At all.

You could safely land a midsized helicopter on the roof—it's big enough and certainly strong enough. That might come in handy if, say, just for discussion, someone, anyone—like a slow-poke carpenter, for example—were to meet with some kind of life-threatening injury, like, oh, a small-caliber gunshot wound or accidentally being set on fire or a high-speed encounter with the business end of a two-by-four, again, just for example, any one of the hundreds of hazards encountered by unbelievably behind-schedule workmen at the hands of irate homeowners any day of the week, well, the medivac guys can land right on that porch roof and haul his carcass out, quick as a bunny.

At this point, even though TCBITW agrees it would have been easier and cheaper to just get the divorce, we think there is hope on the horizon—or at least at the back door. All that remains now is the Installation of the Floor—for which he selected Ipe wood (pronounced ee-pay). It's a beautiful Brazilian hardwood that is so hard it cannot be nailed, termites can't eat it, and it's so heavy and dense it sinks—and the rest of the house will look like a slum compared to the floor of the Divorce Porch.

And that strikes fear into my heart. WHAT, oh, what shall I do if he NOTICES that the rest of the house does not live up to that floor? He might just be moved to begin a remodeling project—INSIDE the house. I could easily be without electricity and plumbing for most of the next decade! And that heliport might get a trial run.

And here we go, fast-forward from there to:

JUNE 2009
My, my, my—how time does fly when one is NOT building a porch. (This state of being is not to be confused with that of persons who, for whatever reason(s), choose to remain porch-less or those who already have porches sufficient to their needs, but rather, it deals with persons, actually, just one specific person who has supposedly, purportedly, and/or allegedly been in the process of building a porch for over four (4) entire YEARS, plus a few months, but spends most—what most?—ALL of his time doing everything in the world BUT building said porch.)

As I said, time does just take wings. It seems like only yesterday I was reporting to you in this space that my husband, The Cutest Boy in the World (albeit The Slowest Porch Builder EV-ER) had been working on that same porch for a little over THREE (3) years (hence the name "Divorce Porch") and—wham! Here we are, another year older and still only half-porched. To be completely fair, and it's important to me to be so, I'd have to say I am actually closer to three-quarters-porched—but it's really a distinction without a difference. What I've GOT is a piece of a porch with piles of unused lumber, tubs of screws and nails, and assorted tools, which could (and may yet) be used as weapons, if the aggravation factor gets much higher around here.

If I'da known it was gonna take four years (and counting), shoot, I could have already whacked him in the head with a two-by-four and done the time for assault with a deadly stick and been out and HIRED me somebody to finish this porch and be sitting there rocking on it right now instead of just thinking about it, which I am—a lot.

With a great deal less deadly force but admittedly a good deal more time and trouble, I coulda divorced him and found somebody else who either already HAD a porch or who could (and would) at least finish THIS one. But this new guy, despite his princely porch proffer, would doubtless be equally derelict in some other crucial and irritating area and there is simply no way he could be anywhere near as cute as the non-completer of my current porch, so I reckon I'll just hang on to him for yet another summer, if for no other reason than to satisfy my own curiosity: Will he EVER finish this porch? How could I leave without knowing the answer to THAT?

Besides, I could name you two-dozen women, right off the top of my head, who would HAPPILY take my place on this half-a porch if The Cutest Boy in the World came with it. And truth be told, I'd rather have him and this half-a porch than George Clooney and the Taj Mahal. I'll just sit myself down and rock on the part that's done and count my blessings—HIM being the mainmost one.

AND TODAY?

As of THIS writing (today is July 11, 2011), all of his porch-building equipment has finally been removed from the center of the backyard—where it has resided, year-round, under a BLUE TARP, since March 2005. One might be tempted to infer from this equipment stowage that the Divorce Porch had finally been completed. One would be mistaken. What one CAN assume is that half of us got sick to death of the BLUE TARP flapping around in the yard and that finally the amount of shit that half of us was willing to dish out and the amount of shit the OTHER half was willing to take in that regard equalized, and thus, the equipment was removed by that other half of us—although it must be noted that this was not accomplished with anything like a cheerful attitude on either side.

So, what I've got today is STILL three-quarters of a Divorce Porch and a big naked spot in the yard where grass oughta be. However, to date, neither of us has consulted an attorney. I would still rather have my piece of a porch and him, and he'd still rather have me haranguing him about it than…whatever he could have instead of that, which I suppose would be pretty much anything he wanted, given that he IS, after all, The Cutest Boy in the World.

Kickin' Off My Travelin' Shoes
As I mentioned, eight book tours have rid me, but good, of any trace of wanderlust that may have ever lurked in a forgotten corner of my heart. Don't get me wrong, I am PROFOUNDLY grateful to my publishers who sent me on those tours, and sent me first class all the way, I might add. Blessings be upon them and their children forevermore for alla dat. BUT.

Yes, there is a BIG BUT coming up here. It has been said to me innumerable times, regarding book tours, "Oh, you get to go so many wonderful places—how exciting!" And yes, that is technically true. I have been to dozens and dozens of what I am sure are absolutely FABULOUS cities—the best cities in America—but I am relying purely on hearsay in that regard.

Here is the sum total of what you see on book tours: airports, hotel rooms (some better than others), and bookstores—all of these stores are absolutely fabulous, I can personally testify to that part. And I must say, I have had the privilege and honor of meeting all manner of innarestin' and entertaining people; I just wish they would all come to Jackson, Mississippi, for me to meet 'em. Not all at once, mind you. I wouldn't mind going into town even two or three days a week, if it meant I got to visit with a delightful crop of Queens. This would suit me so much better than the Book Tour Paradigm, which involves ME going thither, yon, and all points in between to accomplish this.

I remember eagerly anticipating my first book tour for *The Sweet Potato Queens' Book of Love*. The first stop was to be in Atlanta, and I recall looking at the PRINTED schedule of events my publicist, the nefarious Brian Belfiglio, sent to me, and I so vividly recall thinking to myself that there was ALL MANNER of TIME in there—which I could fill with shopping and lunching with friends in the area. The aforementioned evil Mr. Belfiglio had, unbeknownst to me, secured the services of the most sought-after media escort in this hemisphere—the incomparable Esther Levine—and "downtime" does not appear in her handbook. She's never had any, isn't interested in having any, and sees no reason why an author in her care should be doing ANYthing that is not actively selling a book or hundred. I was on every single TV and radio show that was being aired in any time slot in

the Atlanta area in February 1999. Thank God there was no sat-
ellite stuff then, or I never would have survived a day and a half
with Queen Esther. Make no mistake, Esther Levine is as good as
it gets, ever has gotten, or ever will get, and if you are an author,
she is your book's best friend in Atlanta—but you need to train
for a month or so before you get in the car with her.

That was the first inkling I had of what a book tour is REALLY
like—and it was, of course, too late to run away. Here is a typical
book tour day—and keep in mind, this is a VERY GOOD book
tour, one that the publisher has organized and is paying for on
your behalf:

Go to airport at 4:00 a.m. (which implies correctly that you
got UP at 2:30 a.m.). Fly somewhere (first class, if it is available,
but these days, good luck finding a big plane going anywhere—
mostly you will be crammed, like a canned ham, into one of the
ever-tinier seats on a regional jet). Media escort picks you up at
airport and takes you to TV and radio stations to promote your
book signing. Media Escort takes you to bookstore. You speak or
read a little from your book, answer questions, and sign books
(hopefully, a shitload of them). Media escort takes you to your
hotel. Room service quit an hour before you got there. You eat a
can of Pringles and a bag of jelly beans from the minibar. You will
yourself to FALL ASLEEP NOW because you have to get up in
four hours. Room service will not begin operation until an hour
after you have left for the airport. You eat a package of Oreos and
a can of cashews from the minibar. You repack your suitcase and
haul it downstairs to meet your driver who will take you to the
airport so that you can REPEAT THIS whole cycle. You will do
these things—and only these things—for 30 to 60 days. You will
see an airport, a hotel room, assorted TV and radio stations, and
a bookstore—in a different city EVERY day. Even if you are in

a five-star hotel, you will be in that room for no more than six hours. And you will be starving. So glamorous.

Whenever I am on tour, my blessed, loyal Wannabes™ bring me all manner of ho-made foodstuffs to my events. I have often been asked whether or not I actually consume those foods. HELL YES, I EAT THEM! I eat them all and I am so grateful for them I could weep right this second just thinking about it. Genuine Food that a person who cares about me made for me with their own hands in their own kitchen and brought to me? Something that did NOT come out of a minibar refrigerator or an airport concession booth? I can tell you, I have never said grace over any food in my entire life with as much total, heartfelt sincerity as I do over those post-book-signing feasts in my hotel room.

After five book tours done by plane, and time for number six rolled in, I got muley—meaning I sat down in the middle of the road, with my ears back, and refused to move. The Cutest Boy in the World conspired with my publishers to circumvent my best efforts to avoid the book tour altogether by arranging to have me tour by way of a Big-Ass Bus—which accomplished two Highly Desirable Goals. The first, of course, being that it kept me off airplanes, for the most part, and I was more than delighted with that.

TCBITW, as is his custom before embarking on anything, anything at all, did exhaustive(ing) research on Big-Ass Buses and found a willing conspirator in the Quest RV Rental Company in Dallas. These fine folks were willing to rent (to my esteemed publisher) a 43-foot recreational vehicle with every bell, whistle, thing-a-ma-bob and/or -jig you can imagine; they were willing to let TCBITW drive it; AND they didn't mind if we took our only dog, as long as she was one of your "purse-sized" dogs—less than 35 pounds, actually. TCBITW assured them that she was—but he was thinking of MY BIG-ASS MOVIE PURSE at the time, so it wasn't REALLY a complete lie.

TCBITW was so far beside himself he was in another zip code. Being on the road for two months in a Big-Ass Bus was going to require way more preparation than just putting my ass on a plane. It took him three months to amass his "supplies" and an entire week to load it all. Of course, it wouldn't be this way for normal people. They would throw some food in the pantry, sling their clothes in the closet, and hit the road, clam happy. We are NOT normal people. OK, half of us are normal, but that half was not doing the prep work.

If a potential problem could be thought of in that very busy brain of his, the solution to it was packed on the bus—INCLUDING about a gazillion gallons of diesel fuel in gas cans below deck. I was so completely exhausted from watching him load crap onto that bus I didn't think I would be able to make it to the first stop.

After my first signing—which is always here in Jackson, Mississippi, at my "home" bookstore, Lemuria Books—we made our way out to the Big-Ass Bus that was idling in the parking lot, with our three-legged (extra-large) purse dog, Sostie, already perched in the driver's seat. As so often happens on January nights in Mississippi, it was raining at a steady five-inches-per-hour rate, so when we clambered aboard, we were not only tired, we were fairly wet as well. Not an auspicious beginning.

TCBITW was more excited than tired, but in about two seconds, he became way more WET than anything. With all that rain coming down so hard and fast, it had somehow collected in a part of the bus where it really should not have. I'll never really understand HOW this happened, but what did happen was, when we headed out, we were going up a sight incline and we heard an inexplicable "whooshing" sound—like that of a whole big lotta water moving from one place to another—but it made no sense because it seemed to be coming from somewhere REAL close by, like inside the bus somewhere, but we didn't see any water, nor could we imagine where any water could BE. Well, when we topped that little rise and started on the downhill side of it, we found the water. Or rather, it found TCBITW. From wherever it had been, it sprang forth; a great, gushing torrent of it poured directly down on the driver's seat of the Big-Ass Bus, which did contain, of course, the driver—TCBITW. Nonplussed doesn't really get in the ballpark with our feelings about this. WTF was more the question of the moment, and that sentiment was certainly expressed vehemently and repeatedly for some moments, by both of us, to be sure, but clearly, one of us was significantly more upset than the other. The Wet One was reeeally pissed. And reeeally wet.

OK. Now, it's about 10:30 p.m.—we've got to get to Montgomery, Alabama, tonight so I can be on TV at 6:00 a.m. the next morning—and we are still in the parking lot at Lemuria and half of us are drownd-ed. And unbelievably crabby. But he figures out what the Water Issue is, rectifies it somehow (who knows?), stomps to the back, rips off his wet clothes, sticks 'em in the dryer, finds dry stuff, dresses, and stomps back up to the front, where Sostic and I are cowering in fear and dread. We were not wrong in our assessment of the situation as being both fearful and dreadful—as we were about to discover.

Kyle (TCBITW does have a Christian name) settled into his soggy seat, and before relaunching us, he removed his eyeglasses for a final wipe down. Of COURSE, they fell apart in his hands. BUT, not to worry, Mr. Uber-Preparedness simply reached for the SPARE PAIR of spectacles he had purchased JUST IN CASE of this exact kind of bizarro, unexpected (by normal people) emergency and he put them on with a flourish, as if to say to me (the one who would have thrown some crap in the bus and hit the road, willy-nilly), *SEE? It PAYS to be PREPARED.* But what HE had NOT counted on was the optical dispensary fucking up his prescription. He could see better WITHOUT those new glasses than he could with them, and that's saying a lot because I think he's prolly pretty close to legally blind without 'em. So, he's pushed to his very last fallback position, wearing his contacts, which he normally reserves just for water-skiing, but given the recent deluge, maybe it's not such a stretch.

So, finally, finally, FINALLY, we got on the road—the very dark and stormy road—to Montgomery. I sat up front staring out at the wall of water we appeared to be driving through until I couldn't sit up anymore, and I stumbled back to the bedroom and fell (literally, the bus was pitching and rolling) into the bed and, shortly, a deep slumber.

Plenty deep but not nearly long enough. When my alarm went off, I realized we were parked, Kyle was there beside me in the bed, and it was still raining sideways. I could see that we were parked outside the TV station where I was to appear shortly. This was to be the first time I employed my now-standard Early Morning TV Wardrobe Scam.

I got up, which I was loathe to do, having only been asleep about four hours, and there was that lovely sound of rain pounding on the roof of the Big-Ass Bus. No matter that we were parked as close to the door of the building as possible, given the confines of the parking lot and the enormity of the Big-Ass Bus, I was nonetheless painfully aware of the total drenching I was most likely to suffer making the trek from the bus to the building. I was less than thrilled about making this first TV appearance in promotion of this book—given all that would be required to complete it. Enthusiasm for putting a bunch of camera-ready makeup on my sleepy face was impossible to muster. I managed to brush my hair up into a ponytail and clamp on my ubiquitous travel hair (see earlier SPQ™ writings for full explanation), and I dredged up my sequined jacket and my Big-Ass Crown, but I just could not MAKE myself open that cosmetics bag.

I swirled open the tube of my Revlon "Love That Pink" (Pank) lipstick and dabbed some on my cheeks, blending it sufficiently so it passed for "blush," then I liberally smeared my lips with it and put on my SPQ™ rhinestone shades. VOYOLA! Camera ready! As long as I kept those shades on, nobody would know that the face of a mole recently exposed to the noonday sun was lurking underneath.

Kyle opened one eye and surmised my plan. "What if they want you to take off the sunglasses?" he asked. "Way ahead of you," I confidently replied. "They are my trademark; I never take them off. I'm Roy Orbison in pank." He snorted and rolled over as I made my way in the dark to the front door and launched myself out into the storm.

Mere moments later, I was back, having battled my way to the door and succeeded in summoning someone to open it, only to be told that my segment had been canceled in favor of the TORNADO WARNINGS that were in effect for a 200-mile radius.

Are you feeling me here? All of this—just glance back up the page for a recap—ALL for naught. We could have stayed HOME and driven down in the afternoon for the book signing. And this, mind you, was Day 1 on the road in the Big-Ass Bus.

In case you think I'm about to break into song over how everything was FINE from then on—ahem, NO. Soon we were to find ourselves, on yet another dark and stormy night, hurtling down the Pennsylvania Turnpike.

Now, maybe it's just me, but when I hear the words "Pennsylvania Turnpike," I immediately envision a broad, well-lit vista. Clearly, it's just me, because what it IS is a twisty, windy, black-as-the-pit goat trail. But as I was writing this, I thought, *It CAN'T be JUST ME; that is a TERRIBLE, TERRIFYING road.* And so I betook myself to—where else?—GOOGLE.® (What DID we ever do without it?) I instantly found a posting from another motorist who has apparently been equally traumatized traveling on it. Here's what the driver known as "Netzapper" had to say about it:

I hatehatehatehate the PA Turnpike. Even thinking about it right now, my hands and feet went clammy and my heartrate shot up. Why? Because it goes through the mountains with nothing but the barest whisper of a guard rail. And everybody driving through the mountains on the PA Turnpike thinks that they should continue traveling at the 70mph they maintained through Pennsyltucky. And there's so much congestion that you don't have any choice over your own speed. It's the most stressful driving in all the hundreds of thousands of miles I've driven—the only thing that comes close is I-5 around Seattle, but there I'm just concerned for my car, not my life.

THANK YEW, THANK YEW VERAMUCH! My sentiments eggzackly—although I can't really chime in on the Seattle part. I've been there, but not in the Big-Ass Bus.

But then, a little ways down the page of postings, someone named "Loto" totally disagreed with me and Netzapper about the PA Turnpike and he/she really let fly thusly:

Most importantly, when you compare it to I-80 it's like a fucking unicorn shit a road out of gold for you to take to the Care Bear Palace.

While I admire Loto's lyric description, I simply cannot imagine how we have had such vastly different experiences on the same stretch of highway, and I am standing by my own experience—which, for me, is never to be repeated unless I am boxed up in the back of a hearse.

Here's the actual account of the harrowing experience that I wrote as we were attempting to get from Richmond, Virginia, to Pittsburgh:

But anyway, we got on the Pennsylvania Turnpike—which, when I hear that name, I picture a broad, well-lit roadway, for some UNKNOWN reason. On account of it is a skinny-ass, twisty-windy, dark-as-the-pit trail. Thank GOD it is maintained in excellent condition and nobody had car trouble— because there is literally NOWHERE to pull over. Oh, every few miles there's a slightly wider spot in the road where you COULD pull off if you were dying, and as long as you didn't open a door, nobody would hit you and you wouldn't fall off the mountain.

There's not much of a divider and so you constantly have the lights of the oncoming traffic in your eyes—which renders ME completely blind. Fortunately, I am not the one driving. BUT it became MUCH MORE important for me to be able to see jack shit shortly when, in the pitch-black dark (and did I mention the howling wind and driving torrential rain?), the windshield wiper on KYLE'S SIDE just BLEW OFF. OFF, I'm saying. It is somewhere on the hillside of the Pennsylvania Turnpike and it will never wipe another windshield in this life.

SOOOO. What we HAVE NOW is the driver (Kyle) who can see pretty well through GLASS (now that he has GLASSES again)—but not really so hot through glass that is totally obliterated by SHEETS of WATER with thousands of HEADLIGHTS shining through it. And then we have ME, on the other side of the bus, with the one remaining windshield wiper, which is totally moot on account of I cannot see jack shit in the dark with the oncoming headlights.

Not your ideal driving sitchiation.

We limp about 15 miles to a big truck stop—which I note with interest has a sign declaring it to be the LAST EXIT FOR 80 MILES. Thank God in Heaven that wiper took flight when it did—and not 20 miles farther down the road—or we would still be SITTIN' our asses on the Pennsylvania Turnpike.

Kyle managed to flirt with the woman in charge (thank God it was a woman—I was way past Making any Promises by this time) to get her to illegally loan him the station's ladder so he could try to figure out just WHAT, if anything, was to be done. (I myself have taken my own personal measures for dealing with this disaster—I took a XANAX, had some chocolate pie, and called my seester Judy. I ask you, what else COULD I do? I was just grateful I had the pie and the drugs to help me cope! And believe me, it took BOTH.)

I look out the front window of the Big-Ass Bus to see Kyle standing on the very top step of the purloined ladder—you know, the one that says, "NOT A STEP—DO NOT STAND HERE"—and reaching up with both hands, fiddling with the amputated wiper arm thingee. *I am imagining him plunging to his ruin on the greasy truck stop parking lot and me sitting there for the rest of my life with a one-armed Big-Ass Bus and a three-legged dawg.*

But, of course, he was fine. He managed somehow to take the wiper off my side and make it fit on his side. Then he pulled the bus up under a big awning, and once again standing on the Forbidden Ladder Step, he dried off completely the big-ass windshield, then put RAIN-X all over it, and we were back on the road again—only a couple hours later!

It took over a week for the RV folks to get a new wiper blade to us out on the road. So, for all that time, my side of the windshield was just one solid block of ice. It was actually better in some ways that I couldn't see out—I was blissfully ignorant of whatever dangers we were approaching.

This was hardly the last of our Big-Ass Bus mishaps—this was all just the first week of the first of three tours. You can extrapolate from those few tales how the rest of that tour and all the subsequent tours went. We went on to have no power for no apparent reason—in a snowstorm, at night. (The next morning, a banana on the kitchen counter was frozen SOLID.) And also no cell service. Kyle had to stand outside, in the blinding snow, talking to the RV people from a PAY PHONE (who knew they still existed?), trying to figure out why there was no electrical power to anything on the Big-Ass Bus, and that would, of course, include the HEAT. And another time, our water pump froze. I don't know if you have ever been reduced to bathing with wet wipes, but let me assure you that once you HAVE hit that low rung on the ladder, you will never again be able to smell them without a faint wave of nausea. These are just a TINY FEW of the trials and tribulations of RVing.

A word to anybody currently considering buying or renting a Big-Ass Bus for their own personal use: You might be an igmo. No offense, but I know this SEEMS like a swell way to travel, and it actually IS in many ways. It is in EVERY way superior to air travel, let's be clear about THAT. I would rather ride in the luggage compartment of a Big-Ass Bus to anywhere, in the white-hot middle of a Mississippi July, than to ever have to set foot on a commercial aircraft again in this life. I am so over flying. But unless you or somebody else on your bus knows how to fix anything—and I do mean ANY. THING.—and has the tools with which to do that, with them, ON THE BUS, you will spend 99 percent of your time parked either on the side of the road, or if you are blessed beyond any possible deserving, in an RV camp, WAITING for the tow truck or the repair guy, because SOMETHING is going to break every week, and it will be something without which you cannot function.

Oh, and unless they have GREATLY improved the GPS systems on those things, don't even turn them on. Our first two Big-Ass Bus Tours were pre-iPhone, so we had no choice but to rely on the bus's GPS. Such a delight to find oneself in the middle of a bean field at 2:00 a.m. with the GPS lady chirping that "you have arrived at your destination." The iPhone was NEVER WRONG, not once. Yay Apple!

On that first tour in the Big-Ass Bus, in spite of all the mechanical and GPS issues, we never missed or were even late for any of that first tour's 47 events and assorted media stops during 45 days and 15,000 miles on the road—a testament to Being Particular in selecting your traveling companion(s) and RV rental company.

If you do have a resident Handy Andy and are determined to leave home for extended periods of time, then I highly recommend doing so in a Big-Ass Bus from Quest RV. It will be the most comfortable travel experience of your life and no one will pat you down anywhere, unless, of course, you want them to, but that's a whole 'nuther discussion, really. You can park anywhere the big rigs park, truck stops, and the like, and there are some pretty fine RV parks out there as well. Walmarts are nearly always welcoming, and that's real handy for restocking the pantry and anything else, for that matter. But the personal favorite of our crew—which includes me, TCBITW, and by the end of the third Big-Ass Bus Tour, THREE very decidedly NOT purse-size dogs—is, without hesitation or qualification, Cracker Barrel.

At most, you can pull in for the night and have supper. WORD: On Tuesday night, at any Cracker Barrel on the planet, it is BUTTER-BAKED CHICKEN night. That's the only time you can get it and that kills me. I want it every time I see a Cracker Barrel sign. But anyway, you eat, you sack out, you wake up in the morning and go right back in, and somebody in there will make your eggs just for you and just the way you want them. They will also make you pecan pancakes, and their bacon meets with my approval.

Our dogs thought that the whole Big-Ass Bus Tour was our family vacation—planned for and around their comfort and enjoyment—and believe me, to this day, they can spot a Cracker Barrel sign from several miles away. (We brought them their own bacon, morning and night, so you can see how the attachment was formed.)

Just for the record, in (all of) our considered opinions—and this comes after personally visiting pretty close to every Cracker Barrel in the United States east of the Rockies, I believe—THE VERY BEST ONE IN THE WHOLE COUNTRY is the one in SLIDELL, LOUISIANA. You can tell 'em I said so—and of course, we told them so ourselves before we left.

One thing we noticed, though, after living in Cracker Barrels for two months out of every year for three years running, by the last couple weeks of the tour, all the old family photos hanging in there start to look just like people you actually know back home. Kinda creepy.

Etiquette for Recessions/ Depressions/Inflations

I suppose there is a difference in the scenarios listed in the title of this, but danged if I can tell what it is, and frankly, it doesn't much matter to me what the Talking Heads call it. All I know is, I got next to no money, no prospects for gettin' any, and what little I do have won't buy much anymore. I have observed that I am not alone in this predicament, so I wonder if, in the not-too-distant future, Emily Post might see some drastic revisions.

The Green Movement is inescapable, even when it comes to dining, fine and otherwise, so we can't be letting good food go to waste, even if it is on the plates of others. Soon, I expect to see it suggested that if you are dining out during a week that the Dow took a significant tumble, it might be permissible at such times to ask your dinner companions if they are going to eat their fat and/or finish their fries. If all the markets tanked that week, you could extend such a query to patrons at neighboring tables as well. All in the interest of Conservation of Resources—although, having long been of the opinion that Good Manners are the primary source of Grease on Society's Wheels, I fear that there isn't much point in Saving the Planet if it is to be inhabited by boors, churls, louts, and vulgarians. Better that we should all perish properly and politely.

I did actually know a guy once who would totally walk around in NICE restaurants grazing among the plates left by departing diners. In an attempt to place myself at a decent distance from this person, I must say that he was actually the friend of a guy I was dating, which, come to think of it, should have called my DATE into question—first of all, that he was friends with a table scavenger, and furthermore, with advance knowledge of this disgusting habit, he allowed the buzzard to accompany us to the aforementioned NICE restaurant, knowing that I would be forced to witness the scavenging AND, through no fault of my own, have myself associated with him in the minds of other equally victimized patrons.

The events of the evening are seared into my memory: I recall being ushered to our candlelit, cloth-covered table, then the three of us chatting amiably as menus were perused; choices were made by myself and my date and declared to the solicitous waitperson. I do recall a passing moment of mental questioning as our third wheel declined to order anything for himself, but I suppose I dismissed it as acceptable, even if slightly mystifying— I mean, why go out to dinner if not to dine?

Presently, our dinner companion excused himself, politely enough, to visit the facilities, and all seemed deceptively well; however, as he made his return trip through the crowded, but hushed room, my brain refused delivery on the message being sent to it by my very own eyeballs.

What I was seeing—but hardly believing—was our dinner companion making slow progress from the far side of the room, as something seemed to have drawn his attention, causing him to pause by a number of tables that had not yet been bused by service personnel, it being a particularly busy night for this very fine dining establishment. Presently, he began collecting plates from these tables of departed patrons, carrying them expertly balanced on his forearm like a seasoned garçon, and unbelievably bringing them with him to our very table, where he proceeded to grunt to us, his flabbergasted tablemate and my date, his shocking demand that we should make room on the tabletop for all his purloined platters.

Even today, some 35 years later, I can scarcely breathe as I recall the horror of what continued to unfold. Gleefully, he exclaimed over the bounty of leftovers he had recovered from the surrounding tables—"Lookit what all they LEFT!"—as he gobbled furiously and noisily, not unlike the first hog in the trough line.

I was looking around for cameras, certain that this was some kind of prank for a TV show—surely, surely, this guy was not really and truly doing what I was watching him really and truly do. And just what reaction would Good Manners dictate for me and the other hapless onlookers in this situation, hmmm?

Can't say that I've ever seen Miss Manners address this particular situation in her newspaper column, but one can only imagine the ensuing swoonage that would no doubt occur should I pose the question to her. Fearing that, upon reading my query, she might completely fall out and strike her head on the corner of her desk and die, I decided to resort to Google instead.

In a fairly exhaustive(ing) search of the worldwide manners guidelines so handily leaked to all of us common bastids by the fabulous wiki folks, I saw a great many troubling etiquette possibilities discussed. For instance, in Tanzania, it is thought to be rude to show up on time for dinner—best to be 15–30 minutes LATE. I have a good friend who is apparently Tanzanian and I never knew it until today.

Japanese manners say you should wait for your host or hostess to tell you to eat THREE times before you give in and dive in. Gotta tell you, if I had to tell you three times to start eating food I cooked for you, I'd be sorely tempted to snatch your plate away and eat it myownself after the second time.

Some places consider it the height of good manners and a glowing tribute to the hospitality of one's host to eat to the point of explosion, while others think you should just nibble and pick at everything. (I will not be visiting the nibble-and-pick people, of course, but the over-stuffers seem like a congenial lot.)

Rubbing one's chopsticks together is an insult to a Chinese host. Doing so implies that you think the chopsticks are cheap. Who knew? I'm safe on that one—have never been able to master them, anyway, and consider myself lucky to be able to wrangle a fork.

A few countries, including Ethiopia, according to TCBITW, have rules about the use of left hands at the table that are unsavory to ponder—and one has to wonder how a southpaw is supposed to survive over yonder. Some places have rules discouraging the display of the soles of one's feet at the table—can't really argue with that, but surprised that it was necessary to have a stated regulation about it. Whatever. Lord knows, I've seen worse, so I suppose nothing should surprise me.

Every country I read about has rules about talking with a full mouth and/or exposing one's table guests to the sight of the food inside one's mouth. Smacking is NOT well thought of anywhere, but there is a slurping loophole in Japan—albeit for noodles only. I should think that would take a fair amount of skill and control—fine line between slurping and aspirating, after all, with the former allegedly enhancing the flavor and the latter likely to afford one the opportunity for a tracheotomy *sur la table*.

But I could not find one single country in the EN-tire world (at least amongst those that have evolved to the point of compiling Rules of Etiquette and putting them in writing) that even allowed for the POSSIBILITY of Devouring the Leftovers of Unwitting Strangers.

Bonfire of the...Mules?

Money. Lemme tell you something: People who say, "It's only money," HAVE some. The only time po' folks say that is to a TV reporter who caught them as they drove up, in the aftermath of the tornado, WITH their entire family and their dog (alive and unhurt) in the car with them, and they are being interviewed standing in front of the naked foundation of where their mobile home used to be parked. At that moment, they do, in fact, feel with solid conviction that it IS "only money," because everything that really matters to them is standing there with them.

Unfortunately, in a few days, when they are distanced somewhat from their near miss on the casualty list, the major inconveniences of poverty will begin to assert themselves. Of course, they are still profoundly grateful to have their safe, healthy family (and dog), but it sure would be nice to have a place for all of them to live and bathe, a change of clothes, and oh, lunch. Trust me, I have been broke. I've been rich (by my standards, anyway, which means I had enough money piled up at one time to NOT get a tax refund—so you can see the bar is not set all that high where I'm concerned), and with a very high-style daughter in law school, I'm well on my way to being broke again. Rich is better.

"Money won't solve all your problems." That's another one of those things that only ever gets said by people WITH money. It is true, of course, there are all manner of problems for which money is not the solution. However, it must also be said that if what you've got is a MONEY PROBLEM, well, then money is pretty much the only thing that will solve it. Yeppers, money is just the thing for fixing money problems.

My parents had great growing-up-poor stories. Well, Daddy did, anyway. Mama grew up with servants, yacht clubs, and wintering in Florida; she didn't grasp the concept of "making do" until she married Daddy. Daddy grew up barefoot all summer, plowing behind mules, and never left Attala County, Mississippi, until he joined the Navy. Of the two vastly disparate childhoods, Daddy's was by far the happier, so much so that he never outgrew it and never tried, and Mama could not marry into that poverty fast enough. My snooty-ass rich grandmother looked down her witch's nose at Daddy and did everything she could to dissuade Mama from even associating with "that hillbilly," and thank God she did. I'm sure that served only to make the life that Daddy was offering that much more appealing.

The newlyweds lived in Mama's hometown of Detroit for a very brief time. I think my Mississippi daddy could only tolerate one winter there, actually. They had to shop for their groceries every day because they couldn't afford a refrigerator, so Daddy, with the resourcefulness that can only come from cash-poor necessity, figured out a solution: He just raised the kitchen window and put a wooden crate in the opening, then lowered the window to rest on top of the crate—much like a window-unit air conditioner. Since it was prolly three degrees outside, this provided an instant "deep freeze" for food storage. And I suppose it explains why they moved South after the spring thaw.

They lived in Tupelo, Mississippi, for a couple years. (I was actually born there in 1952.) I have Mama's only cookbook—*The Woman's Home Companion* (Garden City Publications, 1946). It no longer has a spine and is held together by a stout rubber band. It is stuffed with additional recipes, some in Mama's own hand, others written out for her by friends over the years. Such a treasure. Stuck in the pages is a yellowed, handwritten grocery receipt from Pannell's Grocery and Market at 447 North Green Street, Tupelo. It's so funny: The store's phone number is printed on the receipt; the number was 982. That's it—982! The receipt is written out to Mrs. Conner:

5 pounds sugar	55 cents	turnip	14 cents
2 quarts sweet milk	50 cents	2 pounds cornmeal	20 cents
1 loaf bread	17 cents	roast beef	59 cents
black-eyed peas	18 cents	5 pounds plain flour	55 cents
green beans	30 cents	6 eggs	28 cents
corn	20 cents	box of cleanser	29 cents

For a grand grocery total of $3.95—plus it says, "Free delivery!" (There was no sales tax on food yet.)

Speaking of taxes, my "cousin" Martin Sennet "Mike" Conner actually kind of "invented" sales tax. When he became governor of Mississippi in the early 1930s, he inherited about a $13 million deficit. Mississippi was one of the first states in the Union to institute a sales tax, and when Mike left office in '36, the state had a surplus. (He also served as the first commissioner of the Southeastern Football Conference, which prolly explains a lot about my autumn proclivities.)

But anyway, a week's worth of groceries for under four bucks? I don't think I have ever spent less than $100 in the grocery store, even if I just stopped in for cat food.

So, Mama didn't have any "poor us" stories until she left home to marry Daddy—but I never heard her tell a single one of them with anything like a mournful tone. When she married him, it was with the "poorer" side of the vow in plain sight and no hint of how and when the "richer" side might top the horizon, but she was a happy woman for all of her 37 years with him and never thought about another man after he died in 1982.

After being passed by a car that had a roller skate (old metal-wheel kind, not in-line) wired onto the tailpipe to keep it from dragging the ground (GENIUS—totally worked!), I asked my friends, "What's the 'brokest' you ever were, and what's the funniest—now that it's OVER—thing you did to 'make do'?"

My own Queen TammyPippa confessed that, when she was in high school, she was inexplicably driving across rice fields in the Mississippi Delta (whatever it was, there was a guy involved somehow, this much we know) and she knocked some important thing off the muffler. "Somehow," she got the guy at the gas station to weld a Maxwell House coffee can on there in place of the knocked-off thing, but he charged her $4 for the job, which she charged to her mama, thereby defeating the whole entire purpose. My question to her was, "Why didn't you 'somehow' get him to waive the four dollars, the same way you got him to do the welding?" She wishes she'da thought of that.

Lots of folks had car stories: Julie's car was so rusted out she had a coffee can holding the tailpipe on, a coat hanger securing the rearview mirror, and anything put in the trunk would fall out the sides. (I cannot even picture this much rust!) But the best part was there was no heat, so she pilfered some candles from an Italian restaurant. (Remember the ones in those glass globes that were in a nylon-net sleeve?) She took some of those, LIT THEM, and put them by her FEET—IN THE CAR.

Connie and her three sisters had a 50-mile round-trip commute to school every day in their decrepit pickup truck. One rainy morning, the rubber on the windshield wiper crumbled, so Connie gave her mama one of her tube socks. Mama pulled it over the wiper blade and…VOYOLA!

Forta and Greer both had cars with broken windshield wiper motors—and both managed to rig up the wipers with string running through the car. Pull the string, wipe the windows. Helped to have passengers to operate that for you, otherwise you really had to have a good sense of rhythm to keep the windows clear and drive, all at the same time.

Sue had a car that leaked so much she bought little kiddie umbrellas for the passengers. Linda said it was too bad Sue didn't have a bunch of those umbrella hats—for hands-free, rain-free cruising.

Kathleen blithely announced that, once, when changing out the brake pads on her truck, she lost the cotter pin and used a heavy-duty paper clip to replace it, which lasted the whole remainder of the life of the truck. I'm going—"WHOA, back up, there, missy! What do you mean YOU were changing out the brake pads on your truck? And what the hell is a cotter pin?" My ability to speak further at that time was torn asunder.

I could much more easily relate to Elizabeth, who confessed to pulling the stems off cherries so she could get more cherries and not pay for the weight of the stems. Even I can find a cherry stem—AND remove it.

Janice's mom took her five kids "midnight shopping"—in corn, strawberry, and tomato fields.

Karen's roommate worked at a really chi-chi restaurant where the chef was a maniac for perfection and any item that did not measure up was discarded. But it all found a good home, of course, with two hungry coeds. Imagine you are Karen's mama for a moment. Karen called her one night, begging for just a little bit of money: "PLEASE, Mama—we are SO SICK of steak and lobster and crab!" Mama's prolly still laughing.

Kimberly admitted that she once counted Tang as a fruit.

Marjo made grilled-cheese sandwiches with her iron.

Jodie and her roommate did not figure out until the last two weeks of their freshman year that they did not actually have to buy their own beer. Duh. Why did they think they let guys in there?

Mare confessed to using Spam to make jambalaya. Denise chimed in with, "SPAMBALAYA." I am certain it's illegal to do that in Louisiana.

Beverly wins a prize for quick thinking on an empty stomach. She was at the hospital visiting a dear friend who was IN A COMA—when what should appear but Coma Girl's LUNCH TRAY. Yup. Beverly ate it. I'm sure, of course, that Coma Girl, loving Beverly so, would not have wanted that lunch to go to waste and Bev to go hungry—but you gotta admit, it's pret-ty funny.

Kathleen said, when she was little, her mama (God rest her soul) wanted a dishwasher in the WORST way. She wanted one so bad she put all her melamine (allegedly unbreakable) dishes in a pillowcase and put them in the CLOTHES WASHER. It should be noted that the melamine shards WERE, in fact, clean, just not, as it turned out, quite so completely UN-breakable, after all.

Kathleen also used to cut the bad legs out of panty hose and put the two good leg parts together to make one good pair. I have done that myownself many times. Works great, and let me tell you, if they happen to be control tops, you could jump on a pogo stick all the way to town and your ass will NOT jiggle.

Bee's water got turned off while her neighbors were out of town on vacation. Bee sorta snuck over there and hooked her water hose up to their faucet and ran it in through her window so she could bathe and flush. She fessed up to the neighbors and offered payment for the pilfered water when they came home—which I thought was Karmically magnificent of her—and they, equally great, refused payment.

Lora tied her swimsuit top together with dental floss when the plastic fastener thing in the back broke, which I thought was pretty quick thinking. Maggie sold all her vinyl record albums to get Laundromat money, but the records were so full of scratches she only got enough to do one load and she had to wear the same clothes for almost a week until she got paid.

Suzanne remembered a time when her family stayed for a good while in a reeeally cheap motel and all she and her sister had to entertain themselves was ONE pair of roller skates. But rather than fight over whose turn it was to skate, they each took ONE and just hopped and rolled all over that motel parking lot—I get tickled just picturing them. That's a coupla good sports, right there.

Melissa's grandmother told her about how poor her family had been: When Granny and her sister were little, their mother would put MOLASSES on the little sister's hands and then stick FEATHERS on them. And the two of them would not move for HOURS; she'd sit right there until she picked off every single feather from her sister's hands. And again, I was speechless for a bit. I'm still not clear if this was meant to be entertainment for the girls or a means of keeping them occupied for long stretches. I think if I'd been the one that got syruped and feathered, I might have run screaming, bouncing off the walls. I have a hard time imagining me and Judy sitting still for hours while Judy picked feathers off my sticky hands. She would have left me stuck to a wall somewhere, I'm sure of it.

A number of my friends sold their blood over and over again. Scott said you could donate plasma every 15 days and get $30 a pop for it, which could keep you fed, PLUS you got cookies and juice. Stephania frequented a higher-class establishment; apparently, they were offering $75 to blood donors. Unfortunately, Steph was even tee-ninier then than she is now and she didn't meet the weight requirements. She would try to stuff her pockets with all manner of things, but they always caught her. Mama tried to sell blood once and they told her she needed to BUY some.

Amanda allows as how she stole toilet paper from the Waffle House—more than once. Beverly—eater of the Coma Girl's lunch—said she and her roommate had two bathrooms, but usually only one roll of toilet paper.

Theresa said, when they were kids, they had to eat their pet pig, and God forgive me, that makes me laugh every time I read it. I'm sorry, Theresa. I don't WANT to laugh. I know it was traumatic but...SNORT! I'm sick. Just sick.

I wish I had a Grand Prize for this, because Mona would absolutely win. She sold all her living room furniture to go to RENO to see WILLIE NELSON. And here we go, this is another one of those times when I just did not get ENOUGH INFO. She did not tell me and I need to know—was she just wild to get to his concert, or did Willie know she was coming? Was this a sorta date she was trying to get there for, and if so, don't we think he coulda sent her a bus ticket or something? Maybe it was when he was having that round with the IRS.

With the economy looking scarier all the time, I thought we might all like to have these tips close at hand—we may be needin' 'em any day now.

In the South, when someone is reeeally rich, it might be said of them, when they are out of earshot, "Whoo-lard, that man's got enough money to burn a wet mule." I have never fully been able to assign an actual dollar figure to that, nor have I ever figured out the point of it. Why would anybody WANT to burn a mule, wet or dry? If there is a point to be made by doing so, it eludes me, other than the ridiculously obvious: This pile of money I've got is big enough to torch an entire mule, even if he's dripping wet.

But then whaddya got, smarty pants? No money and a very large charred carcass—for which there is no use or market under Heaven of which I am aware. Now, a LIVE mule, wet or dry, is a very handy thing to have. A good mule will fetch a handsome price and you could have even more money, if you were of a mind to sell him off. Should you choose to keep him—well, with a live mule, one can haul things, plow fields, make molasses, and/or ride in relative comfort from point A to point B, and no telling what all else. In some countries or under certain dire circumstances, I suppose a cooked mule might be consumed, but your vanity has caused you to overheat your hiney. You deserve to be broke, dumbass.

Like I said, I've had more and I've had less—and more is definitely better. But it's not really what you have or don't have; it's whom you have or don't have it WITH.

Life in Pig Time

*I*have two Favorite Jokes of All Time. One is Cat's On the Roof and I included it in a previous book, and no, I won't tell it again here, and no, I don't remember exactly which book it was in—go read 'em all and you'll find it and it will be Worth It.

Here is my other fave: City Guy is walking down a country road. (We don't know why and it's immaterial.) By and by, he comes upon Farmer Jim, who is holding a fair-sized pig in his arms. City Guy sees that Farmer Jim is holding the pig up to the apple tree while the pig selects a plump, juicy apple and happily gobbles it up. When the pig has finished the apple, Farmer Jim dutifully moves so that the pig can reach the next apple that's caught his eye and so on and so forth. This goes on for at least an hour and City Guy is mesmerized and not a little perplexed by the whole process. Finally, he can bear it no more and he hollers out to Farmer Jim, "Good grief, man, are you CRAZY? Can't you SEE it would be so much FASTER to just throw a bunch of apples on the ground and let the pig walk around and eat them? What you're doing here is just a colossal waste of time!" To which Farmer Jim slowly replied, "Aww, mister, that's the silliest thing I ever heard! What's TIME to a PIG?"

Pigs, in my opinion, seem to have a most excellent sense of Using Time Wisely. You just hardly ever see a pig doing anything that is not absolutely necessary to the immediate comfort and personal peace of mind of that pig. They are not fans of busy-work—or any work, for that matter—other than the never-ending, but always-pleasant pursuit of food. I personally admire that since it's my favorite hobby as well. Me and pigs are like-wise capable of significant ruckus-raising should we be hindered in that pursuit. I concede to porcine superiority in the volume department; they can and do produce shrieks that are at least two decibels louder than a jet engine at takeoff, thus ensuring that the squeaky wheel DOES PROMPTLY get the grease, or in this case, lunch, but I think the pigs would at least consider me a worthy second place here.

However, I digress—time is our subject here, specifically the Prudent Use of It. Time is one of the very few—if not the ONLY—fair thing in the entire universe. Nobody can get any more of it than anybody else—no matter who you are, what you've got, or who your daddy is. Everybody gets the same daily allotment of 86,400 seconds, and the spending of those is our exclusive option and responsibility.

Since no more of it can be gotten, it's best to use it to full advantage. What follows here is the transcript of an actual Girl-on-Boy Pickup Attempt in a bar, as related to me by the Intended Prey, a man I have known to be well above average on the hon-esty scale for at least 35 years. I believe it to be the Gold Standard for any time efficiency test you care to apply.

Woman: You handsome.
Man: Thanks.
Woman: You Indian?
Man: No, Chinese.
Woman: You so FINE.

Man: Thanks.

Woman: You married?

Man: Yes.

Woman: She here?

Man: (We were not privy to the rest of the conversation, but since he was freely telling it, I think we can safely assume that he removed himself from her target zone.)

Let us examine this exchange: She has clearly zeroed in on something that piqued her interest and wasted no time (or excess words) in the pursuit thereof. We can't tell from her question where she stood on the issue of ethnic origin. Was she specifically seeking a liaison with a native of either America or Bombay, or did she have a bias against them? Perhaps she was merely making what she imagined to be polite conversation?

In any event, the answer proved satisfactory since she forged ahead with her efforts. We can't know the reason for her inquiry regarding his marital status, since his affirmative answer was no dissuasion to her pursuit. Or perhaps she was particularly interested in a man so encumbered, thus avoiding the potential for any such encumbrance on her own freedoms?

But above all, you gotta admire the absolute economy of WORDS here. This is an entire "courtship dance," if you will, performed without the use of even a single VERB. Pretty efficient—if they handed out carbon credits for concise communications, she'd be considered pretty "green," I reckon.

In today's world, where just about everybody describes themselves as "crazy busy" (though it often seems to me like there maybe ought to be an "and" in between those two words for a lot of folks), we really don't necessarily want to devote (waste) a lot of time to the slow nurturing and development of relationships. We want to read the first chapter of the book and decide for ourselves what the ending will be and forge ahead, based on pretty much nothing. Or for the really impatient, how 'bout we skip the time-consuming reading part altogether and just go by that cover?

There are far too many times when we blatantly and will-fully ignore the noisy flapping of a thousand red run-from-this-relationship-like-it's-a-festering-boil flags with some guy, but then we hang on until way past the expiration date and the whole thing is just a rotting corpse. Who knows why we do this? But we must admit that we do and it always ends badly but not surpris-ingly. This use of our precious time is puzzling to the extreme.

We seem to be unwilling to allocate any time on the front end of the deal—when we might notice those red flags and choose to move on, unscathed. But then, when we are being bat-tered about the head and body with the flapping flags (or worse), we will often dig in and stay, as if our next complete respiratory cycle could only be granted to us by this, well, for lack of a better word, asshole.

It can be difficult to make the necessary personnel adjust-ments in our personal lives at all—let alone in a timely manner. Enter:

The Terminator.
My friend Adrienne Moncrief Hemphill is a professional ward-robe consultant, which means that, for a very reasonable fee, she will come over to your house, root through your closet, and wrest from you an admission that you have not, in fact, even THOUGHT about wearing that dirndl skirt with the cummerbund in the last five years (for which, let me just say, you are to be congratulated), and then she will FORCE you to get rid of the thing. She will not leave the premises until every single unworn and/or unwearable

item in your closet is GONE—not just relocated to another closet in your house, but actually entirely removed from your possession. The item(s) could be donated to charity, taken to a consignment shop for resale, or relegated directly to the trash—from thence they will be taken to the landfill and burned, which is probably the highest and best use of them by this time—but they will be OUT of your house forever by the end of the day. (And to be clear, Adrienne's cutoff time is TWO years, not five; if you didn't wear it the last two seasons, it's outta there. Once you've experienced your Virgin Purge at her hands, there will never again be any possibility of anything hanging around, unworn, in your closet for five years—SHE will see to THAT.)

If there is an item that can somehow be repurposed or altered in some way so as to render it once again wearable by you, AND if, furthermore, it can be demonstrated that said item will also coordinate pleasingly with at least three (3) OTHER wearable items in your wardrobe, then—and ONLY THEN—will it be allowed to remain.

She is utterly ruthless in this process. Pack rats, like myself, tremble before her because her merciless reputation precedes her. If you still have a crocheted miniskirt from 1971 and you are now 57 years old and 35 pounds overweight, you must make up your mind to crochet a few more rows onto the bottom of it or turn that thing into potholders. Otherwise, it is GOING out the door. I'll just tell you, Adrienne has no patience for your sentimentality or nostalgia and SHE knows you're not about to drop 50 pounds, and even if you do, YOU'RE STILL OVER 50, so wearing that skirt again is really not ever going to be a realistic option for you and she does not shrink from sharing that painful truth with you.

But pack rats, like me, must pay for her services and be prepared to Mind Her, because she can do for us what we cannot do for ourselves: Identify Obsolescence and Obliterate It. (Note to fellow pack rats: Despair not. Just think of the FUN you will have filling up all that newly empty space. The moment she's out the door, you can start gathering more crap. If there's anything we pack rats love more than hoarding, it's acquiring more crap. And you don't have to worry about incurring her wrath for having crapped up your closets again, as she's COUNTING on us to do that very thing—it's her JOB SECURITY, after all! Win/Win.)

I believe there is a huge need in this world for a professional RELATIONSHIP consultant, a variation, if you will, on the theme of what Adrienne does for our closets—only, with PEOPLE. (I am pretty sure I just this second invented the Next Big Thing in Totally Made-up Careers. As a matter of fact, I think I will start an online university offering degrees in this, thus creating a new career for ME as well! PRO-FESSOR!) The Professional Relationship Consultant (PRC) would interview you concerning all the Particularly Bothersome Relationships "taking up space" in your life, "clashing" with whatever Good Relationships you may be lucky enough to have, and causing you to lose sleep as you try to figure out how to avoid dealing with them. The PRC would then, with cool impartiality, assess which ones just Need to GO. (He/she would be especially busy around any and all Holiday Times because that's when the "bothersome" factor of certain individuals seems to reach its zenith.)

There would be a principle similar to the Wardrobe Two-Year Discard Rule: If you cannot recall having had a single ENJOYABLE experience in the company of a particular person during the last two years, that relationship needs and will receive severe scrutiny.

Human trafficking being the huge no-no that it rightfully is, the consignment shop option is not open to you—even if there were a market for asshats, which, I can tell you, there is not. So, just like that crocheted skirt being converted to potholders, one must ask oneself if this relationship could be somehow redesigned—might you be able to just hire this person to come rake your yard, for instance? Or redeemed—might this person be somehow persuaded to stop being such an irredeemable asshat? And if the answer is a double NO, then…PFFFTT! They must be donated to charity, or in those truly unfixable cases, it might be best—and certainly simpler—if they are just thrown into the incinerator. Many charities offer free pickup service, after all, and you certainly can't argue with the no-messy-cleanup aspect of the fiery furnace. So there you go: Two surefire (insert pun-apology here) solutions right there and I'm not even a PRC. (Well, I'd have to admit to having done more than my share of Relationship Consulting over the years—both solicited and un; welcome and, likewise, un—but I certainly have never been paid for it, so that means I'm still an amateur and, as such, would qualify for the Olympics, I suppose, should such a thing ever become a Recognized Sport, and in my opinion, it's way more entertaining than a lot of 'em they currently recognize, like, say, Ping-Pong or curling, but that's just me.)

It is not unusual, in my admittedly amateur, but nonetheless accurate observation, for these Particularly Bothersome People to be members of one's own personal family. In these cases, the professional will no doubt recommend a Family Reduction and/or Remodeling Plan.

In a typical Family Reduction, those members who have, over the years, racked up excessive occurrences of Tedium, Ingratitude, Drama, Irascibility, Fiscal Irresponsibility, Incorrigibility, and/or

Unnecessary Roughness will simply be removed from the game roster. (Note: This is a short list of randomly selected examples of Bothersome Behaviors for illustration purposes only and is not intended to be a full and complete inventory. Personal experiences may vary; such variation does not render them invalid.)

There is a popular misconception that one has no choice but to maintain a close and lifelong association with persons who share one's DNA and/or had the same street address during one's formative years, without regard to any negative life-quality aspects that may have cropped up during or since that time.

I beg to differ.

And I beg you to reconsider.

"Downsizing" has come to be quite the buzzword in our society, so a Particularly Bothersome Person may not be taken utterly by surprise when they learn that they have become such a statistic within the family: "Cuts had to be made, you know, terrible thing, really, but there, off you go, now!" Quite British in its clarity and brevity.

The Common Sense Economic Value of Just Letting Go
Imagine you are in your car. Perhaps it is a big, fine, shiny, and new gas-guzzler of an automobile—with plush leather seats and every imaginable luxurious option. Or maybe it's kind of an old clunker—still runs pretty good, but it could use a paint job. In any event, your car is tied to Something Unbelievably Heavy, and there you sit, in the driver's seat, stomping on the gas, spinning your wheels, trying desperately to drag that Whatever It Is behind your car—and it is s-l-o-w going, if there is any going at all. The more the engine revs and the car frame shudders with the strain, the more you feel it in your own body's responses.

Your heart races and your mind shrieks and your muscles knot up, along with the pit of your stomach.

The Thing you are trying to pull, on the other hand, appears unaffected by all the commotion—totally passive and disinterested. It simply sits there and accepts your Herculean efforts to drag it along with you, wherever it is you're going. It does not care—at all. It doesn't seem to hear the engine, feel the tug, or observe your torment.

Its lack of interest in your efforts only drives you to pull harder. Your spinning tires dig an ever-deepening hole for themselves.

What if the towline were to snap? You'd be loose, but the sudden recoil of that might cause injury to innocent bystanders. No, as much as we think we want solutions to just present themselves spontaneously to us, the best case would be if you were to actually STOP trying to drag The Thing, open the door, get out of the car, walk calmly to the rear of the vehicle, and deliberately unhook that line—ahhh, that would be a glorious thing!

Imagine the difference then, when you climb back in that driver's seat and hit the accelerator—VRRRRRROOOOOOMMMM! OFF you would go, who knows where—but who cares? You're FREE and you're MOVING—forward, onward, ahead—without that big ole heavy load of Whatever that wanted only to stay stuck right where it was forever. And wouldn't you love to have some exciting new Possibilities to look forward to rather than the day-after-day drudgery of endlessly trying to Pull The Thing That Will Not Move?

Just like trying to drag something Immovable burns up not only your car's gas but the very engine itself, keeping yourself chained to Something Crappy in Your Life will sap your energy and have drastic physical repercussions. Whatever It

Is—miserable job, wretched marriage, one-sided friendship—
LET IT GO. And ask yourself, where might you go once you're
out of that mud hole? How fast? How far?

And even more important—ask yourself, what might you
GAIN? What new and wonderful thing might come into your
hands once you relax your grasp on this Bad Thing?

Ties that Bind (and Not in a Fun Way)
Unfortunately, it can be even more bothersome to extricate
oneself from a relationship with a person to whom one is not
related—like a cheating husband, for instance (just picking a
possibility out of a hat, here). But I do have a suggestion:

Move to Hong Kong. Yes, it's far and also unbelievably foreign, BUT I hear they have themselves a handy little law there
that says you may legally kill the bastid. (Although, the law does
state it must be with your bare hands, which, granted, is such
a COMMITMENT—but, really, how hard could that be, given
your level of pissed-offness? It also accurately reveals the true
sincerity of your emotions, I think.) AND—as a bonus and con-
solation prize—for being forced to move to the other side of the
world where nobody knows your name, OR what grits are, just
to avoid a messy (and costly) divorce, you ALSO get to kill the
cheating bastid's lover, by any means that strikes your fancy.

OK, I hear you, and yes, it's going to be expensive to even
GET to Hong Kong, let alone MOVE there (albeit temporarily), but when you factor in a lifetime of lost wages during your
incarceration—should you foolishly decide to select the Double-
Murder Option in THIS country—well, it just becomes a whole
lot more cost-effective to suck it up and go on and relocate to the
Far East for a spell.

In these uncertain financial times, it's important to think such things all the way through and not just give in to your every homicidal whim at the moment that they strike you. You've got to plan your work and then work your plan, as they say.

However, just playing Devil's Advocate here, although your career, whatever it is, will be completely over, you will save 100 percent on your rent, utilities, food, clothing, insurance—hell, you will LITERALLY eliminate ALL EXPENSES from your life if you go to prison. If you look good in either orange or wide horizontal stripes, I'd have to say, it's worth serious consideration. There are, after all, few other opportunities in life that offer such immense personal satisfaction in one's work—work with the security of a guaranteed retirement plan and that requires little or no formal training or expense. (A couple of bullets? A packet of rat poison? An ax? A double murder could be accomplished by even the uneducated with a very modest budget.) Right offhand, I can't even think of a safer financial bet than life imprisonment.

And once there, you could devote your life to working for the betterment of life for all prisoners, yourself included, by writing endless letters to state legislators or even to Congress itself, lobbying for regular manicures and pedicures, as well as more flattering uniform color selections. I mean, ORANGE, really? Only true redheads can successfully wear it—and we all know how rare THEY are. Why must all the other prisoners be forced to appear sallow throughout their unfortunate period of incarceration? Cruel and Unusual, hel-lo?

I think the main thing to keep in mind here is that, no matter how bad things may seem, or actually BE, there are ALWAYS options available to us. And sometimes, just knowing that is enough. We can work our way out of our funk by just IMAGINING how exhilarating it would be to cut off the air supply to the victim of our choice and then what fun it would be to feed the remains to the ever-hungry wood chipper. Tra-la! Yes, there is solace to be gained through this simple act of MEDITATION, and it is 100 percent FREE to all, in every way— dollar-, time-, and energy-wise.

So You Say You're a Sinophobe

That means you're afraid of Chinese people, of which there are a gracious plenty in Hong Kong, so perhaps you won't be murder- ing anybody on the Orient Express or subway. You'll just have to make do with an old-fashioned, stateside D-I-V-O-R-C-E, I reckon. Well, get on with it, then—no sense dillying or dally- ing—and it's not that hard, once you make up your mind and go to it. I've done it lots—piece o' cake, really. Not cheap, but defi- nitely money well spent.

I've been gratified to read that, since the publication of *The Sweet Potato Queens' Wedding Planner and Divorce Guide*, Divorce Parties have become quite the rage, all over the country. I take total credit for this and you're welcome.

I believe we can take the whole Divorce Experience even further, though. After all, it's not just about a good excuse for a party. I think it's time to write, take, and devote oneself to a set of personalized DIVORCE VOWS.

I daresay these may even be perhaps more important than the ones we took pre-Divorce. These are vows we need to make to OURSELVES. If properly made and kept, one might expect to live out the rest of one's days happy—AND unincarcerated.

For instance, we would definitely need to include a solemn— perhaps blood—oath to ourselves that we would absolutely Be MORE Particular in the Future. In that vein, Queen Sheila has publicly sworn that, in the future, she will absolutely abstain and refrain from dating any man who has or does any or all of the following:

- hips wider than his shoulders
- eyes only an inch apart
- is 40 and lives with his mama (and she is NOT an invalid)
- starts sentences with, "I think _you_ (should, are, ought)…"
- has a pet monkey

OR last, but definitely not least, in my opinion:

- walks on his tiptoes (ewww)

Now, she swears that there is positive proof that she did, in fact, encounter these qualities in a man or men (surely, they weren't ALL one guy, because that would beg one helluva question, in my opinion, and I'm sure you agree), but I have not personally seen this proof. Even without photographic evidence, I think we can prolly agree that these traits would and definitely should be sufficient to, at the very least, Give One Pause before accepting attentions and/or invitations from such an individual.

And those erstwhile Wedding Vows? The ones where we promised to love, honor, and cherish that Other Person (who, it should be noted, ALSO promised to do the same for US—and we see how well THAT worked out). What if we were to make and keep those vows—to OURSELVES? Ah, and if we added "Be Particular" to that list, what a wonderful world it would be.

Potholes on Parenthood Road

OK, I CLEARLY wrote the following piece well BEFORE my daughter Bailey's thirteenth birthday! Since then, I find I can still recapture the feeling by looking at her when she's sleeping. Or photos of her when she was a wee little beester. Well, for sure, photos of her when she was a wee little beester, sleeping. Those will do it for me every time.

On The Day You Were Born

Dearest Daughter—On The Day You Were Born I learned that there were deeper meanings to so many words I'd taken for granted for most of the 35 years I'd been around before your arrival. Even the word "dearest" never really lived up to the billing until I saw your face for the very first time.

"Joy" and "fascination" and "devotion," I realized, had been no more than so many consonants and vowels strung together until they put you in my arms.

"Fear" was truly meaningless in my life until I held you to my heart—my heart that was bursting with love for you—and I thought, "What a terrifying thing it is to love this much!" Because, of course, "love" also got a whole new definition On The Day You Were Born. I knew on that Day that everything and everyone I "loved" in my life could go up in a puff of smoke before my very

eyes—and I could somehow bear the pain—as long as YOU were safe.

On *The Day You Were Born* I opened a whole new vein of grief for my own dearly departed daddy. How you two would have loved each other! I believe that God's Timing is perfect—but I have to admit, this one gives me pause.

Dearest Darling Daughter of mine—On *The Day You Were Born* I punched in for the best and clearly most important job I've ever had. Even though the employment package offered literally no vacations (paid or otherwise), no sick leave, not even any coffee breaks, there was no possibility of "advancement." (On the flowchart, who would rank higher than the person responsible not only for 99% of the actual manufacturing of the product but also most of the after-market care of it—forEVER?) And the compensation for the round-the-clock, round-the-calendar hours of work? Ahhh—beyond price. A few weeks into this Motherhood gig, I am sitting on the side of the bed, back aching at 3 a.m., holding you, nursing you, and soothing you back to sleep and—wonder of all wonders that ever were—sharing that first look of soul-deep recognition and receiving, unworthy that I am of such a heart-stopping gift, your very first smile. You smile—for the first time ever on this earth in this life with that precious face—and it is for me alone. I could live a long, long time with only that to sustain me.

I could not know, On *The Day You Were Born,* how many times down the road—in your teenage years—that, some days, that WOULD be all there was to sustain me! I could not know that it would somehow be Enough, the memory of it and the hope for its eventual return one fine day when we know we've both survived—me your adolescence and you my menopause. Behold the Power of God!

On The Day You Were Born so much love filled my heart I could not fathom it. Where did it come from? How could I contain it all? How was I not exploding from it? I could not know, On The Day You Were Born, that it would continue to grow exponentially every minute of every hour of every day that I draw breath— miraculously, somehow, EVEN DURING the time of your hormones waxing and mine waning.

On The Day You Were Born, I believe I got a tiny glimmer of understanding of how much God loves us. And for the first time ever in all my life, On The Day You Were Born, MY MOTHER MADE PERFECT SENSE!

On The Day Your Own Daughter Is Born, only then will you truly know how very much you have been loved and perhaps I will suddenly make sense, too—a mother's fondest dream come true.

And yes, all of that has remained TRUE for her whole entire life, up to and including now; HOWEVER, that is not to say that there have been no times that tried my soul and caused me to ask myself that age-old question that comes to all parents sooner or later. That question being, of course, "WHAT THE HELL WAS I THINKING?"

Children, God's Gift: The Gift that Keeps on Taking
You would be better advised to keep an eye out for the SMOOTH patches in this particular road. I am telling you, it is ALWAYS gonna be SOMEthing. As an old person who is not only still actively engaged in trying to survive the upbringing of my one and only child, but also retaining vivid memories of my own asshatted teenagedness, I enjoy frequent, not-so-secret chuckles whenever I hear a parent verbalizing their belief that all will be well once "X" point is passed in the life of their child/children.

For instance, how relieved they will be when little Willie Steve finally sleeps all night or learns to walk, talk, read, chew with his mouth closed, or drive. THEN the deluded parent postulates that the REST of the way will be nothing but CAVU and foolishly imagines that those letters represent to parental life what they represent in the military: Ceiling and Visibility Unlimited. Experience eventually teaches parents that, in the vernacular of family life, it actually stands for Catastrophic, Awful, and/or Violent Upheaval. Or if you prefer, the more commonly used FUBAR.

We can often take comfort, though, by comparing our own lot to that of others—and find a way to be glad that our kid is either past that stage or has not thus far exhibited signs of moving in that direction. Consider, if you will, these two mother-son conversations:

Mother to Eight-Year-Old Son: Why is there gunpowder in your closet?

Son: I'm building a rocket.

Mother: OUTSIDE—NOW!

Son: It can't get wet, or it won't work!

OK, just some quick figures off the top of my head here: This kid is 8, so we have 10 more years until he's 18 (and not that he's going to improve that much by then, but at least he will be charged as an adult and it will be pretty much off her shoulders at that point), so that's 3,650 days—and we're looking at Xanax at least three times a day, which comes to roughly 10,550 pills that she needs to be getting her hands on PDQ (that's pharmaceutical lingo for RIGHT FUCKING NOW).

Another Mother to Another Kid: Please don't lick the bottom of your shoe.

OK, maybe it's just me here, but to ME, the Big Question that comes to mind is WHY is she saying PLEASE?

Mom I'd Love to Meet ("MILM")

Young teens are in the checkout line behind her. They are being loud and obnoxious, as only young teens can be, and they begin bellyaching about the endless rules and unreasonable expectations and demands of their Truly Terrible Parents. They could not seem to reach an agreement as to which of them had the absolute worst set, but they did agree that all the parents were, indeed, awful and how eerie it was that they were ALL afflicted with this problem—I mean, what are the odds? Finally, MILM could take it no more and felt that she really must speak up on behalf of the PPJTSTTs (Pitiful People Just Trying to Survive Their Teenagers). She turned to them and said, "Just so you know, it IS true: All Moms have a mass meeting once a month so we can plot and plan to ruin your lives. We have nothing better to do with our time or ourselves, and we are organized, so be afraid— be VERY afraid—you little shits." And with that, she paid and strode happily to her minivan.

As I said, I do have an extremely vivid memory of, I believe, ALL of my own personal asshatted teenagedness. If a few instances have fallen out of one of the holes in my old head, there are still a gracious plenty of them in there—haunting me, taunting me. And there is absolutely NOTHING in this WORLD that can produce the level of abjectly contrite, gen-u-wine REMORSE for one's own asshatted teenagedness like becoming a parent. Yes, ma'am, Mama, I SHO' AM sorry NOW. Way too little and decades too late—but Mama was damn glad to get it, I can tell you. As I will be when, one day, God willing, I hear those so-sweet words from my own Devil Spawn.

But aside from the perils and pitfalls of parenthood, there IS a measure of pleasure and joy to be had along the way, and I have had the great big blessing of being on both the receiving and the giving end of this deal.

Anyone who has ever had the dubious distinction of being the Parent of a Teenager will appreciate this: Payback is soooo sweet.

We can all recall times when the public behavior of our off-spring made us look around frantically for a rock with a crawl-space sufficient to conceal us. As they enter their teenage years, of course, our very act of continued respiration is enough to embar-rass our children, but occasionally, life spontaneously affords us an opportunity to reeeeally humiliate them, without even trying. As I have often said, God DOES pay attention.

When my precious darling daughter "BoPeep" was a sixteen-year-old, surly, eye-rolling, constant sigher of exasperated world-weary teenaged sighs, it came to pass that my husband, The Cutest Boy in the World, decided to grill steaks for supper. 'Peep's love for large slabs of nearly raw meat easily overcame her utter distaste for us and she agreed, without even a grudging sigh, to come home for the evening meal.

Now, we do possess an impressively large stainless-steel gas grill—a wedding gift from the beloved Parents of The Cutest Boy in the World—and TCBITW presides over it with absolute authority and something very much like affection. He looooves to wheel that big ole thang out and fire it up. But on this particu-lar occasion, it seems a bunch of stuff had gotten piled up around it in the garage, and since he was in the mood to cook, but not to reorganize the garage, he opted instead to whip out the tee-tiny little charcoal-burning Weber. Truly, it's about the size of a casserole dish on legs.

Picture this: The tee-tiny little grill is blazing away on the driveway behind our house. We've both been working in the yard all afternoon. We're taking a moment to rest while the grill heats up before showering for dinner. What I'm saying is we're in ratty, fairly nasty shorts. I'm pretty sure I was also sporting a tank top—always a good look. We're sweaty looking on account of we actually ARE sweaty. I'm sitting on a cooler, fanning myself with a piece of a cardboard box. TCBITW is sitting, shirtless, on the actual pavement, drinking a beer. We had just remarked and laughed together about how hideous we must have looked, hunkering Neanderthal-like around the fire, when a car—a very shiny, late-model BMW driven by one of BoPeep's similarly surly teenaged girlfriends and carrying a full load of same—inexplicably pulled up and came to a stop by the driveway (which is, as I said, BEHIND the house) and out came a THOROUGHLY mortified BoPeep.

Suh-weet!

The only downside was we got all covered with dirt and leaves and stuff that stuck to our sweaty bodies when we were rolling around on the ground howling laughing.

If you should trouble yourself to Google the term "spoiled rotten," chances are you would find photos of me and my baby girl prominently displayed. It's not my fault. My parents started it. (Yes, I realize that is the Spoiled Kids' Mantra.) We are what would be referred to in these parts as "pure-dee RURNT" (translation: totally ruined), and we are not the least bit chagrinned, unhappy, or dismayed by that fact. Actually, you could color us Pretty Tickled about it all.

I lived at home until I was 25—TWENTY-FIVE! But my friends not only understood it, they wanted to move in, too. You see, my parents were Feeders—they were not truly happy unless they were feeding someone, and I cheerfully made myself readily available for most meals. I am pretty sure there were guys who dated me just so they could eat supper at my parents' house four or five nights a week. My girlfriends still had SLEEPOVERS, for crying out loud, because there would be supper, and then the next morning, there would be breakfast, and if we were to lounge around long enough, there would also be LUNCH! All prepared and lovingly served to us by my parents—we didn't even have to do the dishes. In retrospect, I suppose it would have been the nice and polite thing to at least OFFER to clean up—but, well, I only just now thought of that.

Suffice it to say, none of my friends were happy about my decision to marry and finally leave home, as it affected them all adversely in the free-meal department—an area held sacred by most all young people and not a few older ones.

My parents, God bless 'em, would, every morning for 25 years, come quietly into my room and gently awaken me with a kiss and a soft whisper in my ear, inquiring as to just what I might prefer for my breakfast that particular morning. And then they would betake themselves to the kitchen and serve it up.

I have continued the tradition with my own daughter—even taking it a step further, if you can imagine such a thing. That child has been served breakfast IN BED EVERY DAY OF HER LIFE that she has spent under my roof!

There were the four harsh college years where she lived first in a dorm and then in her own condo, where there was, sadly, no room service in either location. She still shudders at the thought, and we try not to bring it up, in hopes that she will, one day, heal from the trauma. Time is merciful.

And then, of course, NOW she IS back home—attending law school in our hometown—so the Bad Time is definitely over. She can go crawl into her comfy bed at night and sleep like the baby she is, safe in the knowledge that, come morning, there will be a soft kiss on her cheek, a hot cup of coffee on her bedside table, and her breakfast cannot be far behind.

We do sometimes wonder if she will ever leave—and we are not entertaining any bets on that. Perhaps she could marry a chef and both live here? Hope does spring eternal. As much as I have loved being the Spoil-ER, one never really outgrows the love of being the Spoil-EE.

If Art Reflects Life, Then We Must All Be Hookers and Thugs
I think we may need to be preparing ourselves for this prospect, actually. I mean, have you watched TV lately? When I was growing up, pretty much everything available for our viewing pleasure presented us with a united front on the Way Life Should Be. Granted, there were some pretty huge issues regarding the way we were shown the relationships between men and women and the position of women in the home and society and all—HUGE myths and gross misrepresentations of women that had previously only been perpetrated since the beginning of time by the printed and spoken word. But with the magical advent of television, the whole family could (and did) see it acted out before our very eyes on the little black box in our very own living rooms every night.

It's nothing short of astounding to consider the changes that have occurred in the lives of women in less than 100 years—and it's even more astounding to consider what we've done (and not done) with all our progress. In my own mother's lifetime, women in this country got the right to vote. In my own lifetime, we got to serve on juries and have credit in our own names.

Of course, now everybody employs all manner of heaven-and/or earth-moving techniques to try to AVOID jury duty, not even half of us bother to vote, and the whole credit thing has really bitten us in the ass on occasion. When I was 19 and working in the Credit Department at Sears, a woman could not get a charge account in her own name. She had to have a husband, father, uncle, brother, cousin, nephew—some kind of person with a penis attached to 'em—to sign for her. The law changed while I was still working there, and one of the first things women lined up to do was charge a bunch of crap in their own names— for the deadbeat men in their lives who had already ruined their own credit.

I had a turn at that myveryownself. One of those life lessons I so wish I hadn't taken quite so long to learn—coulda done at after the first thousand, say, instead of racking up the full thirty. Some of us do learn real slow—but hopefully, real GOOD.

Anyway, life back then was presented to us by TV as flawless and pure, with a happy ending guaranteed at the end of every half-hour show. Unrealistic and chauvinistic as those early shows were, at least they held up the worthy goal of a life of character and decency. The bad guys never won and it was always perfectly clear which ones were the bad guys.

Now, granted, you might one day come to find out in your own life experience that real-life June really didn't always go along with what real-life Ward thought was best, because on occasion, real-life Ward was an asshat igmo and real-life June could use her own real-life brain and not only see his asshat igmonosity but actually get up on her very own real-life hind legs and not only refuse to go along with it but also tell him to go fuck his real-life self.

You were destined to find out that everything in real life most definitely did NOT have a happy ending. You were going to find out sooner or later that every old aunt who came to live with relatives did not smile, smell, or cook like Aunt Bea. It would become painfully clear that, in real life, nothing about Otis would be cute, funny, or the least bit endearing, and the real-life cops would not hesitate to put his drunk ass in the real-life drunk tank that was really not such a cozy place for sleeping it off.

But even if TV held up an unattainable utopia, at least it was something generally pleasant to shoot for. You wouldn't ever see TV June Cleaver sleeping with TV Fred Rutherford and their TV spouses discovering it and deciding that their best course of action would be to perform a retaliatory hookup and then get drunk and bitch-slap June and Fred at the company picnic. TV Eddie Haskell was a slimeball and everybody knew him to be a slimeball—we weren't ever even subliminally encouraged to aspire to emulate his sliminess. Today, Slimeball would be the name of the lead character and he would have a Twitter® following of several million.

Back then, turning on the TV did not bring with it the risk of beholding the bare behind of the Beaver—or even Whitey or Larry—with a bottle rocket sticking out of it. Nor was there even the chance that we might see the Beaver (or the other guys) then proceed to LIGHT said bottle rocket and scream in a shrill, girl-like fashion as sparks fell on tender flesh while he upside-down-crab-walked all over the screen and a ball of fire shot out of his fully exposed naughty bits in the direction of the drunken, guffawing bystanders—who were NOT Wally, Lumpy, or even Eddie.

And yes, I'm sure the parents of the above-described participants are very proud that, thanks to YouTube®, the whole world can still watch that footage anytime we choose, 24/7/365.

I think we can all agree that the ideals fed to us Boomers by everybody from Cinderella, Betty Crocker, and Donna Reed in the home to Doris Day and Audrey Hepburn in the workplace were seriously flawed in ways too numerous to count. But compare it to what our children are absorbing from *Jackass* (both TV and movie versions), MTV, and the myriad of "reality" shows that depict nothing but the absolute trashiest of all possible "real" scenarios, and the trash is presented as somehow worthy of emulation.

And while we're on the subject of "reality" TV, is there anybody out there who DOES NOT KNOW that ALL of those things are scripted and staged? In terms of "what grown-up people will do on national television for money," reality shows make "scholarship" pageant contestants look like genius-world-peace-making-cancer-curing-child-abuse-stopping NUNS—like if Mother Theresa was a "10" kinda thing—by comparison.

Anyway, I'm afraid that, in our haste to distance ourselves from the fairy tales and antifeminist fluff of the 1950s, we have taken a high dive into the septic tank, and right offhand, it just doesn't seem to be what you'd necessarily call an "improvement," in most cases.

Who's to say? Was it better for June Cleaver to be endlessly acquiescing to Ward, or would we prefer to see her run off with Fred Rutherford (or Miss Landers) and clean out the bank account so that Ward and the boys end up in a homeless shelter smoking crack?

God Wants Us to Eat Up

It's been pretty well established, I think, that the Sweet Potato Queens® are what we in the South call "Good Eaters." By this we mean you can put pretty much anything in front of us and we'll eat it with enthusiasm.

"Picky" eaters are unanimously vilified in Southern states. Nobody wants to cook for them or eat with them; they can and do, as the maxim states, fuck up a sack lunch and pretty much any other mealtime experience. Whiners, they create extra work for cooks and needlessly delay the dining-out experience for their tablemates with their tedious questions and stringent culinary demands. Then when the specially prepared food does arrive, they tend to inspect it as if they were ninth graders about to dissect their first frog, and they eventually eat it with reserve, apparent suspicion, and often thinly veiled revulsion at every bite. They don't LOVE their food. This is inexplicable to us, and therefore, naturally, we hate them. (Please note: We understand and acknowledge the vast and complete difference between a "picky" eater and a person who will actually swell up and die if a pine nut has been in the room with their plate. We hold no grudge against the allergic. Indeed, we are frequently moved to tears of empathy and compassion on their behalf as we dive, carefree and happy, into all manner of nut-bearing delicacies—while at the same time, we must confess to experiencing an undeniable twinge of pleasure at the prospect of, well, More for Us.)

We do, in fact, LOVE food. We love to see it, smell it, taste it, and ultimately, gobble it up in vast quantities. We love to talk about it, watch television shows about it, and write songs about it. I am not alone in the pleasure I derive from reading cookbooks page for page, as if there is a plot to be found between the covers.

We eat at almost any entertainment venue—we eat AS entertainment, no venue required. Any and all special occasions are only made truly special by the menu. Emotional upheavals—regardless of where they fall in the spectrum, from the joyous at one end to the woebegone at the other and all the intervening episodes involving fear, fury, loathing, lovesickness, apathy, aggravation, hopeful, hopeless, sanguine, and/or sleepy—whatever has happened, it has made us hungry.

Eating is required to properly celebrate or commiserate any momentous occasion in the lives of humans, including, if not especially, death. Suffice it to say, unless you are the, shall we say, "honoree" at a Southern funeral, you prolly came primarily for the food.

So, basically, what I'm saying here is we are definitely Pro-Food and we actively resist all efforts by Anti-Food types to foist their ideals upon us, which, if they were to succeed, would result in the fucking up of all manner of lunches, sack and otherwise.

My very first massage therapist used to wonder aloud how it was possible, given the staggering (in his opinion) amount of chocolate I regularly consumed, that my pancreas was not the size of an old VW van and bulging visibly through my clothing? He never failed to ask that rhetorical question at each session, and I never failed to offer the same unacceptable (to him) answer: Chocolate is GOOD for ME—so sorry if it is bad for YOU.

But time passed, research was conducted, and whaddaya know? Turns out chocolate IS O-fficially good for you. Some of us didn't need years of expensive science to tell us that, of course—and to think, if only they'd taken MY word for it, they coulda spent all that money looking for a cure for cancer or even purse-mouth.

Our mealtime enjoyment is enhanced if any (or all!) of the following are true:

1. We didn't have to cook it ourselves.
2. It has a lot of cheese (or bacon or chocolate) in it, on it, and around it, and it also helps if it has fried components.
3. There is a whole big lot of it.

As always, there are those naysayers and killers of joy who try to get between us and our favorite foods. This is really not a safe place for them to be, but there's no running them off or shutting them up, trust me. They just do love to be all up in everybody else's pantry, dictating diets and prophesying doom, but I have just found proof that God Himself has CALLED us to be "Good Eaters."

Don't you just HATE it when people quote Scripture out of context to further their own ends? Yeah, me too—unless, of course, it's ME doing it, in which case I am rejoicing that I have found Divine Support for Whatever It Is I Feel Like Doing at the Moment. And at this particular moment, I have found—in the *Holy Bible*—an Old Testament verse that is making me reeeally happy. I think this just may be the O-fficial Bible verse of the Sweet Potato Queendom: Nehemiah 8:10: "Then he said to them, Go your way, eat the fat, and drink the sweet, and send portions to them for whom nothing is prepared: for this day is holy to our LORD: neither be you sorry; for the joy of the LORD is your strength." Well, amen, my sistas!

I just don't see any other way to interpret that; it's practically a Commandment. God wants us to eat GOOD, and as long as we remember to feed the po' folks, we are cleared for landing at the boo-fay of life.

NOTE: *The following recipes (along with the recipes in all other* Sweet Potato Queens® *books) are poison. If you eat this food all the time, you will die and you will die with a HUGE ASS. However, taken in as much moderation as one can muster, they are GOOD for your disposition, so they are my contribution to World Peace.*

The Much-Touted Five-Minute Chocolate Mug Cake SUCKS

Don't be looking for THAT recipe HERE. Lord knows, you can find it ALL OVER the Internet—and it is a total waste of ingredients. It's not even worth dirtying the mug and the measuring spoon. It's not worth the electricity used to keep the lights on while you read the recipe and cook the mess in the microwave.

This recipe was clearly concocted by those people who regularly put forth all those ridiculous "hints" for killing cravings, controlling one's appetite, and/or losing weight. They chirp away with crap like, "Just really enjoy the FRAGRANCE of nearby fattening foods as you eat your iceberg wedge. You'll never even miss the food—but you'll sure love the calorie-savings!" Or "Just have one small piece of really fine chocolate and savor it slowly." Just the other day I read, "Focus on the number of calories in your available choices and you'll pick the low-cal one every time." Ha. Will NOT.

These are people who do NOT LOVE food. But that is not enough for them—they will not rest content until they at least attempt to make all of US not love it, too. These are NOT Our People. So NOT.

Anyway, this stupid Cake-in-a-Mug recipe is one of the more irritating experiences I've had of late. My dear friend Jeffrey Gross (mostly referred to as "Little Jeffrey," but we can't remember why) was visiting from NYC and we undertook to test a whole bunch of recipes for this book. This stupid five-minute Mug Cake was our first sally and it sucked completely. Right off the bat, I bet you can spot the Fatal Flaw in it if you don't get carried away (like we admittedly did) with the whole convenience and nearly immediate gratification aspects of it. Correct: NO ICING. Duh. WHAT were we THINKING?

Here's how you can save EVEN MORE time and ingredients and have EXACTLY the same result as you can expect with this recipe. You will need two ingredients and no utensils.

Ingredients:
1. Cocoa (any kind—don't waste the Hershey's in the brown box)
2. Kitchen sponge (new, used, doesn't matter if you scrub the toilet with it)

Instructions:
1. Dust sponge with cocoa.
2. Discard.

The Five-Minute Chocolate Cake in a Mug tastes and feels eggzackly like a sponge with cocoa on it. Complete waste of five minutes and a dirty mug.

HOWEVER. Little Jeffrey and I did think that the CONCEPT had definite merit worth further exploration on our part, so when we went to the Kroger for all our test ingredients, we picked up the cheapest brownie mix available. It was a Kroger brand, $1.69. Little Jeffrey mixed it up according to the package instructions, and we put half a cup of the batter into a microwave-safe mug and zapped it for three minutes. Yum.

Then Little Jeffrey wanted to tinker with the texture a bit, so he made another mug and put it in for only one minute. Also yum. This is totally worth doing. Three minutes for a chewy brownie and one minute for more of a ganache. As the two batches cooled (that was the hardest part—waiting), we noted that the chewy one took on an especially pleasing quality: It was as if the entire brownie blob was all "edge." If you are a Brownie Edge Aficionado, this will be particularly enticing for you. It's nice to have two choices because, as WE know, texture is a vitally important aspect of food—especially if one is Eating for Comfort, as one so often is.

Furthermore, we thoroughly appreciate the one-mug serving size. Face it, if you are us and you make an entire pan of brownies, we all know what size the "serving" will be—it's the whole pan. And if you are us, you really do not need to be eating a whole pan of brownies. The one-man/one-mug concept also allows for customizing for each person's desired texture—impossible to do with the whole pan.

But wait! There's more!

Whatever you don't use at the moment, you just freeze it! Then when the brownie urge hits you, scoop out a blob of it, toss it in a mug, and...VOYOLA! No, we did not pour the unused batter into ice cube trays to create perfect portion sizes. That kind of premeditation and orderliness just wears us slap out.

And one more thing: You can ALWAYS just eat the whole bowl of batter raw if it's really an emergency and you can also eat the frozen batter like ice cream if you need to. This is a Perfectly Swell Invention and we are calling it "BIG-ASS BROWNIE BITES." You're welcome.

Things frequently catch my eye on AOL News. You know how it is, you're logging on to check your e-mail and a headline just pops out at you, and before you know it, it's two hours later and you're still reading about celebrity divorces and/or arrests, a fat guy whose ass grew completely around the toilet seat, or a naked guy crashed through somebody's ceiling in the middle of the night. For me, I am receiving far too much information about the celebrities and not nearly enough about the naked guys crashing through ceilings. I have yet to read a satisfactory explanation for those situations and there's never any follow-up. A divorce is a divorce; there's nothing special about it when it happens to a celebrity—boring.

But a naked guy falling through the ceiling? There are just a whole lot of details that need to be shared in this area, in my opinion. That's some NEWS, right there. It happened not too long ago, just about 90 miles down the road from here, in Hattiesburg, Mississippi. In the middle of the night, this rudely awakened woman called the po-lice to report the circumstances of her discourteous rousing. The article in the *Clarion Ledger* (Jackson) said that he demanded that she give him clothes and she refused. We don't know if she had any men's clothes on hand or if he would have preferred something in a nice chiffon.

Of course, he was on probation. Now, I don't know for sure what the terms of his probation actually were, but I'm guessing that they didn't actually SPECIFY, in writing, that crashing naked through a ceiling of a home other than his own would be considered a violation. So how was he to know? Bless his heart, they shoulda TOLD him. Since they didn't even MENTION it, I'm sure he was completely stunned to learn that he was headed back to the pokey—after they picked him up, still naked, in the parking lot.

Speaking of "bless his heart," I had a brief exchange on Facebook this morning with a friend who said it just really fried her when people would say, "Be my guest," and it was perfectly clear from the situation and their tone that they were hardly extending a sincere invitation of any kind. To the contrary, actually. What they really mean is, "Kiss my ass." I suggested to her that "Be my guest" was possibly the secular version of "Bless your heart," although it would not be 100 percent interchangeable. Sometimes we really do mean for your heart to receive a blessing—but you have to know us pretty well to know for sure. Keeps you on your toes and we like that.

ANYWAY, what I started out talking about here is stuff that catches my eye on AOL, and just the other day, I saw this headline: "12 Easy-to-Make Breads to Try This Weekend!" And that just sounds like the makings for one helluva weekend to me—12 different kinds of bread in two days' time? I like wretched excess as much as the next guy and prolly more than most, and I would be happy enough with 12 loaves of the same kind, but this bread smorgasbord idea was just real tempting to me. So far, I've sampled only one of their suggestions, some kind of biscuit, but it was vouched for by two famous chefs, so Little Jeffrey and I thought it worthy of our time and flour. We were very much sorry. We shoulda stuck with the oft-tried and always-true recipe for perfect biscuits, the one we got from Mother Payne.

Carbs are Comfort Food and that is not a misnomer for them. We need carbs and plenty of 'em to keep our serotonin levels soaring, safely out of the range that leads to stuffing troublesome husbands into wood chippers and other surly behaviors. How many lengthy prison sentences could be avoided if we just ate a few more biscuits?

Test this theory for yourself. Keep this recipe handy, and the next time you are tempted to make your own man-mulch, whip up a batch of these and eat them FIRST. If you don't feel completely out of the murder-and-mayhem mood after THAT, well, then your first instincts were prolly right and you should go ahead on—just kidding, sort of. At least you won't be hungry that first night in jail.

Mother Payne's Perfect Biscuits

In a big bowl, pour one cup buttermilk and add one heaping tablespoon of Crisco shortening (don't substitute—Mother Payne never does). Add self-rising flour to that until you have a slightly "separated" dough. Spread a towel on the counter and sprinkle it with flour. Put the dough ball on there and roll it in the flour, flattening it out with your hands. Do NOT overwork the dough, or you'll have crackers, which will still be good but, well, not biscuits. The dough will be lumpy—these are actual biscuits, not those slick whomp things. Cut biscuits with a cookie cutter or a glass—to whatever size you like. Put biscuits on a greased cookie sheet. Dip the back of a teaspoon into the Crisco and put a teeny tiny dot on top of each biscuit. Bake at 425 until light golden brown. Serve hot—with butter and ho-made pear preserves. If you've got something better, bring it here.

High-Octane Mac 'n' Cheese

This was a really nice low-fat recipe (I mean, "nice" as far as low-fat goes, of course) that I had made for years, using ground turkey breast and low-fat cheese. Then, one fine day, I set about to make it and found that I had neither ground turkey nor low-fat cheese, but I did have ground round and habanero cheddar—full fat, naturally. Suffice it to say, I have never again made the low-fat version. This is soooo good AND it takes 20 minutes, I swear.

Boil a pound of penne pasta. This is the most time-consuming part of the whole deal. While that's cooking, brown one and a half pounds ground beef. Let me take a moment here to recommend this Tupperware® thing—the Stack Cooker. I use this thing ALL THE TIME; you should get one. I just dump the ground beef into it and zap it for six or seven minutes—it's done and the grease is all drained out of the meat and into the bottom of the stack. Genius. If you don't have one of these, just brown it in a skillet—the same one you're gonna use for all the rest. You'll just need to drain off the fat when the meat's brown, and then you can add everything else in on top of the meat as you go. Either way, you're gonna need at least a 14-inch skillet—this makes a LOT.

If you're smart and mind me and get a Stack, then while that is doing its thing in the microwave, you can be cooking a cup or so of chopped onions and chopped green bell peppers in a little bit of olive oil. Cook those until tender and add one teaspoon salt, two tablespoons chili powder, one 14.5-ounce can diced tomatoes with jalapenos (plain are fine if you want no spice), one 15-ounce can tomato sauce, and one 7-ounce can chopped chili peppers. Let that simmer for a few minutes while you retrieve your browned beef from the microwave and chop it up into bite-size hunks. Add the beef to the tomato stuff, add one cup water, and let it simmer on low heat while you get the cheese and drain the pasta. Turn off the heat, dump the pasta into the mix, and add two cups shredded habanero cheddar cheese (plain works fine if you don't like heat). Stir it all up until mixed and eat!

IN THEORY, I Hate This Chicken Salad

But in reality, I cannot quit eating it once I start. This is so amazing to me. Historically speaking, when I have been served chicken salad that had what are, in my opinion, ingredients that are extraneous to the dish, I have had a fairly extreme aversion to it. These ingredients would be nuts, grapes, curry, and/or apples. Hate all that in chicken salad, both individually and collectively. So, it should go without saying that I also never considered adding MANGO CHUTNEY to the mix. TCBITW concurs: Blech to all of it. We like our chicken salad to taste like, well, chicken. But then Queen TammyLeigh Redmond brought us a big bucket of this particular concoction once upon a time when I was recovering from something or other, and to be polite and because we were starving, we tasted it. And you know how when you order a chicken salad plate in a restaurant, they bring you a little ice cream scoop of it and that's "lunch" where they're from? We ate JUMBO BOWLFULS of it—it was semi-disgusting, the amount we consumed. So that big bucket—which would have fed at least 25 patrons, one scoop at a time—the two of us polished off in two sittings. When I make it now—which I do often—I double or triple it, just on the off chance that anybody else wants a bite of it.

To make the dressing, mix all this up in a bowl: one cup mayo, half a cup (or more) mango chutney, and one teaspoon curry powder. (Little Jeffrey likes cranberry chutney—sounds good.)

Cook (I boil) and chop eight skinless chicken breasts. Toss together chicken, two stalks chopped celery, half a cup or so Vidalia onion (if not available, use regular onion and sprinkle a teeny bit of Splenda® on it), two peeled and chopped Granny Smith apples, half a cup toasted chopped pecans, and half a cup or more halved red grapes. Dump the dressing on there and stir it up.

I still hate it—in theory—I cannot for the life of me figure out how it is that I love this so much.

Barbara's Beautiful Cornbread

Barbara Whitehead, mother of our very own Shipping Tammy here at the World Wide Sweet Potato Queens® Headquarters, became part of our family when Mama moved into our bedroom for those last few months of her life on this earth. Mama and Barbara would talk for hours about Life Itsownself every day. Barbara made life worth living for all of us in this house during that terrible time. For that, and for this recipe, we are happily in her debt forevermore. She first made this cornbread for us to take for the picnic before we embarked on the Great Gator Hunt. When we unveiled it on the picnic table, everyone there sort of took a breath and then sighed a soft "oh." It was universally acclaimed as The Most Beautiful Cornbread That Anybody Had Ever Seen. We could hardly bear to cut it—but we bucked up somehow and did so, of course. And omigod, I could eat it like CAKE. THIS is the definitive cornbread, amen.

You need a 12-inch cast-iron skillet. Put it in the oven as you preheat it to 350 degrees. While that's heating, mix together three cups white cornmeal mix, one 16-ounce tub sour cream, one-third cup oil, four eggs, two cups shredded sharp cheddar, one 15-ounce can yellow cream corn, one 4-ounce can chopped green chilies, one finely chopped medium onion, and several tablespoons chopped jalapeños. Take your hot skillet out, put a couple tablespoons butter in it, sprinkle a little bit of cornmeal around the bottom of the pan, and put it back in the oven until the butter melts. Take it out, swirl the butter to evenly coat the bottom of the pan, and pour your batter into the hot, buttered skillet. Bake it for around 55 minutes, but good grief, pay attention. Your oven may cook faster or slower, so watch it—you do not want to ruin this cornbread.

Scott-apeno Dip

My sweetie pie, Spud Stud™ Scott Caples from Tupelo, Mississippi—who is the Best Thing That Ever Happened to Me on a Book Tour on account of he is the dearest man to ever draw breath AND he brought major food to at least half a dozen of my events, so I love him and keep him close to me at all times—makes this for me all the time. I nearly always have a tub of it in my freezer, he keeps me so well supplied. I do love him so—and this is not the ONLY reason, either.

In a baking dish, combine 20 ounces sour cream, 16 ounces cream cheese, three jars Armour® dried beef (diced), half a cup chopped jalapeños (canned are fine), and one bunch chopped green onions. Bake it at 350 until it bubbles. Serve with tortilla chips or, my favorite, Fritos Scoops. You will BE popular if you take this to a party.

Make-Believe-You-Can-Cook Pegleg Corn

We're big on imagination and playing pretend—I mean, you've seen our parade outfits, yes? These are most excellent coping tools—right up there with thinking about watermelon, in my opinion. When something is Less Than Desirable, just pretend otherwise and see if it doesn't help.

Once, when my seester Judy was leetle, Daddy had been left in charge of her for a few days while Mama went to Fort Lauderdale to visit her heinous mother. Apparently, groceries ran low—or at least the groceries that four-year-old Judy would deign to consume—and if there was anything Daddy hated more than shopping of any kind, well, I don't know what it was. Judy wanted a bologna sandwich. She had clearly been wanting a lot of them because the bologna supply was gone. So, rather than brave the teeming masses at Pannell's Grocery and Market on a Saturday afternoon, he prepared and gave to her, his only child (at that time), a "MAKE-BELIEVE BALONEY SAMMICH." And she was perfectly happy with it.

Judy was sitting on the stairs outside their apartment and the neighbor lady asked her what she was eating. Judy replied, around the mouthful, "A make-believe baloney sammich—my daddy made it." Neighbor lady could not wait for Mama to return so she could rat Daddy out for feeding Judy mayonnaise sandwiches.

Queen Anna Magdalena of the Drama Queens of the Singing River had heretofore been "the loser who brought the cups and forks or bags of chips" to parties because, while she is an actual bona fide Southern woman, she does not have our typical pathological need to prepare huge vats of fattening foods. It happens, I suppose. At any rate, she hit on this recipe and it is a huge crowd-pleaser and it allows her to pretend to cook on occasion.

All you do is melt together one stick of butter and eight ounces of cream cheese. Dump in two cans of drained white shoepeg corn (or pegleg corn, as Little Jeffrey calls it) and a quarter cup chopped jalapeños. Bake it at 350 until it's bubbly. We made it and found it to be Very Fine, and clearly, it will fool people into thinking you could kinda cook. After we ate some of it, we thought it might be good with bacon—because, after all, what isn't? So we put some in there and reheated it, and yep, we were right—good with bacon. We ate it as a side dish and as a dip with Frito Scoops—both ways highly satisfactory. I think you could also cook some ground beef and put that in there and people would think you could not only cook, but casserole.

Holly Springs Hill County Happycakes

My friend AliceAnd went with me for a Big Fun Weekend in Holly Springs, Mississippi, last year. There are many cool things to see there, not the least of which is GRACELAND, TOO, where it is All Elvis, ALL the Time—and by that I mean 24/7. It never closes. Ever. I don't care where you are in the whole entire WORLD, it would be worth your time to see this because I can, without fear of the slightest contradiction, assure you that you will NOT EVER see anything remotely like it, anywhere, anytime. Holly Springs is also full of lovely people who know how to make oh-so-lovely desserts. From the Millers and the Browns, I received a large quantity of these bars that made me want to kiss everybody in both families, back several generations, full on the mouth, for a long time. I got the recipe from both families, and the only difference is one has coconut and one doesn't. So, if you like coconut, use it, and if you don't, well, I think you can figure out what to do. I can go either way, of course.

Here's how to Get Happy: Line a 13x9x2 pan with whole graham crackers. Melt one and a half sticks butter, then add to it one cup sugar and stir until smooth. Combine one egg with half a cup milk and stir that into the butter stuff. Bring it to a boil, stirring constantly. Take it off the heat and add one cup chopped pecans, one cup graham cracker crumbs, and one cup shredded coconut. Pour alla dat over the grahams in the pan. Cover that with another layer of whole graham crackers. Now, beat together two cups powdered sugar, one running-over teaspoon vanilla, half a stick butter (I just melt it, it's easier), and three tablespoons milk. Spread (or pour) over the top layer of crackers. Chill it for a spell, and then cut into squares after it "sets." It's best at room temperature. Color you Happy.

Redneck Salad

Queen Katherine (adorable, dutiful daughter of Queen Connie) sent me this recipe, and even I could not come up with a better name for it. It has redneck ingredients and it was lapped up by all the rednecks in attendance when Little Jeffrey and I made a test batch of it. So, there you go.

First, you're gonna bake a 13x9x2 pan full of Jiffy® cornbread (two boxes). When that's done, let it cool, and then crumble it up into bite-size chunks. Fry an entire POUND of bacon and do not eat any of it—it all goes in here. Whisk together half a cup dill pickle juice and one and a half cups mayo, then add one finely chopped Vidalia onion (if they're not in season, use a yellow onion and sprinkle some Splenda® over it), one finely chopped green bell pepper, and two diced tomatoes.

In a big pank (if you have one—Little Jeffrey thinks it makes it taste better) bowl, layer one-third of the cornbread, followed by a layer of the dressing—and repeat, filling the bowl. Now, the recipe calls for putting ALL that crumbled-up bacon on the TOP, but that made me and Little Jeffrey nervous, thinking that some unscrupulous diner might skim off excess bacon and leave the supply depleted for others. We thought of that because that's what WE would do, given the chance. So we put bacon in all the layers, just to be safe. Suit yourself—you know yourself and your crowd. This needs to sit in the fridge for at least an hour before serving, and it's actually better the next day.

I-Can't-See-My-Feet-But-Who-Cares Krispy Kreme® Bread Puddin'

Thanks, Queen Maggie, I am now too fat to see my own feet without a mirror, but who cares? What I see in that mirror, besides my highly overrated feet, is the very large and toothy GRIN that comes from eating this bread pudding.

Just when you thought a KRISPY KREME® was as good as it gets…In a big bowl, tear up a dozen regular glazed Krispy Kremes—I know, it's hard to do without just eating them all up, but trust me and carry on. You should know by now I would NEVER steer you wrong where KKs are concerned. Mix together two beaten eggs, one cup milk, and a two-thirds cup sweetened condensed milk and pour that over the doughnut hunks. Add a quarter teaspoon salt, a quarter teaspoon cinnamon, and a running-over half teaspoon vanilla. Put it all in a greased loaf pan and bake it at 350 for around 40 minutes. For the icing, mix half a stick melted butter, one and three-quarter cups confectioner's sugar, and two tablespoons brandy, rum, or any liquid. We just used milk and it was divine. Pour the icing over the hot bread pudding when you take it out of the oven. MUST be eaten warm!

Viney's Floor-of-the-Hilton Minner Cheese

I know, we've had other minner cheese recipes in the past, but this one is our O-fficial Parade Minner Cheese, along with Spud Stud Scott's, but HE didn't send me HIS recipe—so, fine. Every year at the Zippity Doo Dah® Parade, Queen LeighViney, member of the Elite SPQ™ Security Force, gifts us with a loaf of squishy-soft white bread and a vat of her ho-made minner cheese, and we sit around on the floor in our suite and gorge ourselfs with it. It's a tradition. We don't know if it tastes good in chairs, we've only eaten it on the floor. Use your own judgment—we don't mess with tradition.

She hand-grates a block of Cracker Barrel sharp cheddar, adds one very finely minced onion (give or take, suit your own onion taste), and one 4-ounce jar pimientos. To that, she adds one cup Hellman's mayo—to start. She stirs it all up and decides at that time whether it needs more mayo or not. This is purely a personal matter. We like a lot of mayo, because first of all, it's mayo, but also because we like for the finished product to lend itself to easy application to our squishy-soft white bread. Some people fuck it up at this point by adding olives to it—but not if they are bringing it to me. I don't mind if you put some red pepper in it, but if you put olives in it, eat it yourself.

Only Slightly Sinful Sausage Sub

Our peachy Georgian friend, Charlotte Ann, suggests this as a spectacular way to start the day. You have to make it the night before, but you will be glad you did, come morning.

Get a long loaf of good French bread and slice off the top third of it. Hollow out the lower section and tear the excess bread into little pieces. Brown one pound (we LOVE Bryan) sausage, hot or mild, and drain off the fat. Then add half a cup chopped onion and one cup chopped celery to the sausage and cook until tender. In a bowl, mix two eggs, a quarter cup milk, one teaspoon ground sage, and a one-eighth teaspoon black pepper. Dump the bread pieces into that and stir it all up until the bread is all coated, then dump the sausage stuff into that and stir it all up. Melt one stick of butter and brush it all inside the top and bottom of the bread boat. Put the bottom of the boat on a big giant sheet of foil and then fill it with the sausage goo. Put overlapping slices of cheese (I like pepper jack, personally) over the top of the goo, put the top on, and wrap the whole thing up tight in the foil. You can't have it until it has sat in the fridge overnight. In the morning, if you take it out when you first get up and have some coffee and it has time to come to room temp, then you only have to heat it for 40 minutes at 320. If you take it straight out of the fridge, it's gonna take about 55 minutes.

And here's an innovation that Little Jeffrey came up with: Break an egg into a microwave-safe mug (cover with plastic wrap), then zap it in the micro for about 40 seconds. Cut off a hunk of the sub, lift the top, and slide your egg on top of the cheese, replace the top, and chow down. We loooved our breakfast!

Tiny-Weeny Woo-Woo

Queen Pam keeps a gallon jug of this ready-made in her freezer at all times throughout the summer. So, I guess the Party is ALWAYS at Pam's. Stir together one 64-ounce bottle of cran-grape juice, one and a half cups peach schnapps, and one cup orange juice. If you want it "slushie"-style, put it in the freezer for a bit. If you need additional soothing, by all means, add some vodka to it. It also works well as a punch—just throw some orange and lemon slices in the punch bowl with it. I wonder if it shouldn't be called "BIG WHOO-HOO."

Shameful Secret Salad

I thought we'd had some low-rent dishes before—and we certainly have—but I do believe we have a new reigning champion in the Trashy Recipe Department. Little Jeffrey and I agonized over whether we could even bring ourselves to try this one, and to be honest, we only made a third of the recipe—thinking that we did not want to waste the ingredients, which we knew we would enjoy by themselves. See if you don't cringe when you read this: one 8-ounce bucket of Cool Whip, three diced apples, and three regular-sized Snickers candy bars, frozen. Right? Could you die? Our first thought was, "What are the APPLES for?"

But we were on a mission, so we girded our gastronomic loins about us and made a little dab of it. We used a Pink Lady apple because they are my favorite. I peeled it before I chopped it up. It would admittedly be slightly more attractive with the peeling, but who likes apple peeling in stuff? Nobody. It feels like something you need to spit out. So, we used one apple, one-third of the Cool Whip, and one of the Snickers bars. You just stir the apple pieces into the Cool Whip. Then, before you unwrap the frozen Snickers, pound it with a kitchen mallet or other blunt object, to cause it to be broken into fragments. Then stir those into the goo. Let it sit at room temp for 15–20 minutes. Try not to think about what you're about to eat and just get a leetle bit on a spoon and sneak it into your mouth. You will be STUNNED at how good this is. We could not get over it. We ate the whole thing and made the rest of the recipe right then. Will we be cast out of polite society for liking this stuff? Probably. But only if people know what's in it.

Many thanks to Sissy May Lynn (She's a Sissy and She May or She May Not) of the Fabulous Farkleberry Queens.

Armageddon Stew

Since this is a book about coping with the crappy parts of life—a survival manual of sorts, if you will—I felt this recipe from Queen Noelle (former Fried Flamingo Queen, Pep Squad Broad, and Wedding Belle) was an absolute must. After all, if the Big Fan should ever be struck with flying excrement, one must be prepared to somehow provide palatable sustenance for oneself and one's fellow survivors.

When Little Jeffrey and I read the ingredients, we unanimously decreed that it would HAVE TO BE ACTUAL Armageddon before we would be in a frame of mind that would promote a willingness to eat this. It contains not one, but three different CANNED MEATS. I don't know why the thought of canned meats triggers my gag reflex so readily—I admit to a fondness for fried Spam, after all, so you would think I'm fairly bulletproof in this area—but Little Jeffrey had the same response.

We couldn't even FIND canned shredded beef and canned shredded pork. The note on the recipe telling us we would have to "shred the chicken ourselves" was the least of our concerns. The Cutest Boy in the World came to our recipe "rescue" by locating an assortment of canned meats on a "survival and disaster" preparedness website, mredepot.com. (By the way, they are a really great company with which to do business.)

At any rate, in the interest of Total Preparedness and the ability to COPE with whatever crap life hands us, we felt we should attempt this recipe—as written—even though Noelle did tell us that it "works very well with REAL MEAT [emphasis mine] also." I think I'm not alone in experiencing a minor heebie-jeebie at the thought of "real" versus "any other kind" of meat.

Visions of Alpo danced in our heads and were not vanquished at the sight of the contents of the opened cans. We just forged ahead, suspending disbelief, as we assembled this dish that might be the only thing between us and starvation on some dire day down the road. We thought we might have actually found THE food about which that old axiom "Nothing tastes as good as being thin feels" could actually ring TRUE. "Thin" was looking mighty attractive by comparison.

It looked awful in its separate parts, it looked even worse all put together, and it smelled vile as it simmered. We were so NOT looking forward to it being "ready to eat."

BIG SURPRISE—IT WAS GREAT!

This WILL go down in history as The Miracle of the Crock-Pot®. I swear to you, after this stuff cooked overnight, we served it over rice and it was EXCELLENT. I do look forward to trying it with "real meat," however. I am certainly thrilled to HAVE a recipe that would render "emergency meat" not only edible, but tasty—preferring to not only survive, but also to spare suffering by every means possible. And believe me, if this stuff had tasted even remotely like it looked in the assembly stage, there would have been widespread suffering when mealtime rolled around.

If you make this on a day when most of civilization has NOT been wiped out, I strongly urge you to go with the "real meat" option. If, for whatever reason, you are opening the cans, you must TRUST ME—just throw it together with as little visual contact as possible and put the Crock-Pot somewhere where you can minimize exposure to the fragrance as it cooks. It will make it so much easier to bring yourself to take the tasting leap the next day.

Into your trusty Crock-Pot dump one can shredded beef, one can shredded pork, one can chicken (self-shredding required, sigh), three cans creamed corn, two cans stewed tomatoes, half a cup white vinegar, one medium chopped onion—salt and pepper to taste. Noelle said to cook it on low for 24 hours and to drink a pitcher of New Allison's Mambo Margaritas [see *The Sweet Potato Queens' Book of Love*, page 176, and *The Sweet Potato Queens' Big-Ass Cookbook (and Financial Planner)*, page 256] while they cook. But my Crock-Pot only goes to 10 hours and we just went to bed sober. That worked fine for us. As I said, we ate it over rice—and it truly was Very Fine.

Noelle also added the totally unnecessary parting shot that she was certain it would work equally well with possum and/or armadillo. Good Lord, deliver us.

The Holidays: Horrifying Tales of Human Sacrifice

*E*very coin has a flip side—well, except for those trick two-headed coins, but you have to pay extra and have those made special, so they don't really count and are certainly not germane to this discussion. Suffice it to say that just about everything in this world that is making somebody wildly happy is, at the same time, prolly making somebody else equally miserable. It has become my job to identify those things and make fun of them, with the hope of relieving the suffering for even a moment and thereby furthering the cause of my Ultimate Mission in Life, which is, of course, World Peace.

Whatever Human Condition and/or Predicament, I try to assess it honestly and then find some aspect of it that I deem worthy of ridicule. A great deal of territory has already been covered in my previous works: from first love/lust to divorce; from contraception to conception, and from thence to birth and the ensuing fun-, fear-, and fatigue-filled years of child rearing; getting 'round, sooner or later, to death; and of course, what all to eat in the meantime. I'm pretty much your one-trick pony, but lucky for me, I see life as an endless rodeo, meaning personal job security.

Come we now to the Celebration/Desecration/Desolation of Holidays. This could be the most concise thing I've ever written, if I chose to adopt the attitude of the Haters in this regard. It would simply be a matter of issuing a one-line, across-the-board veto of any and all holidays—both now and in the future, forever and ever, amen. But in the belief that laughter—and prayer—can and do cure most anything, and in the interest of furthering not only World Peace (first and foremost with me, always), but also my own personal Plastic Surgery Fund (see previous works for full disclosure of "work" already completed and listing of remaining jobs currently out for bid), I will endeavor to offer my readers an alternative view—more of a Tater than Hater perspective, if you will—and hope to convert the uninitiated totally to Sweet Potato Queenism in the process. After all, if I am willing and able to relieve for an individual a lifetime of recurring Holiday Miseries, would one think it too much to ask of that individual that they help ME, through multiple book and/or merchandise purchases, to finally get my tits hiked up? I should think, and certainly hope, not. Fair is, after all, Fair and all that. ("Tit for tat" would not be inappropriate here, except I guess, technically, it should be "tat for tit." Do we know what a "tat" is, exactly? Or how they came to be redeemable for tits?)

Posing the question "Why Do Christmas Holidays Suck?" is purely rhetorical, of course, because everybody who is capable of unassisted breathing and has even minimal brainstem activity KNOWS the answer. It starts with an "f," ends with a "y," and has an "amil" in the middle—and eeeeeverybody's got one—which means, sooner or later, there WILL be trouble.

Some families create mayhem and misery by their subhuman behavior toward each other only when they're all assembled together in one spot, while others—the really gifted ones—can manage to fuck up one-car funerals from far distant and assorted zip codes. The root cause of most holiday agonies has an extremely high probability of turning out to be some form of Family Crap.

As I told you earlier, our daddy always taught us this: There are very few situations in life that we really and truly can-NOT change, but on those rare occasions when we do encounter One of Those, then the task at hand is to figure out how to either Make Fun OUT of it or Make Fun OF It. This sage advice has served me and my seester Judy quite well, and I feel it would be wrong, on a sin level, even, for me to withhold from you what could and should be life-changing guidance in this regard.

Within these pages, you will find our hopeful attempts at helping you to avail yourself of our Sainted Daddy's Wisdom as it applies to a plague that predictably pops up every single year, without fail, not unlike the ubiquitous and always unpleasant stomach virus (except that, at least with the tummy bug, you do lose a few pounds).

Holidays—specifically those beginning around the end of November and dragging us all through Life's Knothole, side-ways, until the first of January—have for, I suppose, centuries posed just such a seemingly Unavoidable Situation for most of humanity or at least everybody I know.

So, we're gonna have a go at Making Fun OUT of The Holidays. If that fails, we'll move straight on to Making Fun OF Them, and if ALL fails, well, then, at the very least, there is always comfort to be found in the knowledge that One is Not Suffering Alone. (Google "misery loves company.")

OK, first of all, let's take a stab at answering the "Why do the holidays suck?" question. Sooo many possible Sucky Themes here:

Family Crap — Including but not limited to **Sibling Rivalry** — which is never outgrown, even if everybody lives to be 93 and can't remember what they had for breakfast today but can recount, in vivid detail, the list of all the Slights inflicted on them and the Endless Stream of Bonanzas heaped upon The Brothers/Sisters, from 1929 on.

Divorce — Involves the assignation of blame and the taking of sides, which can be entertaining, but only if one is observing from an uninvolved distance.

Remarriage — More blaming and side-taking.

In-Laws — My advice? Try your best to marry an orphan with no living relatives, but failing that, try putting Vaseline on your teeth for mandatory smiling marathons. And there's also alcohol and Xanax, but prolly not together.

Greed — Which you will see firsthand and aplenty if you have CHILDREN and/or SIBLINGS.

Sloth — This term refers specifically to the behavior of Other People; our own is more kindly referred to as Well-Deserved Leisure/Taking Care of Myself. We are not likely to complain that WE have just not been pulling our weight around here.

People-Pleasers — Many individuals hate holidays because they Over-Do—not so much in the sense of physical overexertion as in the way of Doing Way Too Much for Other People Who Don't Particularly Appreciate It But Feel Entitled to It Nonetheless. There is a name for people who repeatedly and consistently Over-Do in this way. Do you know what that name is? CHUMP. That's what we call 'em (ME) in my house, and chances are there's one in your house, too—and it's you. You are The Champ Chump. No wonder you hate holidays. It is not unusual to find that the Chump does not restrict chumping to just one holiday, either; a true Champ Chump is most often going to be a Chump for All Seasons. Chumpdom is more of a lifestyle choice than an isolated incident. (It would be interesting to see the assault and homicide rates among Chumps. That stuff tends to build up and fester over time, I'm just sayin'.)

These are the erstwhile Happy Chumps who continually bustle about for the benefit of unappreciative, often undeserving Others until they wake up one day and perceive their own Chumpdom, and then we find we have a whole new burgeoning crop of Resentment.

It's Christmas and You Don't Celebrate It — I can see that it must be supremely irritating to live in a world that is (on an annual basis) temporarily, but fairly, universally taken over by a theme into which you do not personally buy. I would no doubt feel the same way if, every year of my life, for approximately six months, all the store decorations, catalogs, magazine and TV commercials, radio music—literally every part of the world around me—were a constant barrage of Billy Ray Cyrus or the Real Housewives from Anywhere. Obviously, there is a vast, multifaceted difference between the celebration of the faith of several billion people and a few individuals I personally find either utterly boring or annoying beyond human endurance (Cyrus and all the Housewives), but that is a difference without a distinction for those hapless souls who, while they do not celebrate Christmas along with those of us who do, are nonetheless inescapably TRAPPED INSIDE it, every year, against their will, and I get that. Merchants, believers and non alike, do seem happy enough to rake in the dollars of the faithful, and as a nation, we all do benefit from a healthy holiday shopping season.

However, I suppose, if the months-long Cyrus-Housewives Festival of Awe(ful) came with days off work and fabulous sales, I might allow myself to be somewhat mollified about the whole thing. But perhaps, in the hopes of bridge-building, there should be some attempt to provide some sanity-saving methods for other faiths and/or even your basic heathens, who do, after all, have feelings, too. I don't know what those might be, though— and I've got my own problems to sort out, holiday-wise. Holiday Haters are just gonna have to drink more or something—I can't get involved.

Christmas Parties — This is the time of year when office, neighborhood, clients, and other people with whom you never willingly spend any more time than can be tactfully avoided host holiday galas that must nonetheless be attended and smiled and behaved reasonably well at by you. Personally, I have managed to dodge these by virtue of not having had a job for many years and living in a remote area. Pretty much nobody knows where I am. I recommend this to you. Highly effective.

Christmas Newsletters — I personally LOOOVE these and find them to be ALMOST as good as obituaries, in my opinion, IF you know how to appreciate them. It helps that we have Little Jeffrey to read them aloud to us in the style popularized on the TV show *Def Poetry Jam*, with accompanying urban sign language thrown in for punctuation.

Gifts — There is too much forced giving, and it results in way too much re-gifting, which wouldn't even be necessary if you didn't allow yourself to be trapped into it in the first place. How about you grow a pair (or more, if necessary) and just step up and be the one in your group to STOP THE INSANITY? Nobody needs or wants three votive candles you got at the $1 store (or are re-gifting!), no matter HOW fancy you wrap them—I don't care what Martha Stewart says.

The Cutest Boy in the World and I have hit on the PERFECT solutiontotheannualangstofwhat-the-hell-am-I-gonna-get-him/

her-for-Christmas: We just called "bullshit" on the whole thing; we took our own advice and we do not get each other ANYTHING. He loves me, I love him (arguably and demonstrably MORE, of course), and there is nothing in the world that we need or want, so that right there does create a very real problem in the gift-giving arena. You really cannot imagine how freeing it is to STOP that, and I strongly encourage you to try it for yourselves.

My friends and I made the same move a number of years ago—NO PRESENTS. None. Not allowed. We don't do birthday presents, either. We get together—we laugh, we eat, we drink, we laugh some more—but absolutely no gifts. It is, without a doubt, the BEST gift we ever gave each other.

If it's just "not Christmas without gifts" to you, then, by all means, SHOP! But do it for people who really need stuff and wouldn't have it but for your Christmas spirit. And, of course, kids. The chirren gots to have Santy Claus. I don't care if she's 24; she's the only little chicken I have and she's, by God, GETTIN' Christmas presents. And yes, I'm talking about my own baby girl, and yes, she's utterly spoiled beyond redemption, but that will be somebody else's problem one day. Right now, it's fun for me—so, fine. And, oh, yes, Little Jeffrey must have presents. He came so late in life to Santa but has so joyfully embraced the concept I fear we will all be dead before Little Jeffrey can reasonably be expected to "outgrow" Santa.

I do get fairly fed up with people complaining about the "commercialism of Christmas." Hunny, did you think Mr. Macy was your personal friend? Well, he is a MER-CHANT and he's been pretty up front about that for many decades. He blatantly wants to sell you things, makes no bones about it. See, COMMERCE is where this one group of people has Stuff that this OTHER group of people WANTS and so the first group SELLS the Stuff to the second group and both groups are happy. And that's kinda sorta what makes not only our country, but the whole entire world able to do stuff like feed and clothe ourselves. We all need for the COMMERCE to be big and fat and happy, 'cause when it ain't, we ain't got no jobs and we cain't buy no HD-TeeVee or ramen noodles or nothin'. If you're sick of spending money you don't have on gifts for people you don't care about and/or who don't need or want another "thing" in this whole wide world, but you keep on doing it, year after year, well, that ain't Mr. Macy's fault. You just dumb. But commercialism, just like Christmas itsownself, cannot be in your heart unless you invite it in. So, that's on you, hunny—do something about it or hush.

Decorations — Whoo-Lard, there is a very Deep End here over which many, MANY folks have taken a face dive. What MUST non-Christian people THINK when they see us creating, selling, buying, and DISPLAYING—in our FRONT YARDS— Nativity Scenes, in which ALL the Very Important People are portrayed by dogs or bears or an assortment of Disney characters? I can think of no satisfactory or even reasonable explanation for it, and I've been a Christian for as long as I can remember. I myownself own a ceramic Nativity Scene in which every single character—Mary, Joseph, Baby Jesus, Wise Men, all of 'em—is a CAT. If anything has EVER begged the WTF question, this has GOT to be it. I bought it, of course. How could I NOT? It's hilarious. Little Jeffrey calls it "CAT-IVITY," and every year, it's his special Christmas treat to put it out on the mantle when he arrives at our home on Christmas Eve. Little Jeffrey is Jewish, but he is quite taken with Cativity and, of course, SANTA. Duh. Who doesn't love Santa?

Food/Ten Pounds in Under a Month — Explain to me how it's totally possible to put that ten pounds ON in that time frame, but equally impossible to lose them, quite possibly ever. I do have recipes for stuff that will make you not CARE if you gain that ten and they're totally worth it. But there is some wretchedly awful stuff that inexplicably appears on potluck tables at every family and/or church gathering (usually involving shredded carrots, mini-marshmallows, and Jell-O), and of course, there is that fruitcake and the unbelievable truth that there are People Who Actually EAT It. (I have seen it done—more than once—and there was no wager involved. It was a free-will consumption.)

Does Hanukkah Suck, Too? — I don't know! What ARE "The Holidays" like in Jewish families?

I have to confess here that I feel a bit hamstrung by the fact that only J*ws are allowed to actually use the word "J*w." In case you didn't know this, if a non-Jewish person uses the word, the Jewish person feels insulted. Having many Jewish friends who I would rather chew up my own tongue than insult in any way, I respect this and never use it, but I confess I am confused by it. Admittedly, I have certainly heard it used in horribly derogatory ways, but at the same time, as a Christian, the One we revere above all was, in fact, a J*w, so you see my point. I wish there was a special dispensation for Proper and Appropriate Use of the Word by Gentiles, but there is not, and so I work with "Jew-ish" out of deep love and respect for the Tribe. And I mention this here now in case you've been using the word and you're not in the Tribe—stop that.

Having grown up as the baby in a white, Christian, Southern household, surrounded by other families that were just the same, if not more so, I am pretty well versed in "OUR" holiday drama, intrigue, and angst, but not having even met my First Jewish Person until I was in my twenties, what do I know about the Jewish Holiday Experience? Zip. Furthermore, even my own childhood holidays were tempered somewhat by several modifying details about our family that were slightly unusual for our time and place.

For instance, my mama was not only from Michigan, but she was brought up Lutheran (not one of the Big Ones in the South), and her daddy, who was reputedly the sweetest man ever, had died when she was 17, and she and her sister were left alone in the clutches of their what-passed-for-a mother, who was pretty much universally accepted to be The Meanest Woman Who Ever Lived.

Now, what does that tell you about my formative years?

First of all, I was language conflicted. Torn between a daddy from Ethel, Mississippi, who obviously spoke Southern, meaning that some one-syllable words, like "hey" and "bye," would most often have two syllables—"he-ey" and "by-yy"—and a mama from Grosse Pointe Park, Michigan, who REALLY spoke Yankee, meaning that she would assign two syllables to a whole DIFFERENT set of one-syllable words, for instance, "mule" would be "mu-wul" and "school" was "skoo-ul." It is a wonder I learned to speak at all.

Lutheran. If there was another Lutheran in Jackson, Mississippi, in the 1950s, I never saw or heard of one. And to this day, other than what I've heard from Garrison Keillor, I couldn't tell you anything about them. Mama never talked about it, for reasons unknown to us. (Is there a big, dark Lutheran secret, or is it just boring? No idea.) Daddy, on the other hand, grew up Methodist—which there are a lot of down here, but they're not a loud bunch like the Baptists, and they're not as bossy, so you don't hear near as much about them.

But when Mama and Daddy were newlyweds, living in Tupelo, Mississippi, without a car, it seems that the Presbyterian Church was the only house of worship within walking distance, and so, just like that, we became Presbyterians. And if you think Methodists are quiet, well, let me just tell you, they are a thundering herd, a cacophony of cawing crows, a barnyard of bellowing bovines—combined—compared to the Presbyterians. You could probably have 90 percent of a Presbyterian congregation made up of deaf-mutes and nobody would ever know who was and who wasn't. Pretty quiet bunch and they don't move around a whole lot, either. The term "Frozen Chosen" is not without meaning and/or plenty of substantiation.

As Presbyterians in a veritable sea of Southern Baptists, we were "different." Not nearly as many rules and no mysterious language. Presbyterians could dance, have a cocktail, wear shorts on Sunday afternoons, watch Disney on Sunday nights (no Training Union or Girls' Auxiliary), and watch Red Skelton on Wednesday nights (no Prayer Meeting). For the record, Presbyterian churches offered all manner of services other than the standard Sunday school, followed by church services—but Presbyterians did not fear being whisked immediately off the face of the Earth to the nethermost reaches of Hell, should they fail to attend one (or any) of those. Our God was not such a stickler for attendance as the One Who Governs the Baptists, and we did worship Him for that.

As to the special Baptist lingo, Presbyterians did not/do not get "burdens on their hearts," such as those that are constantly afflicting Baptists, nor were there any self-imposed, God-inspired "convictions"—only the occasional ones occurring within the legal system, which, unlike the former variety that were discussed fervently and endlessly, were rarely mentioned at all and never above a whisper that usually involved spelling out certain words deemed unfit for actual utterance.

No Daddy for Mama meant no Granddaddy for us. And the aforementioned Evil Maternal Presence in her life HARDLY qualified as what one would reasonably expect to call "Mama" in anybody's interpretation and was absolutely, 100 percent unqualified as a suitable grandmother for any creature, save perhaps a particularly malevolent jackal or excessively aggressive wolverine. She was mean, OK? She wasn't anybody's mamaw or grannie or mimi or maw maw or nanny. If she was mentioned at all—and she rarely was—she was "Gaga." Think "gag" and then add a gasping grunt to the end.

Daddy's People were as sweet as any humans could aspire to be, but Daddy's mama died when I was in the third grade, and Daddy's daddy was deaf as a post from the time I first knew him until he died—so there was not a whole lot of grandparently interaction with them in our childhood.

So, my seester Judy and I did not grow up with the traditional Southern massive family gatherings on holidays—or any other times. We visited our grandparents and cousins on Daddy's side of the family—in Attala County, Mississippi—very regularly, but for holidays, we were always at home. Mama's side of the family—our Auntie Marilyn; her husband, Jerry; and their two daughters, Debbie and Wendy—lived in Fort Lauderdale, Florida, not far from the aforementioned heinous Gaga, which was almost exactly 1,000 miles away, one way, and so, while, sadly, we missed really getting to know our Auntie's family, we were also, thankfully, spared very much exposure to the vat of vitriol and venom that was Gaga.

If we'd been forced to spend holidays in her presence, I feel fairly certain that at least one of us would have ended up the subject of a headline reading, "Fiend Seizes Hatchet, Slays Six," sooner or later. (She was mean, OK?)

We had our own Holiday Peculiarities and Peccadilloes that I will discuss at greater length directly, but suffice it to say that, compared to your Typical Christian (especially Southern) Family, Judy and I grew up in a tiny oasis of sanity, surrounded by the Barking Mad. But those tales I've heard all my life—what about the goings on in Jewish families? Who knew?

My first call was to my dear friend—the ever-brilliant Maryln Schwartz, author of the timeless classic *The Southern Belle Primer or Why Princess Margaret Will Never Be A Kappa Kappa Gamma* (Main Street Books, August 1991). (Since the Princess has Left the Building, the book has been re-released, substituting "Paris Hilton" as the no-hopes-of-ever-being-a-Kappa girl. Everybody in the world should read and own this book—there has not ever been, nor will there ever be, a more definitive, insightful book about Southern Women.)

Maryln grew up Jewish in Mobile, Alabama, and one of the first things she ever told me about herself (which she has also *never failed* to work into *any* of our thousands of subsequent conversations over the last ten years) was that SHE had portrayed "Queen Esther" in her Temple's Purim Play AT AGE 8—and never before in the history of the entire Jewish world, living or dead, had it EVER been done by ANYONE under age 11. NEVER!

She and I were once in a Mardi Gras parade together and she made the organizers put that rather lengthy fact beneath her name on the sign on her convertible. Since this took place in a small Texas town, I can only imagine the confusion this caused amongst the townsfolk on account of I seriously doubt that there had ever been a Purim Play in that locale. But Maryln smiled and waved in True Beauty Queen fashion, and THAT they understood plenty, so they smiled and waved back with great enthusiasm.

My relationship with Maryln has been strained over the years by her constant lording over me about the age-eight Queen Esther gig—but since she got her tits, she's nearly unbearable. Having beaten the crap out of breast cancer, as one would, of course, expect of a person who had, after all, been Queen Esther at age eight, Maryln had delayed her breast reconstruction for a few years, but let me tell you, the day they put those new tits on her was a Dark Day for ME. And over time, it has only gotten worse; she is positively insufferable about those tits.

First of all, she KNOWS, as does most of the sighted and/or literate world, that I personally have none and never have, and furthermore, she knows very well that it is a subject worn thin and sore over the many titless years of my existence. And that just makes it that much BETTER for Maryln. SHE'S got them and I DON'T—so, HA.

EV-ER-Y time I speak with her, I am forced, at some point in the conversation, to listen to one more oh-so-casually mentioned reference to Her as Esther at eight and then, again, with 100 percent predictability, some attention called to the fact that "well, after all, SHE's got TITS."

If I were a Baptist, I would suspect that God had put Maryln in my life as a test of my Christian Forbearance—which, it must be said, HAS been truly tested—but I'm not Baptist, so instead, I consider her a pesky blessing with enviable tits, and I do thank God for the great joy and privilege of knowing and loving her, the much-coveted tits notwithstanding.

So, I called up Maryln and asked her to share with me some stories of Jewish Holiday Horrors, if, in fact, there were any. I mean, for all I knew, Jewish people in real life were completely sane, 365 days a year, holidays included—contrary to any depictions otherwise on *Seinfeld*. The non-Jewish readers amongst you will no doubt be as gleeful as I was to learn that they are right up there with us.

Regarding Christmas, Maryln recalls "feeling bad" during that time because there was so much celebration going on all around her that did not include her. (I pointed out to her that SOME people might see a similarity between that experience for HER and MY experience regarding her never-ending victory dance over her tits, and I further noted at least Christmas only comes once a YEAR, where her tit-lording is day in, day out, forever. She willfully failed to see any correlation or similarity whatsoever, and are we surprised?)

But, many years ago, a close friend of her family, a well-to-do lawyer, came to the holiday rescue. It seems that Maryln's mama's birthday was on Christmas Day and so began a fabulously grand and enduring annual December 25 celebration to which many were invited, and it's still celebrated in parts of Mobile to this very day: Giselle Schwartz's Birthday.

One of Maryln's earliest Christmas memories was entering first grade at public school in Mobile, and on the very first day of the first grade, she managed to work into a conversation with a fellow first grader, Lucille Adams, the fact that there is no Santa Claus. We can only imagine the ensuing brouhaha that erupted to the utter bewilderment of young Maryln, who had no earthly idea that this information was, in other segments of society, considered Top Secret—more closely guarded than any other piece of information, with the obvious exception of S-E-X, of course. I'm sure there were many Southern children who did at least hear a rumor concerning "something about birds and bees," long before there was any hint at Santa's true identity. Lucille Adams informed Maryln that she, Maryln, had ruined her, Lucille Adams's, life and has never spoken to her since that day. (Seems particularly unforgiving coming from a Christian child, in my opinion, but perhaps Lucille has gotten a burden on her heart about it since that time and has repented. We can only hope.)

My seester Judy's friend Sue Meyer of New Orleans said that while she is Jewish, as children, her family always had "Santa," just like all her Christian friends. EXCEPT, in SUE'S house, Santa had no rules about crying, pouting, and otherwise behaving badly of which any infraction could result in Santa doing a flyby—a pass over, as it were—and skipping the recalcitrant Jewish child's home in his gift-delivery rounds. No, indeed, at SUE'S house, CHRISTMAS WAS A RULE-FREE TIME. Santa apparently did not care WHAT Jewish children did; he was far too busy watching the brat-nasty CHRISTIAN children, making and double-checking that list, and issuing dire threats. The little Jewish children in SUE'S house could act like hounds from Hell, and Santa would breeze right on in, deposit an embarrassment of kid riches on the living room floor, and fly away home. Sue's childhood clearly made her the envy of MANY children—Jewish and Christian alike.

I spoke with Maryln on New Year's Eve, and she had spent the day pondering over her resolutions for the coming 365, feeling the weighty importance of Using One's Time Wisely and Making a Difference in the World. She finally settled on just one goal for the New Year: She has resolved that THIS Will Be the Year She Sleeps With Sir Paul McCartney. (And she is, of course, certain that her tits will make her irresistible to him.) I did not tell her that my friend Lazy Suzy BonBon has made that same resolution every year of her life since February 1964—they can just duke it out amongst themselves.

BUT FOR ME...

I love Christmas—always have, always will. It's my very favorite time of year, the one most filled with precious memories of my daddy, whose enthusiasm for the season rivaled any eight-year-old's.

For all of the years we had with Daddy, the day after Thanksgiving did not see us hitting the sales in a shopping frenzy. On that special day, we could always be found, usually shivering in a drizzly rain, walking slowly up and down the rows of Christmas trees available for purchase from the local businessmen's civic group, looking for that Tree Amongst Trees—the one that would join our family until New Year's, gracing our living room with its glorious greenness and heavenly scent.

I remember vividly the introduction of the Artificial Christmas Tree into our society. The early ones were, of course, those wretched aluminum abominations that did not stand, proudly bearing strings of lights, before picture windows in stately grandeur, but rather, spun in slow, sickening circles, illuminated by a single spotlight, with a likewise spinning color wheel. My father would have just as soon had a spinning, steaming pile of lighted cow patties in the living room window as an artificial Christmas tree. I naturally share his sentiment to this day.

Daddy's delight on December 25 and the careful selection of the fresh-cut tree to honor the occasion found its double in the heart and soul of Mama, whose passion was for lighting and decorating the evergreen. It was this passion that dictated the type of trees that could even be considered for the job. Sturdy, but well-spaced limbs were required to accommodate the thousands of glass ornaments she spent decades acquiring as well as the dozens of light strings needed for proper illumination of this spectacular spectacle. The eight-foot ceilings of our 1950s ranch house precluded the preferred height—soaring—and necessitated, instead, a sizeable girth in order that ALL of her beloved ornaments be afforded appropriate display space amongst the branches.

Each year, she lovingly unwrapped each and every figurine and greeted them with as much joy as she would the friends who came to breakfast at her table every Christmas morning. Leaving some in the boxes due to "lack of room on the tree" was simply no more an option than leaving folks out in the yard because the breakfast table was crowded.

My parents taught us to reject the notion that Christmas could be "commercialized." Such a thing is simply not possible. Sure, the advertising for Christmas merchandise seems to begin earlier and earlier with the passing years, but as Daddy always pointed out, it should come as no surprise to anyone that merchants want to move their wares—it's sorta what they do, after all. But that's just BUSINESS and that has nothing to do with CHRISTMAS.

Christmas has not changed in over 2,000 years. Christmas has nothing to do with stores and stuff—and if that's what it's become for you, the fault does not lie with any shopping mall. Harlan Miller said, "I wish we could put up some Christmas spirit in jars and open a jar of it every month." I say we don't need no stinkin' jars, just open our hearts. That's where Christmas happens—and could it ever begin "too soon"?

Making All That NOT Suck — It is completely 100 percent possible to achieve this simply by actually employing such brilliantly simple platitudes as "Doing the Same Thing Over and Over and Expecting a Different Result Is the Definition of Insanity, You Igmo," and "You Really Don't Have to Do That," and my personal, lifelong fave, "It Hurts When I Do This—SO DON'T DO THAT." And, of course, when sanity and reason fail, you can always cheerfully resort to Ridicule, which will certainly be easy enough, given the material at hand. And if THAT fails as well, then, well, try to get glad about your own set of problems compared to those of someone else, and if even THAT won't work for you, well, you can maybe at least get happy that other people out there DO HAVE problems. (If you fall into that last group, I gotta tell you, I cannot resist telling you what a colossal asshat you are and suggesting that, perhaps, that is the root of your persistent unhappiness. It might not make you feel any better, but it will considerably perk up your peers.)

And then before you can recover from the December holidays, you've got the one that I personally love to hate: NEW YEAR'S EVE. And it REALLY, REALLY SUCKS. To me, it can pretty much be summed up by this: It Doesn't Matter Whose Vomit It Is, Your Jimmy Choos Are Ruined.

Shortly after New Year's comes a day celebrated worldwide, in perfect harmony. Do I really have to tell you that Elvis Presley was born on January 8? On this day, everyone still living who remembers The King should be required to dye their hair black, wear bedazzled outfits, curl their upper lips, gyrate their pelvises, and say, "Thankyewthankyewveramuch," as they hand out sweaty scarves to youngsters—to preserve His Legacy. Jailhouses should be required to rock, hotels should redouble their efforts to not do anything heartbreaking, hound dogs should be denied rabbits and gestures of friendship, but everybody else should try to love each other tender and true—just for this one day, anyway.

It is also worthy of note that this day also marks the anniversary of the birth of Walterine "Beanie" Odom of Jackson, Mississippi, who is quite frequently and aptly described as "inimitable." People who know Walterbean would agree that Elvis steals a great deal of thunder that should rightfully be attributed to her, but whaddya gonna do? She never had a hit record. But she never had a nasty drug habit, either—so we think she's been robbed.

I think the December/January holidays are the most fraught with peril because they are weighted most heavily in the Expectation Department, but that is not to imply that the rest of the year is worry-free. Not a-tall. Right on the very heels of New Year's Eve comes the Super Bowl. OK, it's not an O-fficial holiday, but it might as well be, and of course, it comes with its own set of anxieties, frustrations, and pitfalls, not the least of which is the stupid GAME itsownself, which 99 percent of the time is the Pillsbury BORE-Off—except for 2010, which was FAB-U-LOUS! That was the year, you will no doubt recall, that the divine NEW ORLEANS SAINTS brought home the Lombardi Trophy and all of us WhoDats ascended to at least the outlying areas of Heaven.

But even though for the other 40+ years of the Super Bowl it has pretty much sucked, there is always a mandatory party that we seem to think must be attended. These things too often end up with the men in one room, watching the game and drinking heavily, and the women in another room, just drinking heavily, watching only the funny commercials, and possibly wondering how many pounds they can possibly pack on in this one afternoon and how one can game last for 18 hours.

I don't have to worry about Super Bowl parties myownself, though, on account of since I just flatly refuse to go to 'em. The Cutest Boy in the World is not particularly interested in spectating much of anything; he's much more hands-on and would prefer to be one of the players BEING watched, so it's not like he's whining to go, or worse, for us to have the Super Bowl party.

I happen to be a football fiend, and I want to see the game, the whole game, and nothing but the game. And then there's the issue of My Language, which can render me unfit or undesirable as a guest in some settings. As you might imagine, this is not the only time in my life that this particular issue IS an issue—but at sporting events it is of special concern if there happens to be other people who can hear who are within earshot. The likelihood of them having their ears spontaneously combust from the stream of invective that spews from me when I witness a bad call or a blown play is extremely high. It's really best if I am contained in a private, enclosed area—alone. My precious iPhone has made it possible for me to share football games, particularly those involving the LSU TIGERS (GEAUX!) and/or the aforementioned SAINTS, via text messaging with my like-minded friend Red. (He was called "Red" from an early age on account of—big surprise—he had red hair. He said he guessed we should start calling him "Gray" now, for the same reason.) A casual scroll through the message history of our exchanges on my phone reads more like an enraged plot to avenge the murder of a family member and a beloved dog than two people watching a football game. And, lordhepme, if South Carolina is playing… Well, for any non–sports fans out there, let me just tell you this: Their mascot is the GAMECOCK. I think you can take it from there.

No sooner have we survived Super Bowl Season than it is February and we all know what THAT means. Fat baby with a bow and arrow. More gratuitous gift-giving—and generally not the kind of gifts I would covet, if I were to feel like ignoring the Tenth Commandment. Who doesn't every now and then? But red roses (blech) and pre-fab candy do not stir such rebellion in my soul. If you got a roomful of peonies and a truckload of truffles from Fifth Avenue Chocolatier, I might—I would tear No. 10 asunder, but who gets that? Lucky for me, nobody I know.

This particular "holiday," however, brings us that unique opportunity to Make All Men Miserable. Valentine's Day does not discriminate, for any reason. There is no escaping its grasp for any man; it does not care about your ethnicity, your religion (or lack thereof), your size, your shape, your sexual orientation, your financial status, your mental state, and/or your geographical location. (If there are any other variables I neglected to name, it doesn't matter—V-Day doesn't care about those, either.)

Whoever, whatever, wherever, however you are—if you ARE a MAN, Valentine's Day is out to get you. Because, without regard to any of the aforementioned potential, but futile exclusions, if you are a MAN, there is a WOMAN (or in some cases, another man, but it matters not, same difference here—and actually, as far as I've been able to determine, it's the same deal for lesbians) out there somewhere who is just WAITING for you to disappoint her (or him) by any one (or more) of any number of ways that you might fail to perform up to expectation on this one stupid, made-up holiday.

It might be your spouse, your life partner, your significant other, somebody you just started dating—it could even be your MOTHER, for goodness' sake—the Day is a total minefield, and the sooner you accept that, the better your odds are for survival.

Oh, she (or he) is not HOPING for your failure. Quite to the contrary, she (or he) is desperately hoping against all hope that you will somehow be magically morphed into Someone Else—Someone Who, While Acknowledging That It's a Totally Made-Up Deal, and Although, Admittedly, It Clearly OUGHT

NOT to Be Such a Big, Fat, Hairy DEAL, Nonetheless Has the Sense to ACCEPT That, Regardless of How Stupid It Is, He Needs to Just Suck It Up and Buy the Stupid Flowers and Does So, Without Whining, With Feigned Sincerity and Enthusiasm Would Be Even Better, If It's Not Asking Too Much.

In the interest of World Peace and Harmony—two things which, as THE Sweet Potato Queen, I do work tirelessly for—I am going to share just the tiniest bit of wisdom with you here, and so if this book ends up on your desk and it just HAPPENS to be opened to this page, we can only hope and pray, for your sake, that you take the five minutes to read it and then MIND ME. February is, after all, only month number two out of the WHOLE YEAR...Igmo.

Diamonds: Hard to go wrong with these, but certainly not impossible. For instance, anything with a LABEL on it that says, "Genuine Diamond," should be avoided.

Roses: Red ones are better than nothing, but they've just been Done to Death. Unless they are the personal favorite of your Beloved/Blackmailer, then go with some other gorgeous color—coral, yellow, fuchsia. Since you have to ask for them specifically, it gives the impression that you actually thought about what you were doing.

Carnations: DON'T YOU DARE.

My dear friend Katie suffered the Ultimate Valentine Humiliation once—and at the bumbling hands of the adorable man she ultimately married—thus demonstrating what a fine, forgiving Christian woman our Katie is. They were dating pretty regular and she was thinking that he just MIGHT be The One, and then what happens but Valentine's Day rolls around, and what does he do? He sends her flowers—to the SCHOOL where she taught (which would be great if it had been the aforementioned roomful of peonies, which would have caused a tidal wave of envy to sweep through the school, which would have been quite thrilling for Katie, naturally, and would have pretty much guaranteed that HE would get a Very Special Valentine hisownself later on). But no. He sent—I can hardly stand to see the words come up on the screen here—red carnations. Did you get that? CARNATIONS! HE SENT CARNATIONS—and the delivery guy walked all over the school with them, looking for Katie's room. He finally found her, and even her sixth-grade students instantly knew this was as Wrong as Wrong Had Ever Been and Could Ever Be. Nobody—neither kids nor fellow teachers—could look her in the eye the rest of the day; the shame just got all over everybody. They should have just dismissed school early—Misery Abatement. And THEN, just in case ANYBODY had missed it, she had to walk out of the school, CARRYING them, so all the Carpool Moms witnessed it and inwardly writhed along with her.

Then, when he came over later, foolishly bounding in the door like a big, happy Labrador thinking you would be so happy with that dead squirrel, she had to sit him down and explain to him—as gently as possible, given the circumstances and her own rumpled up spirit, but with absolute clarity and finality—the EXACT NATURE of his WRONG, lest he bumble around and do the same thing again next year. It took some time—straight men often have trouble with the nuances of flowers—but as I said, she was fond of him and she's an Exceptionally Kind Woman, so she persevered and he did live to redeem himself the next year. Once that was accomplished, she took my advice and officially quit Valentine's Day. I mean, it's just too risky. If a guy has sent carnations one time, there is just no telling what he might be capable of in the future—something "As Seen on TV" could not be ruled out.

Phony, made-up, absolutely unabashedly commercial? Yes. But, really, is it truly such a terrible thing to set aside a special day for a little Public Display of Affection? Surely not—and it just might bode well for a more private display…Couldn't hurt. Igmo.

MARCH is our very fav-o-rite month of the year on account of THAT is when A-L-L-L the Sweet Potato Queen Wannabes™ from A-L-L-L-L over the world convene in my very own home-town of Jackson, Mississippi, for the Zippity Doo Dah® Parade in the funky Fondren District. Yes, for many, many years we were part of the St. Patrick's Day parade, but that became too unwieldy and unsafe for the Queens on foot, and so we teamed up with the folks in Fondren to create a whole new deal.

Some folks were curious as to the choice of Zippity Doo Dah® for the name of the new parade, so here's the deal with that:

When it became apparent to me that the Sweet Potato Queens® needed a new time and place, "Zippity Doo Dah" was the first and only thing that came into my mind. For anybody who has read (and understood) my work (see *The Sweet Potato Queens' Book of Love*, Chapter 11), it required no explanation.

The song "Zippity Doo Dah" is very special in the Queendom—and you either get that…or you don't. When I made the very first announcement of the new parade and its name—at the closing ceremony of our 2010 Queens' Weekend—there was a burst of spontaneous, unanimous understanding, laughter, and applause from the 700 or so attendees from across the country and around the world.

"Zippity Doo Dah" is a Freedom song—about Emancipation—and it resonates on multiple levels with people who understand that my books are funny, but that the humor is just the vehicle by which the Much Greater Message is delivered. (There are blighted individuals who miss that entirely and we are sorry for them, but there's really nothing we can do for them. God knows, we have tried.)

In the Queendom, it's a very personal song. There are those who, through the Sweet Potato Queens®, have rediscovered their God-given capacity for joy and the overwhelming spiritual Power of Play. For some, it represents hard-won freedom from bad relationships in the form of abusive marriages or dead-end jobs. For others, it means finally achieving a lifelong dream, often against staggering odds. And for some, it's about just Still Being HERE, breathing in and breathing out, and living to love and laugh one more moment. And for still others, it stands for the Biggest, Most Precious Gift of ALL: that their CHILD is still breathing in and breathing out, and living to love and laugh—for a lifetime.

But whatever the personal history, we all come together— TOGETHER—for four days of, yes, truly unbelievable hilarity, but with a soul-deep undercurrent of equally unbelievable Power.

We have not found a Line in the Queendom that we do NOT cross. We are women, men, gay, straight, black, white, every other color and combo you can name, every faith (or anti-faith), every economic and social level, young, old, married, single, drunk, sober, and whatever else there may be—we've got it and we're GLAD about it. And we all get together for four days and play like CHILDREN and it is good for our souls.

Children don't care about what the world calls "differences." Children only see "SAME," and they love from that place. That's what happens during our weekend. No matter how "different" we may be in some ways, we have this one overriding SAME, and that is the almost indescribable chord that resonates for us all.

I am a Christian and Jesus Hisveryownself said that we must become as little children to enter the Kingdom of Heaven. We are of many different beliefs in the Queendom, but it is the ability to tap into that childlike capacity to love one another and play together that brings us together in March—and for us, it is, indeed, a heavenly experience.

It is altogether fitting and good that, as we gather to restore our own souls by playing like so many big, giant children, that we remember those actual children who cannot play—who may never get that chance unless there's a place like Blair E. Batson Hospital for Children. A place where every single one of them—regardless of who they are, where they come from, or how much money their parents have or don't have—gets a CHANCE. They get the best chance that human knowledge, skill, and yes, money can give them. And we get to help—by raising money and by spreading the Good Word about Blair E. Batson Children's Hospital so that other people will help, too.

"Zippity Doo Dah" is the PERFECT song for the true nature of this event and the people who come from all over the world to join in its celebration. It's the only song that would do, really, because it invites and allows us all to dance and sing that it is MORNING and the JOY DID COME, that it is MY TURN, that Mr. Bluebird is on MY shoulder, and that there IS PLENTY of Sunshine—for us all.

Come git you some—and remember our motto: "AnyTHANG for the CHIRREN!"

This is a total win for everybody. The other parade can have more floats now that they don't have all of us slowing them down marching leisurely, the Wannabes™ get a lot more attention (which they do loooove), and folks in Jackson have two great weekends. Plus, the Queens were able to raise more money than we ever have before for Blair E. Batson Hospital for Children—nearly $60,000 our very first time. YAY!

ZDD™ is the fourth weekend in March, so mark your calendar and start planning your outfits. Notice I said outfitS, plural—indicating that, yes, you will need more than one. Sign up for my newsletter at sweetpotatoqueens.com and also come join my Facebook fan pages—Jill Conner Browne, author, and of course, Sweet Potato Queens®—and you can follow me on Twitter as well. (I am beginning to master the art of twitting, but it has admittedly been slooow going! Don't expect your inbox to be full of twits from me right off the bat. And yes, I do know that "they" call them "tweets"—I think my version is more accurate, but that's just me.)

Anyway, the Zippity Doo Dah® weekend is JUST what the doctor ordered—assuming your doctor has a lick of sense. By the end of March in Mississippi, the azaleas are blooming and it is warm and beautiful—made more so by the sight of thousands of Queens in full regalia filling the streets.

In 2011, I got new outfits for the Sweet Potato Queens®—from sequinqueen.com, of course. I only wish there had been a hidden camera to capture the reactions of all the seamstresses ("Seamstress" assumes they are all women? What do we call a guy who sews? "Seamster"? Just wondering.) when they opened the box from me containing one of our old outfits—with the enormous UNDERGARMENT that creates that unmistakable Sweet Potato Queen Silhouette. Sequinqueen is in Thailand, which is not exactly the Land of the Giants—most women are around 5'1" and the guys are about 5'4". (I wonder if Thai guys all claim to be 5'9" like they do here. I am 6'1", and if I had a nickel for every guy that told me he was 5'9", as I was looking STRAIGHT DOWN at the very TOP of his head—well, I'd have me a big ole sacka nickels, that's for sure.)

Anyway, Thai folks tend toward tiny—in stature and girth—so I can only imagine the shockwaves when that box was opened and the Queenly boobs and butt sprang forth. I wonder if they tried it on. It would look like they were wearing a Volkswagen.

Anthony at Sequinqueen has overseen the construction of many SPQ™ garments for me, but never before has he attempted THE SPQ™ garment—the PARADE outfit that is so, shall we say, "eye-catching." Everything else they've ever made for us has fit as perfectly as if Cinderella's mice and birds had whipped it up for us theirownselfs. And, it must be said, that MY new parade outfit from Sequinqueen also fit to perfection. HOWEVER…the other Queens? Bwahahaha!

As life has run roughshod over all of us, we find it more and more difficult to get together all at one time. There might be this two or three or that three or four gathered on an occasion, but to get all of us together at the same time, in the same spot, just hardly ever happens anymore. Sometimes, when we meet to dress for the parade itself, THAT will be the first time we've all been in the same room together for months. And so it came to pass that on March 26, 2011, it was the FIRST time that any of the other Queens had seen OR TRIED ON their festive new parade outfits.

Imagine the attitudes and accompanying faces when they put on those new duds and found that, for once, the always-spot-on seamsters and seamstresses from Sequinqueen were NOT spot-on. Way spot-off, actually. The two "best" (meaning unbelievably, hilariously bad) ones were those belonging to the two tiniest SPQs— TammyCynthia and TammyLeigh. These two would look like elves in THAILAND, even—reeeally tiny wimmin, they are. But, here it is, T minus 30 minutes and counting until time to board the buses for the parade, and hold the phone, Houston, we do have a problem.

Well, "we" is not perhaps the correct pronoun. "THEY" would be more like it, because as I said, MY outfit was very glove-like and totally satisfactory—which is, after all is said and done, All That Matters. TammyMelanie and TammyPippa were well fitted, too, BUT there were two sad faces standing out from the others with the tears of laughter streaming down their cheeks as we gazed upon them, or rather, what we could see of them—so dwarfed were they by the dresses. We could see their heads sticking up and their hands could be found, once we pushed the sleeves back enough—we just assumed their legs and feet were still attached under there somewhere since it did appear that they were still standing upright.

PER-FECT! I only wished I had ordered them that way on purpose. I certainly will in the future. And, of course, they THINK I did it on purpose this time, and that's a good thing. One of the secrets to success as a Boss Queen—especially THE Boss Queen—is to maintain a constant state of at least a low-level grade of fear in your Queendom.

Queen TammyLeigh's was easily the bigger of the two misfit outfits. I think the crotch came down to her knees, which meant the hem was about mid-calf—which is SO attractive on a short girl, especially when she's wearing fuchsia majorette boots. She made our Spud Stud Andrew Wallace remove his belt and give it to her—whereupon she hiked up the midsection of her dress, folded it over five or six times, and cinched it with the belt. It held until about five minutes AFTER we got on the float—from then on she was literally dragging ass along the parade route.

But TammyCynthia's was my all-time favorite "look," and her attitude was, as always, "Fuck it! Let's GO!" (SHE would never SAY that, of course, being the very soul of Southern Ladyship—but we do imagine that she's thinking it, and fairly often.) Gotta love that leetle woman! She had a lot more going on with her equipage than just a dress that was several sizes too big for her, though. For some reason, the padding in her undergarment had disintegrated, meaning her gigantic tits and ass were no longer gigantic and thrusting out into the center of everything in the world. They had gone slack and way south—in a BIG way.

So, at the first-ever Zippity Doo Dah® Parade in Fondren, with her very large fake boobs hanging to her waist and her very large fake butt bumping the backs of her tiny little knees, Queen TammyCynthia happily paraded in the guise of "MawMaw Becomes a Sweet Potato Queen."

Here's the really funny part: They both seem to think that their outfits are gonna get fixed before next year's parade! SNORT!

Let me encourage you to join our happy throng: As I said, we are men, women, gay, straight, young, old, black, white, rich, poor, married, single, tipsy, sober, able-bodied, physically challenged, alive, and dead. When I say, "We have not found a line in the Queendom that we do NOT cross," I mean exactly that—there is NO LINE. And yes, I have the ashes of a dearly departed Queen, known to us all as "Dutchy," and she rides in a place of honor on the float every single year. Yep, we parade dead people.

I met a woman recently who told me she'd been left not only widowed but in a shocking state of financial ruin that had apparently been developing for some time, but had been concealed from her by the Departed One. HIS ashes were, she advised me, currently residing in a coffee can under the sink—she had not quite decided what to do with them yet. I told her of Dutchy's honored spot on the front of the float and cheerfully offered to tow him BEHIND it, if that would make her feel any better. It did seem to cheer her tremendously—for the moment, anyway—so I considered my job done.

After the big crescendo of craziness at parade time, the rest of the year seems pretty pale. Easter comes along, which is a Big Day in Christendom—the Biggest, actually—but for some reason, it's never been as fraught with peril as Christmas. I have no idea why. I guess it has to do with the absence of gifts—just not as much riding on the Easter Bunny's deliveries as Santa's. We had a couple of fairly entertaining Easters at our house when my seester Judy and I were little. One year, my maternal grandmother—the dreaded Gaga—somehow contrived to send to us, from her witch's lair in Fort Lauderdale, Florida, two baby-girl guinea pigs. But, in keeping with her lifelong pattern of Evil Doing, of course, one of them grew up to be a BOY guinea pig, and by and by, we had approximately 275 guinea pigs. Now, I'll grant you that guinea pigs are as clean and quiet and sweet an animal as you will find anywhere in the mammal kingdom, but when you get more than a hundred of 'em, it gets unwieldy. They lived in the backyard until, one day, they apparently all ran away to live in the country. Judy and I used to try to visualize them organizing and making good their escape, running en masse on 1,100 or so tiny, silent feet, down our street and through the neighborhood, and ending up who knows where "in the country"—what "country"? We never pushed for too much information on their whereabouts, sensing, I suppose, that we were better off with our imagined version of the truth.

Then there was the year that our daddy got us a couple of those dyed baby chicks. I know it's terrible, but they ARE so very cute when they're little bitty pink, blue, and/or green puffballs. Not much in this world is cuter. And Daddy was so excited to get them for us, too. So excited, in fact, that he got them pretty far in advance of the actual Sunday of Easter—afraid, I suppose, that all the dyed baby chick stores would be sold out if he waited too long. Well, he not only played hell HIDING two baby chicks for several weeks prior to Easter morning, but he also had not recalled from his Attala County, Mississippi, upbringing that CHICKENS GROW REALLY FAST. And so it was that by the time The Time came, the sight that greeted us in the living room of our house in South Jackson, bright and early on Easter Sunday, running around about our brimming Easter baskets, was NOT two tiny puff balls, dyed pink and blue, respectively, but two teenaged PULLETS, with actual gray-and-white FEATHERS and the occasional tag of pink and/or blue puff randomly scattered around their persons—100 percent NOT cute. Big, loud, scary CHICKENS—in the living room. They really did go to live in the country—at my Aunt Moggie's house—where they grew up to be dinner. I have no recollection of how they were transported there, but it could not have been a fun ride for anybody. Chickens do not, as a rule, care for riding in cars, I believe.

Easter is also noteworthy for being Break Out Your White Shoes Day in the South. Eventually, Memorial Day rolls around, which is, of course, White Shoes Day north of the Mason Dixon, but by then, it's practically too hot for shoes in the South.

The phrase you are most likely to hear on July 4 in the South: "Hold my beer and watch this." Phrase you are most likely to hear on July 5 in the South: "You ain't gon' believe this shit." The Fourth of July is pretty stress-free—aside from the uptick in DUI arrests and assorted body parts blown up or off by morons with fireworks, of course—but we make it our policy to try to avoid associating with people who are stupid enough to drink and drive and/or are too stupid to let go of a lit cherry bomb. So, we READ about those people, but we're not usually involved in their mayhem, which is good, because mayhem, bloodshed, and the like do so mess up a picnic. We do not like to be distracted from our barbecued ribs, watermelon, or ho-made ice cream by calls from the county jail or the emergency room (it's just off-putting), and if you are responsible for us being called away from our food to come bail your ass out or go hunt for some far-flung body part of yours when we are just sitting on the porch under a ceiling fan minding our own bidness (that bidness being the consumption of our pic-a-nic goodies), well, you won't be invited back, I can tell you that for sure.

I do not understand why folks continue to drink and drive—especially since most of the ones I know who do it should not even be allowed to drink and TALK.

Statistically, I think more *People of Walmart* photos are taken on July 4 than on any other single day of the year. It's probably the first day of the year when it's warm enough everywhere, even in Anchorage, Alaska, for folks to turn out in their tank tops and cutoffs—hairy beer bellies, fat arms, and lardy legs notwithstanding—and since it's an official picnic day, supplies must be laid in. It's hot and it's a holiday; let's get weird and go to Walmart!

Halloween is clearly the new Christmas—at least as far as advance marketing and competitive outdoor decorations are concerned. As soon as the red, white, and blue is marked down in July, the black and orange comes out, and I must say, I have been surprised at how easily people have been persuaded to devote so much cash, time, energy, and effort to covering their homes, lawns, and even trees with massive motorized, lavishly lighted outdoor displays, formerly reserved for Santa, Snoopy, the Seven Dwarves, and the Holy Family. It's like folks were just looking for another way to spend money, while mounting rickety ladders and risking electrocution and/or spinal cord injuries.

I grew up in a Halloween household, for sure. My parents LOVED to trick-or-treat. Daddy just loved to play, period—whatever was going on, he was up for it and usually one up on it—and Mama loved Daddy and she enthusiastically aided and abetted him in all his shenanigans. The two of them dressed up every year for as far back as I can remember—in order to "take the young'uns trick 'r' treatin'." Mmm-hmm. It was ALL and ONLY for the chirren—that being me and my seester Judy. That line worked and made them look like saints amongst the neighborhood parents and kids alike—until Judy and I were, oh, 24 and 18, respectively, HARDLY needing parental accompaniment or supervision any longer, at least not while on our own STREET. Even though Judy and I had outgrown trick-or-treating altogether, Mama was still excitedly shopping for Halloween masks every single year—for herself and Daddy.

They got new masks every year, until one very special year when Mama really scored a hideously horrible Halloween bonanza. For herself, she found this semi-opaque mask that allowed traces of her own features to be seen, but distorted them into a really scary and alarmingly real-looking face. But for Daddy? Oh my.

For Daddy's "outfit," Mama got this whole head thing that was enormous, and it remains THE scariest-looking thing I have ever seen in my life. It was big, with splotches of grizzled gray hair on the head and chin. The eyebrows were overhanging and bushy. The nose was bulbous and warty. Wrinkles and hairy moles were everywhere. The lips looked like, well, if we're telling the truth here, they looked like my grandmother's—the very mean and awful GAGA'S lips—which is to say thick and slobbery and kind of like two slabs of bleached liver pulled into a menacing grimace. Daddy loved it on sight and never wore another mask but that one as long as he lived.

At dusk, the first thing he and Mama would do is put on their beloved masks and go up the street to the Peshons' house to literally scare the pee outta Mrs. Peshon. I don't know where Mr. Peshon was, but he wasn't ever home at dusk on Halloween, because every year, Mama and Daddy would put on their very terrible masks and ring Mrs. Peshon's doorbell. She was a little bitty woman, as I recall, and she always sounded kinda breathless. They could hear her tiny footsteps on the hardwood floor as she approached the front door and they would hide—in a slightly different place every year. She would open the door, expecting neighborhood kids hollering "trick or treat," and there would be nobody there. EVERY TIME, she would come out on the porch and look around, and EVERY TIME, Daddy would pop out at her with his very terrible old-man mask, and EVERY TIME, she would squeal and wet her pants, and EVERY TIME, Mama would come out of her hiding place, with her mask pushed up on top of her head, tears streaming down her face as she laughed at Mrs. Peshon's pissed-on pants and porch—until, EVERY TIME, Mama wet her own pants laughing. And then they would ALL laugh a whole lot and Mrs. Peshon would whack Daddy on the arm and tell him how bad he was, and how COULD he do that to her AGAIN? And Mama would laugh and allow as how she "certainly couldn't do anything with him, he was just BAD."

And by then it would be "good dark," so Mama and Daddy would go on back down the street to our house, where Daddy would set himself up on the front porch, with a candlelit jack-o-lantern dimly illuminating him in his very terrible old-man mask. He would sit, still as a statue, while the kids came up and rang the doorbell, and then he would come to life and scare the crap outta them, and their parents, too. Ahhh, good times. Yes, Halloween was always a special time at our house.

The passing of a goodly number of years has had an impact on my own Halloween habits. As you have no doubt surmised, I do enjoy playing "dress up" whenever the opportunity presents itself, and I have even been known to create such opportunities for myownself when none showed up on their own—so I'm down with Halloween, Big Time. Back when I was first old enough to go out to parties and legally consume the alcoholic beverages being dispensed—and, indeed, for many years after that—my costumes always had a central unifying theme: trashy. Whatever I was supposed to be, I was a trashy version of it. There was always a lot, a lot of hookerish makeup and big, big hair involved—but fabric? Eh, not so much.

For years, there was a HUGE costume party at a place called Costas Lodge. I still to this day have no idea WHOSE party it was—but whoever it was, they sure did throw a swell soiree. One year, I went as a skunk, and I bet you think it's difficult to make a skunk outfit trashy. And you would be right—if you were to WEAR the BOTTOMS to the outfit, which I naturally replaced with black fishnet tights and extremely high black pumps. There you go…VOYOLA! Cute into trashy in one simple step.

And one year I went as Tina Turner—which involved a wig, a hot-pank "disco" dress that I purchased especially for the occasion, and the requisite hooker heels. The dress was two sizes smaller than everything I planned to put inside it, and it was, in my opinion and for my purposes, about a foot too long, which was easily remedied. There was also a lot of mandatory ass-shaking that is required of one masquerading as Queen Tina. I say, if you don't want to be called upon to shake your ass, dress as Joni Mitchell. Ass-shaking is a lot more than just second nature to me. I wouldn't necessarily say it has defined me and my life—definition might be overstating it—but you could safely say that, at some point in time, it has been all the parts of speech from noun to verb, and all points in between, including the gerund, as we've just seen. (When is the last time YOU used "gerund" in a sentence—or even thought about one, for that matter?)

Costumes of my creation could be counted on to be too short, too tight, and too low-cut—and oh, how I lament the loss of the body that could carry that off! Sigh. Do you even KNOW what I dressed as last Halloween? I wore a gray wig, with a hairnet, and I had both pulled down to a most unflattering place in the middle of my forehead. My eyebrows were painted to the size of merkins (look it up) and they were so close together as to nearly be united as one on what was still visible of my forehead. I wore a pair of SPQ™ rhinestone shades—with the shady lenses popped out so they just looked like glasses. I carried myself in such a way as to suggest that not only was I completely cowed by the entire world at large, but I also had more than a hint of a dowager's hump. And what, you might ask, would be needed to complete this ensemble? A bright-blue, but well-worn, O-FFICIAL WALMART GREETER'S VEST. All I did all night long was schlep around and sidle up to people and say, "Weh-cum to WAWLMARK." Yes, in Mississippi, the name of the world's largest retailer ends in a "k."

Not satisfied with the rendering of myownpersonalself into a hideous crone, I also undertook the transformation of my husband, Kyle, who is known far and wide, and for good reason, as "The Cutest Boy in the World," or for efficiency's sake, simply TCBITW. Being pretty far down Crone Road in real life, my own metamorphosis hardly even made a dent in my eyebrow pencil, but to take the magnificent Kyle and transmogrify him from TCBITW into my COWORKER at the Wawlmark—well, that took some doing.

First of all, I got the largest of the O-FFICIAL SPQ™ undergarments that we have in stock, and I put him in that. From there, I felt like I had a pretty good launching pad for his cliff dive off the pinnacle of Cute, where he usually resides. Some black stretch pants were perfect—they clung to that enormous ass with sickening realism, as did his knit top to the big, giant boobs. He got one of our O-FFICIAL SPQ™ wigs—in our signature red—WITH the hairnet left on, naturally. Who knows when one will be called upon to man a cafeteria line? Then I put makeup on that hawk-like face. Oh my. Cutest Boy in the World he may well be, but he ain't a purdy girl and there ain't nuthin' in this universe to be done about that. Anything you TRY to do only makes it worse. Mascara and lipstick on that face are deeply, deeply disturbing. Bless his heart, he is just plain HOMELY as a girl. But he was HAP-PY! Just a big ole ugly ray of sunshine because HE got to wear the Really Special Wawlmark Vest—it was burgundy (which is hideous on everybody, of course) and it had GOLD imbrawd-ree (kinda like "embroidery," only too ticky-tacky) and it identified him/her as the "STAR CASHIER." He was QUITE the star that night, for sure.

Can't tell you where I got the two vests—a truly Loyal Queen gifted me with them when she learned of my longing for them. I hadn't really BEEN longing for them until I talked to my dear friend Queen TammyEllyn, of Pendleton, Oregon, and SHE was DYING for a Wawlmark Greeter Vest and she told me that they were like GOLD or URANIUM or something. Nobody could get one—not nobody, not nohow. They were the Holy Grail (albeit of

Useless Items, since unless you work there, why would you need one?), and they simply Could Not Be Had for Any Price for Any Reason. So, naturally, I was dead for one—if for no other reason than taunting Ellyn. What do I mean, "if for no other reason"? That WAS the ONLY reason I wanted it.

So, I simply stated my desire on Facebook, and within MINUTES, my wish was the command of this Most Precious Queen Who Shall Remain Nameless but Well Thanked, Nonetheless. You cannot even imagine my glee when I received the package and it contained not ONLY the gen-u-wine Wawlmark Greeter Vest, but the unbelievable bonus of the Star Cashier Vest as well.

How fast did I get Ellyn on the phone? Pretty damn fast, I tell you. And was she sufficiently green with envy? Well, hell, I reckon she WAS. Most gratifying. But, being the good Christian woman that I AM, I did send 'em both off to let her have a turn with 'em for the NEXT Halloween. I swear, I am astounded at my own goodness sometimes—really, I am.

No sooner have we packed away our costumes and scoured off all our makeup than it's time, as citizens of the United States, to celebrate our acquisition of our own favorite part of the North American Continent, albeit by less than totally honorable means. The late, great *Pogo* comic strip used to call it "ThanksGRABBING," which is actually kinda sorta true, when you think about it, especially if you're Native American. But, well, we do have this swell country now and we also get time off work for the sole purpose of gathering together for gobbling and giving thanks. And there's a swell parade on TV, and the next day, there's bargain-hunting for the mentally impaired.

The most important thing to remember about Thanksgiving is that this is the O-fficial Start of the CHRISTMAS Craziness—which is where we started with all this. For future reference, Thanksgiving is the time of year by which you should have concocted and memorized your excuse for Why You Won't Be Around for Christmas.

At our house, of course, it was just another excuse for excessive eating, which always put all of us in a really good mood. Plus, there was just me and my seester Judy growing up, and we had no responsibility other than to come to the table and eat ourselves into a stupor, which we were more than happy to do on any and every day, really. There were no in-laws or outlaws joining us at the table, so it was always peaceful and quiet, except for the repetitive sounds of enthusiastic gulping, mastication, and swallowing that could go on for some time. Mama and Daddy always cooked together, every meal, three meals a day—except for the days when Daddy went out of town for work. But on holidays, the two of them were ALWAYS in the kitchen together. There were things that Daddy cooked and things that Mama cooked, and they never seemed to get tired of it or each other.

Daddy made the cornbread; Mama made the dressing. Mama made the gravy; Daddy cooked the lima beans and okra. They were both on turkey detail. It was a tiny kitchen, with about three feet of counter space, but they navigated around each other as smoothly as a dance, with never a cross word between them.

From the time I was a senior in high school until, oh, I guess until Daddy died in 1982, my parents also undertook the Thanksgiving dinner for my best friend Allison. They loved her, and Daddy always called her "AliceAnd"—we don't know why. But anyway, on Thanksgiving morning, Mama and Daddy would get up early, early, and in that teeny tiny kitchen with the one oven and negligible countertops, they would make TWO Thanksgiving dinners. They'd get AliceAnd's ready first and call her to come pick it up, and then they would start on our own. So when they weren't scaring the piss outta the neighbor lady, they were pretty sweet people, I reckon—which is a good example of how people OUGHT TO BEHAVE, holidays or not.

"27" Is the New "39"

$\mathcal{B}$ irthdays are not public holidays and therein lies the problem for some people, I believe. My friend Skippy Nessel is a completely adorable dollbuggy for days 1–364 each and every year, but when his birthday rolls around, he sulls up and shuts down—nobody gets in. No one knows why. Many people have tried (and failed utterly) over the years to jolly him out of this, with gifts, trips, parties, sexual favors, and the like—all to no avail. (Although I think he prolly doesn't turn down the favors.) Skippy prefers to pout on his Special Day, so we pretty much leave him to it, experience being the excellent instructor that it is and all.

I still gird my loins, muster up my courage, and make every effort to contact him by phone on his Special Pouty Day (SPD), though, and I don't take it to heart if all I'm able to do is leave him a voice mail. It's his day—if he wants to be a butthead, so be it. But this year, he answered on the first ring and sounded so perky I thought I must have dialed the wrong number or perhaps miscalculated on the day. But no. It was, in fact, the birthday boy himself, and it was, in fact, the SPD of Sir Nessel, so naturally, I wondered what was up with the cheerful demeanor.

I was soon to learn the source of this surprisingly sunny side of Skippy. It seems that the younger of the two beloved Nessel heirs had suffered a freak accident at a fraternity party (what are the odds?) the night before, resulting in a BROKEN NECK for the young squire. The reason Skippy was so deliriously happy—on this, his SPD—was that he had just learned that his baby boy was going to be 100 percent FINE, basically unscathed other than some bed rest and physical therapy. I nearly wept with joy for him, and I couldn't resist saying, "Wow. You will never get to be crabby on your birthday again in your whole LIFE after this!"

Skippy, being Skippy, allowed as how he has, in his words, "a mercurial temperament" and that he will no doubt find a way to simply "amortize it over time" from now on. I think we know better. In the coming years, I fully expect him to be breaking out the champagne, cake, and confetti—nothing but HAPPY birthdays for him from now on.

The Queens are not reluctant to celebrate birthdays, their own or otherwise. We are a celebratory lot, for the most part—any excuse is plenty good enough. Queen TammyPippa, always the extremist, adopted the month-long PippaFest plan for her own celebration. And Queen TammyMelanie has certainly never been one to pass up a party.

As the natal day of Queen TammyMelanie approached, I inquired of her as to her desire for a celebratory cake for the occasion, and she advised me in the affirmative regarding same. Yes, indeedy-do, she would be wanting her a REAL birthday cake, meaning "store bought," with tons of sickly sweet icing flowers. OK, did she want any "reading" on the top of it or just the obligatory edible floral decorations? Yes, of course, she wanted it to SAY, "Happy Birthday, Melanie," on it—but no age. So, she didn't want it to say, for example, "Happy 27th Birthday, Melanie"—not saying she IS 27, not saying she isn't, just a random number there for the sake of the example.

I've got my cake instructions and also that she would like to be taken to the Cherokee Drive Inn for Birthday Burgers, and from there, she would like to go "Mystic Bowling," which is when you bowl in the dark with only black lights for illumination. I will say that I don't bowl any worse in the dark than I do in broad daylight. But I also wouldn't bowl any worse if I did it with my left hand and my eyes closed. When you suck, you suck—degrees of suck aren't really important.

Calling around for store-bought birthday cake recommendations, the consensus quickly revealed itself: You just can't beat Walmart Bakery for a tasty, yet economical birthday cake. So, I called 'em up and placed my order—taking great care to communicate EXACTLY the wishes of the Birthday Girl, regarding her cake. I told them it was to be yellow cake with chocolate icing. It was to have a superabundance of flowers and fancy stuff, and it was to say, "Happy Birthday, Melanie," with NO AGE on there. And the Walmart Bakery girl read my order back to me—just as I had said to her. Or so I thought.

I will swear on anything you trot out here that this is 100 percent the truth: When we arrived at the Cherokee for Queen TammyMelanie's Birthday Burgers, I carried in the box containing the store-bought Walmart Bakery birthday cake and I set it on the table. Melanie came in and immediately demanded to be shown her cake, and so I carefully slit the tape holding the box shut and lifted the lid to reveal the top of the cake, which did have the requested superabundance of icing flowers. And it READ, just like this, "APPY BIRTDAY, MELANIE!"

You see what happened, yes? What the Walmart Bakery girl THOUGHT I said was, "Happy Birthday, Melanie—with no 'H.'" Now WHY she thought we would be so dead set against the presence of an "H" on our cake, I cannot begin to imagine, but that is, by golly, what we got. "APPY BIRTDAY, MELANIE," bigger'n Dallas. Yes, we do have photos.

Ally Ally In Come Free!

I recently celebrated my 27th birthday. OK, that's not entirely true. FINE! I was 58. And, admittedly, I was recovering from hip repair surgery, so there wasn't much in the way of celebrating—I hardly knew it was DAY, let alone MY day. But none of that is the point of this. The point is that The Cutest Boy in the World, being also The Most Thoughtful Boy in the World, pondered long and hard until he came up with The Best 27th Birthday Present EV-ER for me, the lucky object of all his love and devotion.

Yessireebobtailcat, he REALLY nailed it on this one. It is absolutely uncanny how he comes up with JUST what I was longing for, every time. He is one swell gift-picker-outter, he is. Nobody even comes close—he's THAT good.

At least, that's his story and he's sticking to it.

You see, we can't really offer any CONCRETE evidence to support this particular claim of Superb Present-Picking. (There is plenty of proof of past performances in this area, but that won't help him NOW, I assure you.) On account of if there is ONE THING that TCBITW does BETTER than selecting superlative surprises, it's HIDING them once he's got them.

That's right. He hid my birthday present—sometime around the first of November 2010—and here it is, July 2011, and he has not been able to FIND it YET. (When it surfaces, I will immediately send out a newsletter, post it on Facebook, and I'll "twit" about it, so be sure you sign up for alla dat. You won't want to miss this news.)

Despite devoting many (as in lots more than one) whole entire days—long ones, at that—say from around 4:00 a.m. until

8:00 p.m., pausing only for meals and potty breaks, rambling and running from one end of the house to the other, ransacking every area, top to bottom, only to reveal: NOTHING, except perhaps a larger command of four-letter words than either I or his mama had previously been aware.

He did find PART of it. Apparently, it arrived in separate parcels, so he does have possession of some accessory to the main gift and he has offered (begged) to give me that portion, in hopes of convincing me that, yes, Virginia, there REALLY IS a birthday present (although he does know better than to call me by the wrong name). But I have refused on the grounds that it will just "spoil the surprise" of the whole thing if I have PART of it, and since it's not the main part, it would be utterly useless to me, anyway.

So, back he goes, on the hunt—in the attic, in the boathouse, in his truck, in all the closets, in the freezer…you get the picture—and even though he's already looked in ALL those places, he looks again…and again…and again.

Someone (who obviously doesn't know him very well) suggested that perhaps there never WAS a real present, that he forgot and he's just going through all this to save his hide. Well! As I said, they don't know him at all; lying for any reason, ever, is just not in his DNA. He's just not made that way—thank God and The Cutest Parents in the World. Also, I am NOT FIVE. It wouldn't have been a deal at all—big or otherwise—if he HAD forgotten my birthday. I mean, he was waiting on me hand, foot, and hip after my surgery—the guy's perfect. So, no, there REALLY IS a birthday present and it really is MIA.

But, I gotta tell you, no matter WHAT it turns out to be—and sooner or later (obviously, at this point, LATER is our only option) it WILL BE FOUND—I don't see how it could have brought me any more laughs than I have had watching him tear the house apart for going on eight months now.

Whatever your "birthday style," pouter or partier, pick your poison—whether you need a little pick-me-up or a little calm-me-down—get as happy as you can manage about the fact that you are still HAVING a birthday. The American Cancer Society thinks that they're pretty important; that's their whole mission statement—"Official Sponsor of Birthdays."

Whenever I get really down—and yes, I do that—sooner or later, I remember my dear friend Cindy Holmes who fought cancer with every fiber of her tiny being and wanted so MUCH to live. I remember her blind fury when we learned that another friend of ours had committed suicide. For Cindy, it was just the ultimate insult. She could not even bring herself to go to the funeral she was so full of rage. HOW could he so blithely THROW AWAY what she was literally crawling through Hell to try to hang onto for another year, or month, or week.

Life. It's your birthday present. Open it up and play with it. Act like you like it. (The One who gave it to you is watching, after all. Don't wanna hurt His feelings.) And if you don't like your life, CHANGE IT. It is all yours.

Faith in Times of Stress: Religious Tolerance

$\mathcal{Y}$ou may recall from one of my earlier writings the favorite asseveration of a certain old coot from Attala County, Mississippi. Whenever he REALLY wanted to drive his point home, he would close with, "And if that ain't so, then God's a possum." Which never failed to convince his audience that he was at least personally convinced of the veracity of his statement—else he would not have dared to drag God into it at all, let alone suggest the possibility that He might be a garbage-eating, naked-tailed, tragically unattractive marsupial. It also never failed to draw at least one or two gasps from the Baptists in the group. Baptists live their lives on full alert, just waiting for lightning to strike—they're easily spooked.

I do believe that there is One God and that He always speaks the language that can be understood and I accept that I do not understand all of those languages—indeed, I cannot even begin to comprehend them. I must confess that I have serious doubts within my own personal soul as to whether or not some things perpetrated in the Name of Anybody's God are actually in any way pleasing to Him. While some must certainly be as confusing to Him as they are to me, a mere mortal, I think a great many of them must really piss Him off royally. (And I've occasionally wondered what that means, exactly. If one is royally pissed off, how is that quantified, exactly?)

Take, for instance, the big, giant JESUS SAVES bull on Highway 49, south of my hometown, Jackson, Mississippi. Oh, I can hear you thinking, *What's so unusual about a big, giant JESUS SAVES bull?* They are no doubt liberally dotting the landscape where you live and, thus, seem commonplace, even humdrum to you. Allow me to elaborate. This is no ordinary JESUS SAVES bull. Not by a long shot.

First of all, it is easily four times the size of any real-life bull I ever saw, which, if you have even a rudimentary familiarity with bovines, you would realize is fairly enormous. Second, it is standing on its forelegs with its hind legs thrust high in the air, and it has a most fierce expression on its big, beefy face. I have not ever seen a real live Angus, or even one of the more outlandish Longhorns doing a handstand. It's just one of your typical cow moves. Did I mention it's made of cement, or as it would be said in these parts, "cee-ment"? Third, it is painted a brilliant TAXI-CAB YELLOW, and it says, as previously mentioned, "JESUS SAVES!" on its midsection.

I just don't know what to tell you about that. I don't even know what to THINK about that. Every time I drive by it I have the same reaction and I say the same thing. I see it. I can't believe that I am seeing it. I can't think of any way in the world to EXPLAIN it. I say, out loud, whether accompanied or alone, a very emphatic, albeit confused, "HUH." I expect the Heavens resound with the same thing every time God looks at it.

I wonder if there is any correlation between the Big Yellow Jesus Saves Bull and the biblically famous Golden Calf. Surely not.

The Jesus Saves Bull is way more confusing to me than Big Butter Jesus. The first book tour I made on the Big-Ass Bus with The Cutest Boy in the World for my driver, we were ambling through Ohio one clear wintry night, and what should suddenly appear to us, just off the side of the interstate, but an enormous Jesus—well, actually, HALF an enormous Jesus—sticking out of a pond that, if the rest of Him were actually in there, would have had to have been at least 150 feet deep, although it looked like it was only about 30 feet wide.

"Way out of proportion" seems about the most charitable thing to say. Tiny reflecting pond, biggest Jesus EVER sticking halfway out of it, arms stretched Heavenward, lit up like God's own Christmas tree—well, let's just say, it's not ever going to be what you expect to see on the side of any highway in the middle of the night. But, even though He's huge and very startling, He IS in front of a church. Granted, the church is about half His size and it's a puzzlement what exactly He's supposed to be DOING, off in the pond like that, but at least the passerby can make the connection between the big, giant Jesus and the church building behind him and his tiny pond. (Incidentally, I can take no credit for naming him "Big Butter Jesus"; that came from Heywood Banks, who is also responsible for the catchy song by the same name. And yes, now that Mr. Banks has mentioned it, sung about it, no less, it DOES look like He's carved out of butter—something about the lighting, I suppose. Go check Him out on YouTube—see for yourownself.)

I figger God has got a pretty good sense of humor. (I think that every time I look in the mirror.) And so, I reckon He gets a kick out of Big Butter Jesus being so much bigger than the pond He sits in and/or the church He sits in front of and looking like He's made out of butter and all—but I'm betting He's as confused as I know I am by that JESUS SAVES bull. As many questions as we will surely all have for the Almighty upon our arrival up yonder, I expect God will have at least ONE Hisownself: "DUDE, what was UP with that BULL?"

Our brilliant forefathers could not have foreseen the Big Yellow Jesus Saves Bull or Big Butter Jesus, specifically, but they certainly did their best to create a safe environment for both. I'm just grateful to live in a country where we are ALL STILL FREE to worship whatever God we choose, by whatever means we choose, no matter how bizarre it may appear to our fellow citizens, as long as we can refrain from trying to cram it down their throats.

My mother is from a time and culture that did not exactly embrace diversity. For her, "Different" equals "Bad," actually, but I was heartened to see that, when some of those beliefs were gently challenged, she was still able to allow her mind to be changed. Fairly miraculous in a person of any age, at any time, but she was 84 when this conversation took place.

We were having a discussion about Prayer in the Schools—a popular platform for some—the position being that All Our Problems Started When "They" Took Prayer Out of the Classroom, and furthermore, All Our Problems Would Be Solved IF ONLY "They" Would Bring It Back. Mother was taking the position that this was absolutely 100 percent true and the answer to Everything. I did not agree. A fistfight could easily have ensued, but luckily, cooler heads prevailed. I suggested that perhaps what she was maybe more interested in was having school-wide prayer that was acceptable to HER—as opposed to say, God. She was properly horrified at such a thought. Oh, really?

I asked her to recall when she was in school, and even when I was in school; both were times when everybody in those schools was The Same—white and Protestant. All schools in those days were legislated to be segregated by race, of course, but they were also very much segregated by religion. Catholics were Different (and therefore suspect) and went to their own schools by their own choice—lest they be corrupted by the Baptists. There weren't any other variations. I never even knew a Jewish person until I was out of school—why would a Jewish family want to live in South Jackson? North Jackson had attitude even way back then. And in the neighborhood where Mother grew up—Grosse Pointe Park in Detroit, Michigan—Jewish people were simply not allowed.

So, in Mother's mind, "public prayer in schools" reflected only one experience and belief: Protestant. I asked if she had noticed that our country was experiencing an unprecedented growth in the Hispanic population, and she said, yes, she knew that. I asked if she would be surprised to know that, probably during our lifetimes, this country might become predominantly Hispanic, and she said, no, that would not surprise her.

I said, OK, then if we become mostly Hispanic and "they" are in charge of everything, and we go back to having mandatory public prayers in school, then THAT could mean that the prayers would be CATHOLIC prayers! OMIGOD—WHAT THEN? Or what if we had a predominantly Jewish Congress and they legislated that there would be mandatory public prayers at school—and they were JEWISH prayers? What if Jehovah's Witnesses took over the country and we all had to start going door to door, hounding everybody else? What if the Pentecostals confiscated all the cosmetics? The Mormons would have all the hot, young guys dressed in awful black shoes and riding bicycles all over the country—the dating pool would quickly stagnate. If the Baptists were the Boss of Everything, we would all have to drink in the closet and *Dancing with the Stars* would be canceled. I couldn't even bring up Islam to her without fear of pushing her completely over the edge. She'd trip and fall on a burka the first day. And it's a point of pride that no one in our family has ever been beheaded, stoned to death, or even flogged, so far; furthermore, all our women can drive, work outside the home, and marry and divorce at will—even willy-nilly, if so desired. (And yes, I know that Islam is a religion of peace, but there ARE, one must admit, those bad seeds out there. Just like there ARE "tolerant Baptists"—somewhere, I'm told—but who isn't at least a little afraid of the fundamentalist brand…of any religion?)

I assured her that it was 100 percent safe for us all to pray, all day, every day, no matter where we are, and that all the little schoolchildren could do the same—even to the point of completely ignoring their lessons by being so deeply immersed in prayer, if they were so inclined—but it would not ever be safe for anybody to make it a mandatory public kinda thing.

And so it came to pass that Mama could finally accept that it was, in fact, a good thing to keep the Church and the State apart—on account of there is just NO TELLING WHO will end up in charge. It's one thing for the guy next door to erect a Big Yellow Jesus Saves Bull in his yard—and quite another to require all to follow suit. We must all be diligent in protecting not only his right to have the Bull, but our own to respectfully abstain from availing ourselves of the incredible opportunity.

Amen.

Prayer Is Power

It doesn't matter who you are or to whom or what you pray—it's a powerful thing and we all need to do more of it.

In Alcoholics Anonymous, references are simply made to a "Higher Power" and it is up to the individual to determine what, for them, that HP might be. This is a pretty inclusive mindset. For some, at times, that Higher Power is simply the collective consciousness of the group—the acknowledgment that, SURELY, this many people cannot be WRONG, all at the same time, when they tell me that I am fucking-up BigTime, and so maybe I need to listen to them and just try doing something different for a change. I know an awful lot of people who actually stumbled on God Himself this way. Whatever works.

What Difference Does It Make What Anybody Believes In?
We can take that at least two ways. The first, most obvious, being that it ain't nonna my bidness WHAT you believe; it's my job to look after what I believe. If you express any interest in hearing about what I believe, fine, I'm happy to tell you, but I don't think it's my job to attempt spiritual assault on you. Mutual respect is a very fine thing.

I think there's a more important way to hear that question, and that is, what difference DOES someone's belief make in the way they live their lives? If we truly believe something, it ought to be readily observable by any and all—by our ACTIONS, not our words. Words don't mean boo-diddly-squat if the actions don't match up. Talk is not just cheap, it's FREE, and if it's not backed up with a fair amount of Walk, it's also completely worthless.

Although I've not been what you would call a Great Student of any religion, I've at least a cursory knowledge of most of the Big Ones, and I gotta tell you, I have not ever found anything in any of 'em that put more emphasis on its followers minding the affairs of others than it did on sweeping around their own back doors and getting the two-by-four out of their own eyeballs before they worried about the dust speck in their neighbor's.

I wish I COULD find a religion that wanted ME to be the Boss of Everybody else, 'cause Lord knows, I sure do have an OPINION about what-all THEY oughta be doin', and it is infinitely more entertaining to identify and enumerate THEIR endless string of faults and even to outline, in minute detail, the steps they should be taking to correct some—as opposed to examining and/or modifying any of my own personal character defects, if I had any. If I could be the High Priestess of the Church of All Y'all Have to Do Whatever I Say and Pay No Attention to What I DO, I would be one happy high priestess. And if there were positions of authority within that church to be had that would offer to others the opportunity to meddle in the affairs of their fellow church members, I bet we'd have us a big-ass cathedral built in no time. And talk about a tele-ministry! Whoo-boy-hidee, we'd have checks comin' in so fast we'd have to rent a dumpster for a mailbox.

You Just Can't Count on Dying Young

I don't know anybody still living who isn't surprised by it. Nobody really thought they'd ever make it to 21, let alone 30, or good Lord, 60—and beyond! And with the way some of us carried on along the way, I guess it is pretty much a shocker that we're not off in a ditch somewhere. Eubie Blake said—on what everybody thought was his 100th birthday, but turns out, he was "only" 96—"If I'd known I was gonna live so long, I'da taken better care of myself." Well, yeah, that hindsight will bite you in the ass every dang time.

And now, it is WAY too late to for us to "die young and leave a beautiful corpse." We are left with mandatory closed caskets and/or cremation. People can hardly stand to look at us alive, the shape we're in, we're hardly gonna look better dead. Although, silly putty and theatrical makeup, coupled with lying perfectly still and flat on your back with good lighting—those things would definitely help. If we could count on people's eyes being sufficiently blurred with tears, it would be a huge help. (I look pretty good blurry, although, as always, complete darkness is still best.) It'd be a stretch to think of what could make it any WORSE.

I'll tell you what could make it worse: If we don't hurry up and die, it will get a lot worse. It is getting worse ever' damn DAY that we are above ground. So, it comes down to two choices: Die Soon or Do Something About Ourselfs.

Since it doesn't appear that sudden death is a good bet, I think it's time we figure out a plan for doing something about, you know, all of That.

If you're under 40, it doesn't apply to you yet, but you can go on and read this next part—you should, actually, and you need to try to remember it for your not-too-distant future. Here you go: If you're over 50, it's prolly time for a haircut. Let me suggest an exercise for you: Go look up a photo of Hillary during the 2008 campaign. Fabulous. Great haircut, she looked like several million. Look at any photo of her in 2011. Only three years in actual time and aging, but that hair makes her look haggard—as in "like Merle"—and with emphasis on the first syllable. Block out the 2011 hair, and her face and skin still have that 2008 star quality. Word.

It's part of the whole "65 is actually a really cute, fun age" fantasy we (the Boomers) have got going, and at some point, it happens to us all. We suddenly realize that we are NOT 25, nor will we ever be again, and we think, *Omigod, this is my LAST CHANCE to have long hair,* and we grow it out and it is just wrong. Our last chance to have it—and look GOOD in it—was actually some several decades ago. Long hair on older women makes them (us) look older. If you can't bear to cut it off, can't afford a haircut, or you're Pentecostal, put it up—you'll look like you had a face lift.

But should you decide to do the whack job on your ponytail, it's prolly a good idea to ease into the transition a little bit at a time. Especially if you consider going really short, you're gonna want to sneak up on your head and check it out pretty thoroughly before you just lay the whole thing bare before the world. You haven't seen your neck since grade school, and it's a good idea to survey the area before you remove all the ground cover. Just recently, I saw in my very own Kroger (grocery store), in person, a short-haired woman with a roll of neck fat that was bigger than my gut. I'm guessing she HAD to wear her hair that short to keep it from getting caught in the neck fat and giving her whiplash.

When Daddy was growing up in rural Mississippi, women still mostly kept their hair long their whole lives, but they wore it up once they reached adulthood, except for country singers and the like. It was unusual to see a woman with extremely short hair in Ethel, Mississippi, in the late 1920s, early 1930s. So, when the woman who played piano at the Methodist church cut all her hair OFF, it was the talk of the town for weeks. Daddy said he remembered most distinctly when he first learned there was a New Haircut in Town.

Back then, on Saturdays, everybody for miles around went into town for supplies. The town square would be jammed with mule-drawn wagons and folks on foot—not a whole lot of cars then. You could learn all the news of the community just by sitting still and being quiet in the General Store for a few minutes—which is how Daddy came to learn of the shocking new "do." A gaggle of women gathered, and at least one of them was a Methodist, so she had the scoop, and Daddy heard the announcement delivered in those hushed tones that always accompany the very juiciest tidbits of gossip—so he knew this was Big.

Mrs. Ramsay silenced the Baptists with one phrase.

"Did y'all hear about Zellene Champion's hair?"

"NO! What happened? Did it all fall out?"

"She cut it ALL OFF—it's just like a BOY'S BEHIND!"

Now, what she MEANT was that the hair was cut very short—as short as a boy's—IN THE BACK. But that is not at all what Daddy heard and he made sure he was in the FRONT row at church the next week; he wanted to see if the back of Zellene Champion's head did, in fact, look like the buttocks of a young male.

So, of course, for me and Judy—our whole entire lives—if somebody got a short haircut, Daddy would say, "It's cut off just like a boy's behind." I admit, it took me a while to figure it out myownself. I thought for the longest time that Daddy just thought the back of women's necks were best covered up. So, what we're shooting for here is a flattering style, somewhere between a boy's behind and Lo-retta Lynn.

I've been pondering on the whole question of makeup for some time now. Too much of it on an old face looks freaky, but with too little, you kinda disappear. I look at my daughter Bailey ("BoPeep"), who is in her early twenties and gorgeous. Makeup is a waste on her. You cannot improve on the perfection that is youth—a lily in no need of gilding. Bailey and her friends would have had such an easy time being Most Beautiful during the Depression. I do think that her generation is the most beautiful one that has ever walked the earth. They even looked good in JUNIOR HIGH—how is that possible?

This is a group of young, gorgeous women who could have successfully used burnt matchsticks for eyebrow pencils and vanilla extract for perfume. Pinching those flawless cheeks would achieve the perfect glow—no blusher or bronzer needed. Past a Certain Age, you absolutely cannot use that method: If you pinch old cheeks, they stay pinched. The skin will remain bunched up together in creepy little bundles so it will look like the bags under your eyes gave birth.

Have you quit smoking yet? YOU. MUST. DO. THIS. I know that Carrie Bradshaw looks totally hot doing it. She also looks like her feet don't hurt in those ridiculous shoes, and you KNOW that ain't so. But if we were to see Carrie's MOTHER and GRANDMOTHER smoking (and hobbling around in that silly footwear), it would be a horrifying spectacle.

OK, if the thought of permanent purse-mouth and skin that looks like beef jerky doesn't scare you enough, try THIS on: I personally know a person—in his thirties—who was recently told by his periodontist that if he didn't quit smoking, forever, THAT DAY, they would be PULLING ALL HIS TEETH BY THE END OF THE YEAR. OK, let that sink in. All his teeth...PULLED OUT...OF HIS HEAD. No teeth left.

Maybe you don't suffer from dental phobia like I do, but lemme tell you, if somebody told me that if I didn't turn into a spider monkey, they were gonna yank a single tooth outta my head, I would start running up the walls, swinging from the lamps, flinging poo, and howling. I can tell you without a doubt or a moment's hesitation that the threat of having all my teeth pulled would absolutely put an immediate end to my smoking career, mostly because I would be to afraid to breathe, even, let alone create and inhale smoke. So, suck on that cig, why don't you? And you know what they say about a BIG SMILE being your most important beauty accessory—well, you'll have a REALLY big one with your shiny new choppers!

Health is an area where it's really dangerous to employ our favorite coping mechanism—that being "denial," of course. We all take good health totally for granted, and we just blithely go about our igmo business and keep right on doing stupid stuff like smoking, or baking in tanning beds, or not wearing seatbelts—you know, stupid stuff—because SO FAR, nothing bad has happened to us, personally, and statistics are not nearly as compelling to us as our own momentary whims.

Normally, I love denial, as you know, but we just can't afford it when it comes to this stuff, so to help you grasp my point, here's what I want you to do: Go home and put on a pair of shoes at least two sizes too small. Just cram your feet in there somehow and walk around in them for an afternoon. When you cannot stand it one more second, I want you to imagine what it would be like to suffer that level of discomfort—on a permanent basis—all because of something STUPID that you CHOSE to do. Now straighten up and act right.

If I Hate the Bishop, Will I Go to Hell?

I had lunch this week with an amazing woman who happens to be a Bishop in the United Methodist Church. She has the enthusiasm, joyful anticipation, and wonder about all of life—also the body of a much younger woman. Disgusting. I could hardly eat, so filled with envy was I, but of course, I did manage somehow—it was lunchtime, after all. But over the sound of the voices in my head that were shrieking, *LOOK AT HER SKIN! LOOK AT HER EYES! LOOK AT HER ARMS! SHE HAS ON A SLEEVELESS BLOUSE—DIE, BITCH!* I did somehow manage to hear her relating to me the story of a fascinating woman she and her husband encountered on a visit to Prague.

They just happened to meet this very curiously dressed woman while waiting for the bus to a World War II museum. She was dressed in what appeared to be hiking gear from another era. It turned out that the woman was also on her way to the same museum—to speak to schoolchildren there about her experiences as a young Jewish woman interned in one of the Nazi Death Camps. The woman was 90 years old and had survived the Death Camps—but here she was all these years later, and not only was she still alive, but she had walked however many miles there to catch the bus, and she was on her way to the museum to talk to school kids about the Holocaust. The Way Too Cute Bishop was agog, as was I, hearing about it. But, at the same time, the voices in my head were saying, *Well, hell, I don't know why SHE'S surprised at that, SHE'LL prolly be hiking the Grand Canyon and baptizing people in the river at the bottom when she's 105—would you just LOOK at her?* It was a tough lunch.

Anyway, The Way Too Cute Bishop went on to say that she would be turning 60 before too long—which only increased my internal fury and covetousness—and she and a friend had been talking about How They Wanted to Spend This 3rd Third of Their Lives. (And I'm going, *See? She's already PLANNING for what all she's gonna be doing when she's 90. Hate her—I'm having dessert.*)

But, later, when my indigestion cleared up and I managed to exorcise from my soul the green-eyed monster, I reflected on what a truly remarkable, if way too cute, woman that little Bishop is. And I began to think about my own 3rd Third.

When Kyle and I were in Los Angeles a number of years ago, we met a darling woman who told us she had ridden her BICYCLE from LA to Jackson, Mississippi, just to parade with us in the Million Queen March™ the year before. She also rode that same bicycle back to LA, post-parade. We were pretty impressed at the whole thing, but then she turned out to be 72, and as we say Down Here, we like to fell out. (This means we nearly fainted with shock.)

I used to have these really old neighbors—Mr. and Mrs. Jones. They were in their late eighties and they looked it, but Mr. Jones still pushed the lawn mower all over their yard—and on the city-owned lot across the street. I went outside one day and saw a ladder leaned up against their house, and there was Mr. Jones, up on the roof, sweeping off the pine straw. Later, when he got down, he washed and waxed all three of their cars—none of which Mrs. Jones could drive. She never learned.

That evening, I noticed Mr. Jones loading one of the cars, as if they were going on a trip, so I asked if this were so and if they needed me to feed their cats or anything. He allowed as how, yes, they were going out of town—they had to go check on Mrs. Jones's MOTHER, who was "not doing well."

I remember thinking at that very moment, *Dear Godinheaven, if I get to be 85 and my MOTHER is still alive, I WILL shoot us both.*

As I thought about the very old Holocaust survivor, the 70-something cross-country bicycle Queen, Mr. Jones's manual labor, and Mrs. Jones's thousand-year-old mother, I also pondered on The Way Too Cute Bishop and her friend and how they were thoughtfully and prayerfully planning for THEIR OWN "3rd Thirds," and I contrasted all of that with the recollection of my own immediate thoughts of dread and murder/suicide, should Mama and I manage to coexist for so long.

So, right off, we see why SHE'S the Bishop and I'm not, right? OK, but accepting that I am shallow and mean and totally lacking in ambition and just moving on from THAT, and also accepting that I don't seem to be on the verge of imminent death, it appears incumbent upon me to consider What I Might Do With My Own 3rd Third of Life. And so I've considered that, and upon consideration, I decided that, for whatever I end up attempting in this upcoming Third, I do know that I will want to have the ability to move about freely, under my own steam, on my own feet, even, if you will. I don't know exactly WHAT I want to do, but I DO KNOW that I want to be AMBULATORY for it.

So, it's a start.

As the saying goes, "You gotta start SOMEwhere." And when you're gonna start something, WHERE is not really optional—the only place you CAN start is where you ARE. You can't start where you want to BE—which is so irritating and time-consuming. You have to start at the stupid beginning. I hate that. Whenever I look at a magazine, I ALWAYS open it to the last page and look at it backward from there. It drives Kyle crazy. I'm very goal-oriented, so if the goal is X, then I prefer to start there, without the bother of all that ABCDEFGHIJKLMNOPQ and R on the front end of the thing.

It should be noted that just because that is the way I would LIKE to do things, it does not actually work that way. Ever. For anything. It especially does not work that way for, say, losing weight and/or getting in shape. What I would LIKE, now that I have seen The Way Too Cute Bishop, is to look like HER—with her cute haircut and her perfect arms and her size-little-bitty everything else. And with the exception of needing to be about 10 inches shorter, that's in the realm of Doable—I could be her taller twin. One day. But not TO-DAY.

Now, at least since I have been mostly full grown, I have actually loved to exercise. Remember, I worked for the YMCA for about a hundred years. I was the very first women's program director for the YMCA in the state of Mississippi, as a matter of fact. (When I first started working for them, it was still an all-male organization, nationally and, most assuredly, locally.) Anyway, I just worked out nonstop from about 1977 until around 1999, and I was in way better shape at 30 than I had ever thought about being when I was 18. Sigh. The last time I did a serious workout at the "Y," I could curl 30-pound dumbbells—that's 30 pounds in EACH hand. Bigger sigh.

First, book tours ruined my life. It is impossible to work out on book tours; there is simply no time. There is also no time to eat, sleep, and/or bathe, so you can see how treadmill time just goes by the wayside in a hurry. That's two months out of the year, right there. I typically toured in January and February, so by the time I got back, I hit the ground in full-PARADE-mode. OK, so now it's APRIL and I haven't worked out once yet. You see where this is going, right?

The years are whizzing by and I am getting slower and fatter in exponential increments. Then I got a gimp hip. No idea how, but somehow I managed to tear the labrum in my hip. First of all, I had no knowledge that I was in possession of any labrums (labri?), and I have no recollection of tearing one, and it would seem to me that one would remember such a thing. But I didn't. All I know is, my hip, it lit into hurting and I tried everything. Massage. Acupuncture. Physical Therapy. Water exercise. Rest— oh, Lord, yes, lots and LOTS of rest. Nothing helped. I Googled the surgery they wanted to do to repair it, and under all the "comments," I could not find a single happy patient, which did not fill me with enthusiasm or confidence at the thought of going under the knife for something that, first of all, was not even going to SHOW (like on my face or bosoms), and second, everybody I could find who'd had it was miserable.

Before I could make up my mind about THAT surgery, though, I had a bad mammogram. So, you know the drill. You get the callback for another screening. They don't like that, either. You go for a needle biopsy. They don't like that, EITHER. So you go for a lumpectomy. I was lucky and unlucky in this process. I was lucky that it was atypical but not malignant and they got it all (thank you, God). I was unlucky that the needle biopsy, which should have taken 20–30 minutes, took about three hours. If you've never had one, I'll tell you the needle part is nothing—big whoop. But lying perfectly still, flat on your face, on a stainless-steel table with your arms in impossible positions—for THAT part, they should be handing out Valium, Xanax, and Percoset by the handfuls. Which, of course, they are NOT. And, duh, pad the damn table. I posited to the doctor that if this were a TESTICLE TABLE instead of a TIT TABLE, it would be tricked out like a La-Z-Boy. She did not disagree. Lucky for me—what with the bad hip and all—I was "holding" and was thus well prepared to self-medicate, which I DID, I assure you, after the first HOUR.

I told 'em to let me up, which they did, and I CHEWED, I swear to you, one of EACH of my little friends. Told the doc to give me just a very few minutes (until all that kicked in—which it did, like a fair-sized MULE) and I would be good to go. Furthermore, I would be good for pretty much anything else they could think of that did not require mental or visual acuity or standing upright or operating machinery or making complete sentences or breathing with my mouth closed. (If you're scheduled for one of these procedures, DON'T PANIC. Mine was a totally bizarre case—it NEVER takes that long. And as I said, the needle part was a nonevent. Relax. You'll be fine.)

So, I've still got the screwed-up hip at this point and now I do NOT have breast cancer—YAY—but I do have, like, one and a half tits after the lumpectomy. If I have to have another one on that side sometime, it will effectively BE a mastectomy—I really only HAD the ONE "lump-worth" of boob on that side. Too bad it wasn't on the other side, which has always been bigger after breastfeeding, but whatever…I DON'T HAVE CANCER. So I'm limping and I've got lopsided bosoms, but I DO NOT CARE AT ALL. This is a Major Win, of course.

But I've got a screwed-up shoulder now, too—from the over-long time on the steel table in the awkward position. I am just a MESS, and a big fat one, at that, since any form of exercise is now impossible for me. I have had shoulder surgery before, on the other side, and although it was 100 percent successful and I have great range of motion on that arm, the physical therapy for recovery after that was beyond the limits of human endurance. I literally had projectile tears flying out of my eyeballs at every session. I was nearly ready to just accept having one functional arm for the rest of my life as opposed to signing up for more shoulder surgery.

Somebody told me about medical massage and suggested that it might be worth a try to avoid surgery. If they had suggested having the car run over it as opposed to surgery, I'da given that serious consideration. I found a medical massage therapist and presented myself for treatment. Holy Mother. Don't be fooled by the inclusion of the word "massage" in the description of what these folks do to you. It is in no way even distantly related to a "massage." It is way more like being run over by the car, or dragged behind it—for a long way. Ridiculously painful. But it WORKED unbelievably fast. Literally, after the first "treatment," I had over a 50 percent increase in my range of motion. And that was THE ONLY reason I ever came BACK for another treatment, I can assure you. It was not an easy thing to voluntarily get on that table again—knowing what was coming. But seeing the positive result so immediately was irresistible. Hideous pain, but instant gratification once it was over. Fully recovered from that with no surgery, so I thankyewveramuch.

BUT still no exercise program because I've still got the bum hip and it is getting worse all the time. My consumption of Percoset was reaching peak capacity and it really wasn't helping anymore. The last time I went to the grocery store (before I gave up and had the surgery), it flared up so bad I thought I was going to have to get IN the cart and have the bag boy push me to the car.

I went to see my orthopod and told him that I had been looking online at this surgery he was proposing, and well, I could not personally locate ANY satisfied customers—did he have any hisownself? I allowed as how I also understood that it was possible that the only people who bothered to post anything about their surgery were whiners—but I was really curious to know if he personally had made ANYBODY happy with this procedure. So, he went right outside the exam room and got one and dragged him in there to give me his testimony. It was one of the baby doctors they have hanging around, learning stuff, and the young man swore to me that he had been every bit as crippled up as I was—and he was only about 12, from the looks of him—but that our good doc right here had fixed it up right and he showed me how he could walk and skip and run like the other children now, and I signed up.

Now, I am pissed that I waited so long! From the moment I woke up from the surgery, the pain was gone. I am healed, I tell you, healed! I am ready to take up my bed and walk! However, it has now been over 10 years since the last time I exercised. Groan.

I remember the last time I took a break from exercise. It was when I was pregnant with BoPeep—who, you will recall, is now in her midtwenties. I was inactive for approximately 11 months at that time. So, that was my previous "break," 11 months, give or take, and I thought I was gonna die when I started back. This time, it's been over a DECADE—I'll be stunned if I DON'T die. But I am finally ready to BEGIN. Break time is over and I feel like I need to hurry up before some other part of my body fucks up.

Our friend Randy "Kiltboy" Wallace is pretty much an exercise fiend and he told us he had been doing P90X—you know, from the infomercials on TV. I looked at it online and saw all those tragic "befores"—with which I could totally identify—and the amazing "AFTERS." Oh, I wanna be an "after" sooo bad!

So we ordered off and got us the whole P90X system, and be danged if we ain't TRYIN' to do it! Truth be told, I am forced to do a whole lot of the recommended "just keep moving" stuff during parts that are not just "too strenuous" for me, but are actually more along the lines of "the HELL you say!"

The Cutest Boy in the World is doing it with me, and of course, HE looked like an "AFTER" before we ever started—which is just every kind of WRONG. Granted, he is 10 years younger than I am (gag), but he has not exercised in 19 YEARS! I've only been off for 10. There is just no justice in this universe, I swear.

I'll keep you posted on this as it develops. Should I morph into any kind of "AFTER," I assure you, I will purchase billboard space to showcase that—but no, there WILL BE NO "BEFORE" shots.

I Was Nice Last Year, Too Bad You Missed It!

For this "3rd Third" of my life, I have no desire to repeat much, if anything, from the first two Thirds—other than the aforementioned walking upright and feeding and grooming myself. I'd like to keep on doing those things right up until it's time for the big box or the bonfire, but quite frankly, I'm thrilled that a whole bunch of stuff is DONE and that I don't HAVE to do it, ever. I am free to NOT go to Bonnaroo, for example, and I count that as one of the truly great blessings of being Full Grown. I am also free to wear comfy shoes and big giant panties—although decorum dictates that the outfit be a bit more complete, but it could all be commodious clothing, to be sure. I have *been* drunk—check that off, don't have to do that again. I no longer have to smoke to be cool, which is good because who can afford cigarettes today?

I am NEARLY old enough that, pretty soon, I can stop even attempting to be nice and I'll be considered a funny, cantankerous old lady—that will be a dream come true.

"You're only young once." So true. And once that part is over, it becomes important to have a stable of OTHER excuses for whatever it is that you're doing that you would formerly have been able to justify, rationalize, or receive pardon for due to your youth. However, it occurs to me that if you are a Boomer, currently living by the "60 is the new 40" credo, then you ought to be able to go right on claiming the "only young once" clause. On the other hand, it appears to me that old people get even more latitude than kids. You can certainly SAY just about anything to anybody with impunity.

For example, a very small-breasted friend of mine was attempting to purchase "cute" undies from a Cute Undie store with little success. She had dragged every small-cup bra in the store into the dressing room and an older lady was attempting to help her. Finally, the lady decided it was time for some straight talk and she just came right on in there with her and said, "Look here, sweetie, I don't know WHO tole you you was a thirty-six B—you no mor'n a double A at best. Them thangs just sittin' there in that big ole B like they's waitin' on a elevator—you gon' hafta go ta SEARS."

My own personal mother got a way early jump on Saying Hideous Things to People and Getting Away with It. By the time BoPeep came along, my seester Judy and I were so inured to it we had no sympathy left to offer her when BoPeep wailed to us, "My friend asked how she was doing, and Mawmaw said she'd had the squirts all day!" That right there is a level of transparency I'm just not sure I can ever aspire to—nobody had any secrets when she was around, including her.

Party Party Party

Not having been exactly a party animal in my first two Thirds, I cannot imagine that I will morph into one for the 3rd Third. One of the absolute WORST things you can do to me is somehow contrive to make me go to a cocktail party. Right offhand, I can't really think of anything WORSE you could do, actually, short of setting me on fire. But if I had to pick one of those two, it wouldn't be a snap decision, I can tell you that.

I am no fonder of clambakes on my home turf, either. This is largely due to the fact that I am easily the worst housekeeper ever, in the history of the EN-tire world, living or dead. And that is no exaggeration—you can ask anybody who knows me. I have an extremely high tolerance for dog hair, coupled with no motivation for performing tasks that won't stay done. This is a dangerous combination. Also, every time I throw something out, I need it the very next week—without exception. We're hot on the trail of a recipe for disaster here. Don't drop by my house is what I'm telling you; it is a mess—always. On my BEST day, I would still be a candidate for the *Hoarders* TV show by a popular vote. To have invited guests on purpose requires renting a track hoe to clear a path.

Whenever I go to anybody else's house, I am always amazed by their neatness and apparent lack of stuff. Where is all their stuff? You know, the piles of crap that accumulate unaided in MY house—where do y'all keep yours? Really. I wonder about it.

And you know those "reality" shows where the professional organizer person comes in to the hoarder's house to show her "just a few simple tips" to "declutter" and keep everything hunky-dory, spic and span—what-EVER the hell THAT means? It makes me INSANE to watch those things—or to see the print equivalent in magazines. They show the "BEFORE" house, where you cannot see the floors or the walls, just an endless sea of crap—that part, I totally GET. But the "AFTER" is the same room, WITH NO CRAP and three baskets on a shelf that are what the organizer woman claims were the "key" to the whole thing. I'm looking at it, screaming, "WHERE IS ALL THE SHIT? Those baskets are EMPTY, and even if they were overflowing, they would not BEGIN to hold all the crap that was in that room!" Organizer Woman did not organize JACK—she just threw it all OUT and stuck three baskets in there.

I used to think my friend Blanche had THE Cleanest House in North America. Blanche buys Clorox like most people buy Cokes—by the case. I have seen her make three trips from the car, toting in NOTHING BUT gallon jugs of Clorox. Everything in that house is subject to being bleached at any time of the day or night. If Blanche can't sleep, she gets up and bleaches something—linens, area rugs, floors. I don't think she bleaches the cats, but she does have them bathed every week. Who bathes a cat? Blanche, for one. Well, she causes them to be bathed, and there is a nice, freshly bleached kitty bed waiting for each of them when they come home from the beauty pah-lor.

But Blanche is a total slacker, a slob, a bandersnatch, if you will, compared to Mrs. Abby Jim Payne of Philadelphia, Mississippi. I will not reveal her age, but only say that she is, in my opinion, way past the point where she COULD be sitting back, on her laurels, as it were, and never lifting a finger or a broom again in this lifetime. "Mother Payne" is responsible for giving the world the inimitable and fastidious Allen Glen Payne, about whom you have read much in my books. Allen is partner to Little Jeffrey—who is also inimitable but not fastidious. At all. When we all gather at Mother Payne's for a meal, first of all, we all wear the closest thing we can find to actual Pajama Jeans. We may have to avail ourselves of those soon—specifically for mealtimes at her house. It is not unusual for her to have prepared fried chicken, pork roast, AND pot roast, plus sweet potato casserole, fried okra, broccoli salad (that weird stuff with the raisins and three pounds of bacon—looove that), cornbread dressing (made two ways because Allen is finicky), fresh green beans, homegrown tomatoes, and (just for me) deviled eggs. There is always cracklin' cornbread. Plus, there are always two pans of homemade yeast rolls, one of which, although seemingly perfect, will be denounced by Mother Payne as cold, flat, or in some other way defective, and another pan is coming straight out of the oven to replace the inferior ones. We always eat them all, of course. Then there will always be a caramel cake, a coconut cake, and a red velvet cake—all of which will be greatly apologized over for various and sundry reasons by Mother Payne, and all of which will be eaten in their entirety by me, Little Jeffrey, and Allen. The Cutest Boy in the World does not CARE about sweets. Hmph. I care about so little else.

At any rate, when Little Jeffrey, TCBITW, and I arrive at Chez Payne for our modest repast, we are always regaled with the tales of What All Got Cleaned Around There That Day. Little Jeffrey and I are always wondering when any dust particle has ever been there, where it came from, and how it got in.

Once, Kyle and I were in town for a funeral, and since the cemetery is within blocks of Mother Payne's house, we stopped by—DROPPED IN, as in unannounced, without prior warning, and/advance notice—to see her. She knew about the funeral and therefore thought there was at least a chance that we might be attending it, so naturally, she had made a pie for us—just in case we stopped by afterward. And our stopping by was equally natural, betting, as we were, or at least I was, on the off chance that she might have thought there was a chance of us stopping by and thus made a pie for us (me) in order to be prepared for that possibility. I do love a wager when both sides are able to win—so rare.

While we were there, visiting and receiving pie, I availed myself of the facilities and I nearly fainted from shock. There was a TOWEL draped over the side of the bathtub that, from its slightly damp appearance would indicate to the casual observer, had been USED. Never, in the nearly 25 years of our visits to the home of Mother Payne, has there EVER been ANY evidence of anything in the house having been used prior to our arrival—and most assuredly, not anything in the BATHROOM. We've often thought that perhaps she actually has another house somewhere nearby where she actually lives and that she just maintains this one for "company." If my doorbell ever rang unexpectedly and I was able to discern that it was Mother Payne dropping by MY house, I would immediately run out into the backyard and shoot myself in the eye before I would allow her to see the normal state of affairs in our house. Better that I should fall on my sword than be the cause of the sudden heart failure of this lady, most beloved. Nor could I bear up under her gaze when it moved, as it surely would, from the giant drifts of dog hair, piles of junk mail, and unfolded laundry, to my lazy-ass, good-for-nothing, guilty face. It kinda makes my throat close up a little bit to even think about it.

As soon as we were a safe distance away from the house, I called Little Jeffrey and reported The Towel Incident. Little Jeffrey is even more cowed by Mother Payne's superlative housekeeping skills than I am, since if you can even imagine it, his dirtball-ness is at least equal to, if not greater than, my own. Little Jeffrey found The Towel Story to be shocking, bordering on the outside of credibility, even. He challenged my observation repeatedly, to the point that I began to wish I had taken a photograph of the offending terry cloth, but he would have sworn I staged it to support this fish tale with which I was bending his ear.

Finally, Little Jeffrey was convinced of the veracity of my story when I thrust the phone up to Kyle's ear and demanded that he back me up. With a slightly derisive glance in my direction, he sighed and spoke in the general direction of my iPhone: "Yes, there was a TOWEL." With a triumphant "HA!" that drowned out the rest of Kyle's words that indicated a somewhat lowered opinion of both Little Jeffrey and me, I whipped the phone back to me and resumed my conversation with a totally bumfuzzled Little Jeffrey.

"What," he wondered aloud, "could account for this utter deterioration of Mother Payne's vigilance? Had there possibly been a catastrophic health event or an earthquake or something that temporarily distracted her from the usual maintenance of her domicile?" The concern in his voice was palpable. I could tell he was wondering if we should tell Allen—not wanting to alarm him unduly, of course, but certainly not wanting to withhold evidence of what could be a pending disaster at home. How to break it to him, this only child, living far, far away from his precious mama? "Sit down, Allen. We have something to tell you. We don't want you to get upset, and we think it's probably nothing, really, but well, we found a towel. It was only the ONE but…Well, it was damp. We just thought you needed to know."

I assured Little Jeffrey that there was NOTHING, absolutely NO-THING, to be worried about where this towel was concerned. We already knew the circumstances leading up to this Incident. Shortly before we arrived for our spontaneous visit, Mother Payne had, in fact, been about her usual business—the immaculation of her residence. A particular job had been on her mind when she awakened that morning, and so working back from the time of the funeral and when she might expect us to unexpectedly drop by, she knew she had to make that pie, but it was mandatory that this other urgent task be completed before our anticipated unanticipated visit. Because if it were not completed by then, she might miss us altogether, not being able, as it were, to hear the doorbell—from UNDER THE HOUSE.

Yes, ma'am, it was that time, once AGAIN, to CLEAN UNDERNEATH the house. And she, in fact, DID get her little self under that house and clean it. No, I have no idea what that involves. Obviously, from the state of my own house ABOVEGROUND, one can infer most appropriately that I would have no concept of cleaning its underside. And note that I did say "AGAIN," and yes, that would indicate that this task has been performed by her not only more than once, but on a regular basis. I was, and I remain, agog.

But I could not WAIT to share that bit of Cleaning Lore with my dear friend Bleaching Blanche, who was duly impressed, and I could tell that her mind made an immediate leap to the question of the underbelly of her own house. In a mere second, I could tell that I had raised an issue with her: There was a slight gasp as she considered the possibility of there being DIRT under her own house at this very moment, and then I could see her face relax as she remembered that her house is built on a slab. She could breathe again and focus solely on appreciating the artistry of another and acknowledging the superiority of Mother Payne's housekeeping over her own—while enjoying having a higher mark to aim for in the future. Only a true draggletail like myself could enjoy a bit of third-person one-upmanship like this. How pathetic does one have to be to derive pleasure from taunting one domestic goddess with the prowess of another, while dwelling in utter squalor onesownself? I have only to look in the mirror to answer that one.

When we were young(er) and somebody moved into a newly rented hovel, they would often host "painting" parties at which guests were provided with paintbrushes or rollers (and paint, of course) and were expected to help the tenant buff up the new digs. Sometimes beer was provided. Oh, there was always beer INVOLVED—but if the "host" was particularly poor (usually was), "guests" were encouraged to pack provisions. Of course, that always meant that there would be some equally impoverished guests who would drink up YOUR beer when you weren't paying attention. This impelled some painters to arrive pre-drunk as a cost-saving measure.

In any event, it made for some pretty impressive paint jobs. Not to say "GOOD" ones, just impressive. Especially if my friend the diminutive Brenda Avery was on the guest list. She is the Reigning World Champion Horrible Painter—if there is a competition out there for this, we should enter her, bet large, and retire on the winnings. NOBODY comes close, I'm telling you. I have seen this woman—on more than one occasion—stand up, with an extended roller, to paint a perfectly flat piece of plywood that was lying perfectly flat on the FLOOR and end up with paint on her own back. She's got a knack.

In keeping with the painting parties of yore and given my own apparent lack of even the most cursory cleaning capabilities, my brilliant seester Judy came up with the perfect party solution for me. I am happy to ply the guests with alcoholic beverages and nabs. (We call any food "nabs," but particularly party food. It's the name of a snack cracker and people in the South call all snack crackers "nabs," but Judy and I have further bastardized the term to cover all food. Just FYI.) I enjoy feeding people. Judy's suggestion was, instead of asking them to come paint, to have everybody bring their own DUSTBUSTER and assign them an area to vacuum. Featherduster Fest. Scrubbing Soiree. Drunk Dusting. I don't know, we'll come up with something. I think this could really catch on—I may be the biggest slob, but I'm by no means the only one.

A Fire Truck or an Indian

Here we are, many pages later, and I am still no closer to identifying What to Do With the 3rd Third of My Life. Lots of stuff I DON'T want to do—I have a great deal of negative ambition, I suppose. How's that for a positive spin on "hopeless slackass"?

There used to be a local TV show, back in my first Third, hosted by "Captain" Dick Miller, and they would have scads of little kids on there every week for…I don't know what for, just so they could be on TV, I guess. Cartoons were aired, and in between *Popeye* and *Mighty Mouse*, Captain Dick would interview the young'uns, who always had smart things to say and astute observations to offer. As all adults will do when forced to converse with small children with whom they are not well acquainted, Captain Dick would ask the kid crop du jour "what they wanted to be when they grew up." My all-time favorite was the little boy who said he wanted to either be a fire truck or an Indian, he hadn't quite made up his mind good yet. But at least he was, like, four. I saw a "scholarship" pageant contestant who said she wanted to be BOTH a pop singer AND a gynecologist. I've often wondered if either of them achieved their goals.

I've got until November 23, 2012, to make a plan for my 3rd Third. Your suggestions are welcomed: hrhjill@sweetpotato-queens.com. Drop me a line with your ideas—for either your OWN 3rd Third or for mine.

Kumbaya, Already

*N*ot since I wrote *God Save The Sweet Potato Queens* have I been so reluctant to write the final chapter of a book. If my absolute drop-dead deadline for this manuscript were not breathing so hotly down my neck, I imagine this book would be 1,000 pages long. I would just keep writing OTHER stuff—to avoid this part. But this book purports to be about surviving the Crappy Parts of Life and not all of those can be laughed or denied away, unfortunately. Well, actually, I believe they CAN, but first, they must be FACED—and sometimes, we just don't want to do that.

The last several years have been easily the most difficult of my life so far. I say "so far" in a pathetic attempt to persuade Karma to put me down gently and leave me alone for a little while, knowing that there is plenty more bad stuff that is available out there for distribution.

So many Faces of Loss have shown themselves to me—some belong to those things we, on some level, expect to face one day, but when we finally do, we find we are nonetheless just as unprepared for them as if they had been a low-hanging branch that clocked us between the eyes or an unseen hole off into which we have plunged, free-falling to the big bone-crushing crash at the bottom. Even when the Loss means the end of an episode so painful that we pray for it, beg for it, rail hourly against the delay of it, we are not ready for it when it finally arrives. The reality, the seeming finality of Loss, the very real Absence—you can't "get ready" for that. Our minds just do NOT really grasp Gone.

Mama's death was like that for me. Some part of your heart, mind, and soul KNOWS that the odds are in favor of your out-living your parents and there is some degree of acceptance that comes with that. When Daddy died of a heart attack at 62 (62!), Judy and I thought he had lived a good life, and although we cer-tainly wanted MORE time, we didn't feel cheated—on account of him being "so old" and all. Snort. Now that I am 59 and Judy is 65, and we realize that Mama was only 58 when he died, suffice it to say, our perspective on how OLD he was has changed sig-nificantly. We now know that we were all ROBBED—Daddy and all of us, equally—and we are retroactively pissed off about it. He has not, by the way, weighed in on the matter, as of yet.

In March 2009, Mama rode in that fabulous Rolls-Royce convertible with the Queen Mothers and Used-to-Bes of the Sweet Potato Queens,® and the very next week, she fell and her dominoes began to slowly fall with her. She was in and out of hospitals and rehabs for weeks on end and finally ended up in a "nursing" home that summer. I put nursing in quotes because there was precious little of it going on that I could see.

As a family, we have always prided ourselves on being "good" patients. I have stated in my books many times the importance of Always Being Nice to Nurses, Waiters, and Bartenders—since they have power over your pain meds, food, and beverages. Our comportment as a group in the nursing home did not stray from this maxim. We did not try to be LOW maintenance; we aimed for NO maintenance, doing everything possible for her without "troubling" the staff. So, I can honestly say that we did not bring mistreatment on ourselves. It was part of the "service" for all, apparently. I thought we would be the favorite patients—since we did everything for her ourselves, they didn't have to fool with us much. Kyle said, no, we were actually their worst nightmare—because we were THERE all the time, and even worse, we paid attention.

From a nurse dispensing meds without her reading glasses (and trying to give Mama the wrong drug as a result) to pleas for potty assistance that went unanswered for over an hour (we didn't make Mama wait all that time—we helped her ourselves, of course) to our alleged "attending" physician, who never bothered to come into Mama's room once during her stay and who never even looked up from his paperwork as he told me that my mother was dying.

I had tracked HIM down and introduced myself—as he busily signed charts, perhaps for other patients he had also not visited. I asked him if he had a prognosis for Mama, and he said, as he admired his signature, eyes on the charts, "She's dying." I stood there, incredulous, looking at the top of his head, and asked if he could give me any sense of how much time we had. Still, without pausing in his signatures and without glancing up at me, he said to me one word: "Days." I remained planted there for some moments until it became awkward, just staring at the top of his head, then I sort of stumbled down the hall to her room, stunned—more by his callous behavior than by the news he so flatly delivered. It's hard to have a snappy comeback for somebody like that—even for me.

So many wonderful friends called and e-mailed, praying for Mama and asking for reports on her, I sent out an update about her:

JUNE 2009

Well, I am sorry to report that my mama is Not Doing Well—not well a-tall. Hard to believe that this same woman was riding in the lead convertible for the Million Queen March,™ and now, as I said, she is just right poorly. I can't even count all the Near Misses we've had with Mama lately. I swear, she is AT Death's Very Door— and she just keeps turning around and coming back. Yesterday, she was nearly comatose all day and I had a long talk with her, because I know she can hear me, and I told her that God's Timing is Perfect and we are trusting that. I said, "We are taking care of you AS IF you will be here with us for the next 30 years—but if you're tired and want to go on Home, that is fine." Told her not only had she done her job, she'd done a DAMN FINE JOB, and we would be right beside her, every minute, she could just relax, and we would follow her cue. Told her we were even thankful for these most recent days, although sorry for any physical suffering she has had, that we counted the opportunity to care for her so completely as a JOY and a privilege, thankful for the chance to, in some way, repay ALL she's done for us, and that it was kinda like having a baby—a lotta work, but a total joy—and she smiled and nodded.

After that, I just sat, in the near darkness of her room (lights bother her)—sat right by the bed and held her hand—and told her I wasn't leaving. An hour may have passed, and suddenly, out of the dark silence came a Voice. The Voice said, "LET'S SIT UP AND EAT!" It was Mama. I couldn't have been much more surprised if it'd been an angel or a spider monkey. So, I sat her up and fed her—actual food as well as mucho dessertos—and then Kyle came back and she wanted to GET UP OUTTA BED and sit in her wheelchair and feel her feet on the floor! So we did THAT!

Then she was ready to sleep, so Kyle put her back in the bed and we tried to sleep, too. I actually did a pretty good job of it until

I got the worst charley horse in the history of legs in my right calf. Kyle said Mama had awakened HIM 3 times during the night: once for a back rub, once for a drink of water, but she made him search until he found the RIGHT SIZE water bottle to suit her (?), and the last time, she called him over and said something he couldn't hear. Never knowing if she's got something Important to Say to Us, he leaned in and asked her to repeat it, so she did. She said, "I'M THE BIGGEST."

So, yeah, even as dark as these days have been, we ARE having a FEW laughs. We would appreciate your prayers for Mama—and for us—as we walk this Road. Confident in the words that tell us we walk THROUGH the Valley—NOT TO the Valley—we are pretty much living on prayers right now, although, truth be told, I am personally supplementing those with a large chocolate milk shake, EVER' DANG DAY! Somewhat more fattening than Xanax—but every bit as effective, in my opinion.

That was written the first week of June when we were told we had "days." Mama apparently did not get the memo from Dr. Death on account of she did NOT die on schedule as forecasted. When she failed to go to The Light, clearly preferring to remain here with us, in the dark, we decided to move her home with us. Since, due to the complete lack of care and/or caring at the "nursing" facility, WE were staying with her 24/7 and doing literally everything for her—and when I say EVERYTHING, trust me, I know what that means (now), and yes, we were doing it—we said, "Well, hell, if WE are doing all the caregiving, why are we even staying in the same building with these assholes? We can take her HOME, do the same things for her there that we're doing here, and sleep—or rather, NOT sleep, but in our own bed at least."

I bought the best hospital bed available and The Cutest Boy in the World took it home, put it together, and set it up, in our bedroom, literally right beside our own bed. Weird, I know, but it was our best option. We only have the one bedroom downstairs—we knew we couldn't get her up and down the stairs, plus we'd been staying in the same room with her for months, as it was. And this way we would be free of the nursing home hellions and we wouldn't have to drive all over creation every night and day to make sure nobody was torturing her.

We sacked her up and fled those premises, but I must confess, I did "act ugly" before we made good our escape. Since everybody reading this is NOT from the South, I suppose I need to pause a moment and explain about our use of the word "ugly."

See if this helps: I recently received a query from a Queen in Central Florida who freely acknowledged that while, technically, she had for some years made her home in a southern location, that didn't qualify her as Southern. I applauded her for knowing the difference. It's the whole kittens-in-the-oven-ain't-exactly-biscuits mistake that many Individuals Geographically Marooned Outside the South (IGMOS) often make. This Queen had the grace to at least know what she didn't know, and so she came to the Font of All Wisdom—me, of course—for an explanation of the Southern usage of the word "ugly."

She had encountered a group of women crowded together in a small area where many were vying for space and more were expected to arrive momentarily. One particular woman in the group kept remarking on how tight the quarters were and expressing her irritation at the anticipated advent of newcomers. Her complaining grew more intense, and as it did so, she began prefacing her venomous statements with the phrase, "Now, I don't want to be ugly..." Or she would go on ranting at some length and then close with, "...but I don't want to be ugly."

Queenie was nonplussed. WHO would WANT to BE UGLY? Why should it ever be necessary to state out loud for the benefit of others that one, in fact, did not harbor any secret hankerings to be deemed unattractive? Queenie was so distressed by the woman's continued disclaimer that she finally felt moved to speak up and assure the woman that she need have no fear, as she was really quite fetching and in no danger whatsoever of being thought unfortunate looking—not even plain. "You're really cute," she said reassuringly.

And so Queenie was even more confused by the look she got in response to her kind offer of affirmation: "I couldn't tell if she thought I was stupid, rude, or out of my mind, but she clearly did not appreciate my attempt to bolster her confidence in her appearance."

"And then what happened," I wanted to know. Queenie said she left to go to the bar after the woman Blessed Her Heart and everybody else looked real uncomfortable.

Oh my. Poor Queenie. She had no idea what just happened to her. I explained to her that what the woman had been doing was venting her spleen about the poor planning that caused the overcrowded conditions and she was affixing the blame for her discomfort to a certain person or persons, but she was not sufficiently displeased as to be willing to confront the planners face-to-face about the situation, nor did she wish to be quoted on the matter, and thus, the all-purpose Southern anti-venom: "I don't want to be ugly, but..."

"Ugly" in this case is not describing an unattractive physical appearance. It means being "unkind" or "unpleasant," and with it, if one is Southern, one can freely SAY all the unkind, unpleasant—indeed, snipy and downright snarky—things one wants to say about another and then totally defuse it by assuring one's listeners that one "doesn't want to be ugly" about it.

About the heart blessing, I asked Queenie, "Did she laugh and give you a hug when she said it?"

"No," Queenie said.

The woman gave her a pitying look, patted her hand, and said, "Bless your heart, hunny."

"Was that bad?" she asked.

Oh mercy. I knew instantly why the rest of the group had fallen into an uncomfortable silence. Queenie had just been dog-cussed by the quintessential Southern Woman—who still didn't want to be ugly.

This stuff cannot be taught, can it? Y'all saw it coming from the first paragraph—and she STILL doesn't know what hit her. Bless her little heart.

So, I hope that clarifies things—if not, well, it would seem that I cannot help you. Bless your heart.

At any rate, I did, in fact, act ugly before we left the nursing home. I tried not to. I tried to adhere to our strict "be nice to them folks" policy, but they forced my hand. They sat me down and gave me "sympathetic" looks and very sweetly and quietly told me that they "understood how upset I must be," what with Mama about to die and all. And that just TORE IT for me.

Lemme ask you this: Has a guy ever done something—no, a whole BUNCH of things—so stupid and irritating and ass-headed that you just wanted to stab him in the eye with a fork, and then, when you showed REMARKABLE restraint and only beefed him out about it, HE asked if YOU were "PMSing"? And when he said that, did you not wish you HAD stabbed him in the eye with that fork and think that perhaps it was not too late to go with that option, after all?

Well, after all they had done to Mama (and all they had NOT done FOR her), to have them pat my hand and talk all sweet to me about how THEY KNOW what a STRESSFUL TIME this was for me—well, I was wishing for a fork, lemme tell you. I did not, unfortunately, have a fork with me, so I took a very deep breath and paused—just to see if my fury MIGHT subside enough for me to just walk out. Ummm, no. I took another deep breath, and I smiled at them, and very quietly, I said, "I am not strrrresssssed because my mother is dying; I am strrrressssed because YOU motherfuckers are making it WORSE." And then I left. (Note: I neither prefaced nor closed with any mention of not wanting to be ugly. I DID want to be SO ugly.)

Now, I gotta tell you, as bad as my language admittedly is, I have not ever, in all my LIFE, called ANYBODY that name—to their FACE. Never. Ever. I have never actually cussed somebody out. Oh, I've said plenty in the car driving away or retelling it later, but I just don't lose my temper. Haven't allowed myself to lose it since I was a kid. Neighborhood kids used to get in little tiffs when we were little, "acting ugly," and I would always be so totally consumed with remorse almost immediately after that I would be running down the street after them to apologize, and they would be running back to me, and we would have big bawling Lucy and Ethel make-up scenes out there. It was easier and more dignified for me to just stop letting my temper get away from me. But I did let it fly that day, and I don't mind telling you, I was not sorry.

I confessed it to Mama when I went back to her room to get her. I leaned down right by her ear and said, "Mama, we're taking you home now—and I just talked real ugly to all those people. And I am NOT SORRY." She didn't open her eyes, but she grinned and patted my face. Thank God she didn't tell me I had to go say I was sorry. Because I wasn't and I'm still not.

It took Mama four more months to die, and it was so not pretty. At first, she was able to get up several times each day. Well, I say "she was able to," but that's not completely accurate. Kyle would lift her, bodily, from the bed and put her in her wheelchair. What "she was able" to do was sit up in that chair, once ensconced, but she was not able to lend the slightest bit of assistance to that process.

In the mornings, before the heat became intolerable for her, we would wheel her out on the Divorce Porch to look at the morning light on the lake and the flowers. After a short sit, it would be back to bed for breakfast and then a nap. Before lunch, Kyle would again lift her from the bed and get in the shower with her in his arms. I would join them and bathe her while he held her. A video of that would not be unamusing, I imagine. Three enormous people in a shower—the holder, the bather, and the bathee—with water going in every direction. The holder and bather are both in sopping-wet gym shorts; the bathee is appropriately dressed for taking (or in this case, receiving) a shower. Unfortunately, none of us were particularly appreciative of the humorous side of the situation at the time.

A shiny, clean Mama would be returned to her bed, have a new nighty put on, and then she would order up Whatever She Could Think Of for lunch. I poached countless eggs and cooked gallons of custard over those months—whatever she wanted, whatever she would eat a mouthful of, I made. Our dear friend Barbara Whitehead, who came every morning, would usually feed Mama her breakfast and lunch, and then they would talk until Mama drifted off. After her post-lunch nap, Mama would want to look at old photographs—luckily, I have thousands.

Not too long after supper, we would collapse into our bed—which was less than two feet away from hers—and all watch something mindless on TV until we fell asleep, praying that we would all stay that way until the sun came up.

Those were the "good" days in the Beginning of the End. I shrink from detailing the real deterioration—it is just too raw, still. Some comparisons can be made to caring for a tiny infant. Although, it must be said that a grown-up person can lose the ability to do even things that newborns do for themselves, and when that happens, it must still be done—by the caregiver. However, when you are caring for an infant, while you do get just as "used-up" exhausted, underneath the exhaustion is the knowledge that, with every passing day, that infant is learning and growing and moving ever toward independence, and you are reinvigorated for the journey with each new success your baby achieves.

When your parent becomes your child, there is no such bright glow on the horizon to yearn for and struggle toward together. Well, there is a Light off in the distance, but you're not the one who can see it, and as she moves closer to The Light, your task of caring for the body that she is ever so slowly inching away from becomes more and more demanding—and truly horrifying, if you allow yourself to consider it. You just have to DO it and not think about it and try to help her to not think about it, either.

On the one hand, this is the person who gave me life and love every day of that life, who cared for my every need, above her own, for she was a Good Mother, so I was honored and happy to give it all back to her for as long as she needed it. But it is one thing to say that—and even mean it. It is quite another to Do

It. I was not able to care for her with perfect patience—and that haunts me now. No matter what I tell myself about her own occasional—perhaps, at times, even frequent—impatience with me when I was growing up, no matter that I can recall times when I was equally impatient with my own daughter, I still am wracked with guilt over the times that I failed with Mama. Why is that?

As is so often the case, it is when we are helping OTHERS cope with something that we realize the comforting words we are offering to THEM would or could serve US just as well. And so it was that my dear friend Blanche was suffering a bout of guilt over a bout of impatience with her mama, the ineffable Big L, and she called me, wailing over it and berating herself harshly for it.

"Baby Girl," I said to her, "you are becoming the parent here, and it is a hard job—no matter who is doing it. And as much as we love and admire Big L for all she has done and is doing in her life, I think we can acknowledge that there WERE times when she was WAY less than patient with YOU, was she not?" Blanche did admit that this was so. "So, it's just the same, only reversed now—and you WON'T do it perfectly—but you WILL do it with LOVE, and that's all that matters." Blanche agreed, but I could tell she was still harboring some guilt over her behavior. "OK," I said, "the big difference here is that when SHE got angry with YOU, she could and did SMACK you! Have you taken to hitting her yet?" Blanche snorted. "Have you sent her out in the yard to PICK HER OWN SWITCH YET?" That did it—guffaws ensued. I told her to tell Big L if she didn't straighten up and mind the doctors, we were gonna have to send her out in the yard to pick us a switch.

I prayed every day for God to take Mama, and she just lingered on and on. And I hate that because she lingered long enough for me to get so tired I couldn't think, and it just got harder and harder for all of us. Every day, it would seem that she could not possibly live through it—it also began to be doubtful that we could. I had said yes to every single speaking engagement request for that summer, and I was unable to fulfill a single one. I just could not leave when The End seemed so near.

All the hospice literature told me that, when folks linger, they will ultimately leave on their terms and in their own time—some will wait for family to arrive and others will wait for them to leave. I believe it is a holy thing to help someone have a peaceful death and I very much wanted to be with Mama, so I canceled event after event, all summer—waiting, hoping to have a repeat of that one beautiful moment we had in June when we thought she was dying.

Marie, our precious home hospice nurse, told me on September 28 that Mama had settled into a kind of groove and that, barring some kind of "event," she was likely to be with us for quite some time yet. I cannot tell you how that thought made me feel—a million different emotions, but none of them particularly positive—but I couldn't imagine how WE could survive her living much longer in this condition.

Midmorning, Kyle got a phone call from the Susan G. Komen Foundation of Northwest Arkansas. Their biggest annual fundraiser was two days away and their featured speaker had just been hospitalized for a recurrence of her cancer—was there any way on earth that I could come and fill in? Kyle explained that we were pretty much on a 24/7 Death Watch around here, but that we had just been told to prepare for the haul to be much longer—so maybe; he'd call them back.

He came to me with it and said they would arrange to get me there and back in 24 hours, and he asked if I wanted to do it. I try to do anything I can for Komen, and with Mama looking like a long-term roommate, I said OK. So the next morning, I kissed her good-bye and told her I'd be "right back," and off I went.

After an easy flight, I checked into the hotel and collapsed. I don't think I even rolled over in my sleep. I woke up, showered, and began dressing for the event. Kyle and I spoke briefly—nothing out of the ordinary. I told him I would call him after my speech, when I was on my way to the airport. Just a few minutes later, he called back—to tell me that Mama was gone. He had gone in the bedroom to see if she wanted breakfast and she had left the building.

When he had spoken to me the first time, he knew this, but he also knew that I was minutes away from walking in front of 700 women to make a speech and he thought that perhaps it was not the BEST time for me to receive such news. And let's face it, the news was certainly not going to be any DIFFERENT in a couple hours. But his mama told him to call me right back, that I absolutely needed to know the truth, and she was right.

I couldn't believe it. I had not left the house in literally MONTHS, and I leave for 24 hours and this is what she does? I am praying every day for God to take her—and He waits until I'm 500 miles away to pay attention?

I know God must get completely worn out with us, always asking for stuff—for the same stuff—over and over again, as IF He has no Plan and needs our input. I imagine it to be a lot like when my three dogs have decided that it's Time for Their Daily Ice Cream—but I've got 14 other things going on at that precise moment, all of which must be done BEFORE I can give them their ice cream. I AM GOING TO GIVE THEM THE FREAKIN' ICE CREAM—as soon as I do this other stuff. I look at them and I say, "INNA MINIT—I'll get your ice cream IN. A. MINUTE." Moral of this story: Much like WE seem to struggle with the ultimate truth that God's Timing IS PERFECT, dogs simply do not grasp the concept of INNA MINIT. Poor God. I know how He feels. But I forget.

So. My escorts arrive to take me to the meeting hall and Kyle has already called them. They are looking at me as if I might fly off into space at any moment, and that's prolly how I looked, actually. I asked them to please let me handle it. I knew if anybody said anything sweet to me, that would be it, I'd dissolve, and there would be no reassembling me.

I began my speech by telling them that, for the last six months, my mama had been dying by inches and that while it was, indeed, my honor, privilege, and joy to give anything back to the woman who had given me EVERYTHING—that being said, it was, at the very same time, pretty much like being pecked to death by a duck. And, of course, everybody laughed, including me. Then I said, "So, now that we have had a good laugh over that, I know you're gonna feel bad when I tell you that she just this minute DIED"—HUGE GASP in the room—"but don't, because I have prayed for this every single day since we found out that she couldn't get better. Now, I haven't left her side for the last six months and she didn't even know I was coming here—but as soon as she figured out that I wasn't coming right back, she left. Clearly, she did not want to die with me there—and this was Her Journey, so all is well. God's got her and He's got me, too. Y'all pray me through this and we'll make it—and have a good time, too, even."

While I was speaking, my hostesses secured a private plane to fly me directly home the minute I was finished, and they even flew with me—what a Godsend. It was so very odd to come home to...just home. No oxygen tanks, no Hoyer lift, no hospital bed, no wheelchair—no Mama. To go from being on duty all day and all night, every day and every night, for months and months, to having nothing at all to do is a transition for which one cannot really prepare.

I went to see Mama at the funeral home because she wanted to be cremated, and I just needed to see her one more time. I'm so glad I did because she looked absolutely BEAUTIFUL. I was sorely tempted to ignore her wishes and have an open-casket funeral, just so everybody could see how fabulous her skin was— there was not a single line remaining in her face. I know she would want you to know about and be envious of her gorgeous skin. So, there you have it.

When our daddy died, we were so shocked my seester Judy and I completely failed him in the Obituary Department, something we have always regretted, because as you should know by now, we do LOVE us a good obit. We vowed we'd not make that same mistake with Mama, and we did have such a FINE time writing hers. It evidently struck quite a chord with other Obit Fans out there because it went viral on the Internet—an NPR station in San Francisco even read it on the air. Mama woulda been so pleased. In case you missed it, here it is:

Janice "Jan" Louise Wendt Conner, wife of the late and much lamented John A. Conner of Ethel, Mississippi, died peacefully at the Lake Caroline home of her favorite daughter, Jill Conner Browne, on Wednesday, September 30, 2009.

Mrs. Conner grew up in Grosse Pointe, Michigan, the daughter of the late Mr. & Mrs. Walter Wendt. As a young woman, her statuesque beauty won her a spot among the models at the John Robert Powers Agency, but her mother disapproved of that career, and so she became a buyer for the J. L. Hudson stores. During World War II, she and many of her friends worked tirelessly at the

USO, where she met the only man she ever really loved, her sailor boy, John Conner.

She became a devoted Southerner by choice when she finally defied the wishes of her mother (who was, by all accounts and evidence, the Meanest Woman Who Ever Lived), by marrying and following "that hillbilly" back to Mississippi, where they lived happily until Mr. Conner's untimely death in 1982, after which Mrs. Conner never gave so much as a thought to another man.

The Conners' home was a haven for all the children in the surrounding neighborhoods, having a wide-open, fully stocked kitchen, a refrigerator full of Cokes, and the only swimming pool for miles around. (It should be noted that the 20'x40', 7-foot-deep hole for this pool was personally dug, with picks and shovels, by the two of them. If you've ever tried to dig even a small hole in Yazoo clay, the extent of the Conners' devotion to their children can be extrapolated from that endeavor. It should also be noted that this pool was the pet project of Mrs. Conner and there was no peace for Mr. Conner until it was completed. He might have initially thought that she would be discouraged when she saw first-hand how difficult the digging proved to be—one of the many, but more significant times He Was Wrong.)

They were active members of the Alta Woods Presbyterian Church, where they, for more than 50 years, provided thousands of cookies as Sunday bribes to the children of the church.

Mrs. Conner's daughters, the aforementioned Jill and that other one, Judy, were finally sources of pride for Jan, as they both became best-selling authors. It did remain a lifelong disappointment to her, however, that neither of them ever chose to pursue the career she would have preferred for them: writing messages for greeting cards.

Both daughters give much credit to their mother for spending countless hours reading to them until they finally started reading for themselves. Mrs. Conner also taught her grandchildren to read and to love it. Blessed be her name for that.

Jan's only two grandchildren—Trevor Palmer and Bailey Conner Browne—were born 23 years apart; thus, each was able to enjoy the many benefits of being "the only grandchild," a position both exploited to the fullest and with great felicity to all parties.

Mrs. Conner was well known in her younger years for adopting families in need and browbeating them into prosperity via the many donors she "persuaded" to join the effort and her relentless and most often successful attempts at placing them in gainful employment—often without any particular desire or willingness on their part. She would and often did give "the shirt off her back" to someone, but if her own didn't happen to fit the need, she had no qualms about obtaining, by whatever means necessary, the more suitable shirt off someone else's back. Her daughters dreaded the annual Christmas Flooding of the town of Flowood, knowing that the pantry would be emptied and their own closets would be raided, in support of the victims.

Jan Conner was an advocate of the homeless—be they human or otherwise—long before it became fashionable. She never passed a panhandler without giving him something (along with an admonition to "go eat something") and she never turned away a hungry creature of any species. She basically, over time, stole the neighbor's nondescript brown dog, Rascal, and was somehow able to elicit from him that, although before moving in with us he had considered himself fortunate to get a dab of dog food now and again, all he truly liked to eat was chicken livers and that furthermore he only liked them fried very brown and crispy. Rascal ate crispy brown chicken livers every day of his 10 years with us. Whenever Jan left town, it was only after giving John strict instructions on

How to Cook the Chicken Livers for the Dog, lest he (the dog) suffer in her absence.

To this day, Mrs. Conner's entire family has an inordinate fondness for Brown Dogs.

Mrs. Conner is widely known as a world traveler, as she frequently arranged group trips, which she sometimes guided or at least herded. A most interesting aspect about all of Jan's travels was her high and constant level of disdain for Other Countries, or at least all of Europe. She did love a cruise, though—anytime, anywhere—which accounted for her enjoying 50 or so of them. As much as she disparaged all of Europe, she loved Alaska and anything west of Hawaii. All things Asian were wonderful to her and she made numerous trips to the Far East.

The latter years of her life were spent joyfully at The Waterford on Highland Colony with her many friends, especially the rowdy bunch on the Second Floor North. She declared that living at the Waterford was "like being on a cruise, every day."

Since 1999, no St. Paddy's parade was complete without the lead car carrying "The Queen Mothers of the Sweet Potato Queens,®" and while she shared this title with dear friend and fellow Queen Mum, Caroline Hewes of Gulfport, it cannot escape attention that Jan always rode in the front seat.

Jan is survived by the aforementioned favorite daughter, Jill Conner Browne, and husband Kyle Jennings, and that other one—Judy Conner Palmer of New Orleans—granddaughter Bailey Conner Browne of Oxford, and grandson Trevor Palmer and his wife RuthAnna and their daughter Riley and sons Conner and Mason, of New Orleans.

The family wishes to lovingly thank Barbara Whitehead for her devotion and support to us all and to Marie Fenton of Hospice Ministries for her sensitive care to Jan and to us.

No flowers, please. Mrs. Conner was allergic. Because of Jan's lifelong propensity for taking in strays, be they four-legged or two, she would love for you to make a very generous donation in her name to the only no-kill animal shelter in Rankin County— Animal Rescue Fund of Mississippi, founded by Sweet Potato Queen Elizabeth (Pippa) Jackson, located at 1963 Holly Bush Road, Pelahatchie, Mississippi 39145 or www.arfms.com.

There will be a mercifully brief and joyous Memorial Service on Monday, October 5, 2009, at 5:30 p.m., at Wright & Ferguson on Highland Colony Parkway, Ridgeland, followed by a Celebration of a Life Beautifully Lived and a Very Fun Reception, until around 7 p.m.

Judy and I were quite pleased with ourselves, but we admit we were given pause when we saw it printed in the newspaper and it filled nearly half a page. We thought it might easily take every dime Mama had left to pay for her obituary, which we quickly decided would be entirely worth it. Then we saw, with horror, that in the headline of her column it listed her as hailing from ETHEL, MISSISSIPPI, and we thought, "Oh dear God, thank goodness she is dead. If she saw that, she WOULD DIE." Daddy was from Ethel; MAMA was from Grosse Pointe, Michigan.

Oh, and I should explain "that other one." Judy actually put that in there, but here's where it came from: Most of the time, Mama was perfectly lucid, but not always. On one of her "foggy" days, she called me over to her and said, "I've just been lying here thinking and it is driving me crazy—I can't remember my young'uns NAMES." And I leaned down and asked her if she knew that she had some, and she said yes, and I asked her if she knew that they loved her, and she said, "Oh, yes, of course," and I said, "Well then, Mama, it doesn't really matter what you call us, but I'M JILL and I'm your favorite—and that other one is JUDY and she lives in New Orleans."

Judy and I had many guffaws over that and she insisted we include it in the obit, which I was perfectly happy to do.

Since Judy has lived out of state for many years and thus was not necessarily still a familiar face to some, at the memorial service, she wore a large name tag that identified her simply as "That Other One." Snort.

Mama's memorial service was perfect except for me. In retrospect, I think I must have had post-traumatic Tourette's—I vaguely recall babbling a great deal more than usual and with far less lucidity.

The folks at Wright & Ferguson Funeral Home were beyond accommodating. We planned the service for 5:30 p.m. on a weekday so that people could just come by after work. There were no other "clients" in the building that evening, so we were able to have, well, a nice party. A bagpiper opened the service for us with "Amazing Grace," and then Lelon Thompson—with the angel voice—sang for us and led us all in song as well. One of Mama's favorite songs was "God Bless America," which is not so unusual, I suppose, but she particularly loved to hear it sung by Kate Smith. (If you're under 50, Google it.) So, as Lelon asked everybody to stand and sing it, one of my Tourette's moments was to bellow out that everybody should try to imagine that they were Kate Smith as they sang and everybody laughed. But this image shook Lelon so much that I thought for a moment he would not be able to sing.

Keith Tonkel, pastor of my home church, Wells United Methodist, was, at the time, walking through that same Valley with his precious wife, Pat, but he was there for us, every step of our Journey. Mama's good friend Albert Butler prayed the most magnificent prayer for us. Jamie Ward dismissed us with Mama and Daddy's "special song," which was "Don't Fence Me In," and it was just supposed to be Jamie playing the piano, but everybody apparently wanted to sing it, which is funny because none of us knew more than a few words to it—but we all seemed to know a different few words—so it was like the song was being sung by a small swarm of bees that was moving around the room, until we came to the last line and everybody got to holler out the "DON'T FENCE ME IN" part.

Other than my own bizarre and inexplicable outbursts here and there during the service, it was pretty swell, I must say. Then my dear, lifelong friend Debbie Rankin catered for us, so we had great food and an abundance of champagne and the whole thing was so much FUN that the funeral home folks said they just wished everybody would do it this way. My friend Fran brought her six-year-old daughter, Juliette, who had such a fine time she said she thought they oughta go to funerals more often. Fran felt it necessary to caution her that this experience was really not indicative of most funerals. My feeling is that, as Christians, if we believe what we say we do, we ought never to do it any other way. It SHOULD be a party. God love her, Mama was FREE AT LAST, and this was a celebration, not only of a life so wonderfully lived—but also of her Great Escape. Hallelujah, indeed.

As I said, Loss has visited me so many times in the last several years. I've lost Mama and way too many other precious people to death—one, my darling Dennis Black, took his own life, which truly did and does break my heart. I've lost work relationships and dear friends to "divorce," for lack of a better word, which, in many ways, is even more painful than death.

The only way to heal from any loss is to grieve, but the only way to grieve is to accept the loss. The only way to accept the loss is to look at it—and that also includes reliving all the things that one knows one did wrong. And who wants to do that? Who is ABLE to do that? What is more painful than that?

Sometimes, it hurts too much to even think about it—because it's DONE, we can't change it, and that is maddening. We want so much to go back, to get that moment back and do it right—NOT react that way, NOT say that mean thing, say the sweet thing, slow down, and spend more time. Bells cannot be un-rung, nor can they be rung once the time for bell-ringing has passed.

Things happen that can't be fixed. Relationships are ended by death, or maybe nobody's dead, but the relationship might be ruined beyond repair. Sucks. Just make sure you don't lose the LESSON, too—because there was one, every time.

If you feel REGRET about anything, there's a lesson there for you. If there is anything in your life that, when you think about it, you would give ANYTHING to be able to redo it, there's your lesson. Pay attention—because it WILL come around again. Not in the same way—obviously, some people are dead and gone, can't fix that, and other stuff is just over and there's no resurrecting it—but we do have opportunities to get it more right, more often, with other people, every single day. That's the way life works and it's where peace lies.

Forgiveness—such a wonderful thing to give and to receive. We just have to remember to start that process in front of the mirror—you gotta give it to yourself and allow yourself to receive it before you can go any further with it.

If you keep one foot in yesterday and one foot in tomorrow, ALL you can DO is make a very unfortunate mess all over today. And today is all ANY-body has ever got. Let go of yesterday, quit worrying about tomorrow—grab hold of today and get your money's worth out of it. See if you can make only NEW mistakes today and be grateful for the goodness of the moment.

This one's been kind of a life-changer for me. I offer it for your consideration:

> *What if, when you woke up in the morning,*
> *ALL you had LEFT was what you had thanked God for*
> *the night before?*

About the Author

Jill Conner Browne is the *New York Times*–bestselling author of nine Sweet Potato Queens˙ books, which are being developed into a Broadway musical with Grammy Award–winning singer/songwriter Melissa Manchester, Oscar nominee and Nashville Songwriters Hall of Fame inductee Sharon Vaughn, and Tony Award–winning playwright Rupert Holmes. She has been featured in such publications as *USA Today*, *Newsweek*, *People*, *Los Angeles Times*, and the *Washington Post*. Her books have inspired more than 6,200 Sweet Potato Queen Wannabe˜ Chapter Groups in thirty-seven countries. When she is not writing, hosting Jackson, Mississippi's Annual Zippity Doo Dah˙ Parade Weekend Festivities benefiting Blair E. Batson Hospital for Children, or speaking at fundraising events around the country, Jill lives and reigns in Jackson with her three cats, a three-legged girl dog, a big boy dog, her daughter's rescued mutt, and her husband. And no, he's not the Sweet Potato King.